Tim—

THANK YOU FOR YOUR LOYAL
FRIENDSHIP FOR 20 YEARS! I
APPRECIATE HAVING YOU AS
A JESUS WARRIOR BROTHER!

God Bless Team Mohns,

Hutch

JESUS

His Life, His Love, His Promise

A FATHER'S NOTEBOOK TO HIS KIDS

JEFF HUTCHISON

Jesus: His Life, His Love, His Promise

A Father's Notebook To His Kids

Jeff Hutchison

ISBN: 978-1-66788-953-5

To Jake, Sam, and Julianne

This book is a gift to you,
as you were a gift to me from God.

I love you.

Dad

GOOD MORNING!

This book was never supposed to be written.
I wrote it for my three kids, Jake, Sam, and Julianne.
This is a Father's notebook to his children.
Here is the backstory.

In 2016, three friends invited me to listen to the Gospel of John with them over the course of a week. Even though I had grown up in the Church, that sounded like a very big project for me because I had never really "read" the Bible, much less listened to it. So, I accepted the challenge. I lasted two days. I have a very short attention span and I get distracted quite easily and I absolutely do not process information by hearing it. Ask my wife, Jean, and she will confirm! I told my friend that I would read the gospel while they listened to it. I was surprised to learn that the Gospel of John is only about 20-30 pages, depending on your Bible. I think I believed the Gospels were a lot longer than they really are. Reading the Bible the first time, word by word was quite a challenge for me. In truth, I finished that exercise with more questions than answers. I thought to myself, "I wonder what else is in here". I decided to read Matthew, Mark, and Luke as well. While it was a gratifying experience, I can't say that I enjoyed it all that much the first time I did it. It just felt like something I was doing because I said I would do it. When I finished the Gospels, I figured it only made sense to keep going, so I read the rest of the New Testament. I must say that the first time I read all of Paul's letters in their entirety, I was moved. The depth of his commitment, despite being imprisoned, beaten, and tortured was so inspiring. I began to enjoy the process of reading scripture, so I thought I would start all over again. This time, I decided to make notes in the margin of my Bible as I read through the New Testament for the second time. What I found, is that it is exactly like your favorite movie that you have seen so many times that you can't turn off when you see it is on TV. (I've seen Forrest Gump at least 50 times!). I was surprised to see how much more I enjoyed my second journey through the Gospels and Letters. And my Bible was filling up with notes. I read it again, and again, and again. And my Bible had even more notes in it. Between 2016 and 2020, I read the New Testament 12 times. Please know, I don't share that statistic with you to brag. ("none is righteous, no not one" Romans 3:10). I share that statistic because I found every time I read a story, I picked up things that I never saw before. The colors got brighter, the messages from Jesus resonated stronger. And most importantly, the story of Jesus got so vivid, I couldn't take my eyes off the story. So I kept reading. As I thought about my Bible that included all my notes, I said to myself "someday, I'm going to give this Bible to my kids, so they know what I thought about all of this". The pandemic hit in March of 2020, and it shut the world down. For the first time in our lives, we were told so many things we could not do, like go to work, go to school, go to shops or restaurants, or travel. I posted something on social media that essentially said, "in this moment of being told the things we can't do, here are 10 things you can do". One of those things was encouraging people to read the Bible. I was blown away to discover that post got over a million views. I asked myself if I'm encouraging others to read the Bible, and I've done that, what should I do? And then it hit me. "What if I actually wrote all of this down? All of it. Then I could give THAT book to my kids". I'm a person that learns by doing, watching, reading, writing, speaking, and listening, in that order. Writing things after I read them helps me comprehend and stay focused. So, in January of 2021, I decided to rewrite the New Testament. I started in Matthew Chapter 1, and I rewrote verses, summarized stories, and shared quotes from Jesus from all 26 Books in the New Testament. I rewrote it all by hand in a journal. (This book does not include Revelation because I'm still trying to figure it out!) I felt like Forrest Gump when he ran across the country and just kept "running and running and running". I just kept "writing and writing and writing". By the end of that year, I had written 630 handwritten pages in two completely filled journals had completed my 13th trip through the New Testament. What I learned is that the journey of reading the Bible gets better every time, without exception. It starts out as a challenge to read it, and it becomes a habit, then it becomes something that you can't live without because it is so fun, so enlightening, and so important to your daily life. No matter how many times I read these books in the Bible, new things jump off the page every single time. It is like food and water, which Jesus told us it would be. After decades of people telling me what Jesus said, and what they thought about what he said, it was so nice to actually read what he said. There is no need to speculate as to the life of Jesus. It's all written down.

I told a few people I was writing this book for my kids, and they told me that I should publish it. And I told them that I couldn't because it was just for my kids. Folks continued to push, as did my family. I asked my kids, Jake, Sam and Julianne if they minded if I published something that was supposed to be a gift from me to them, and they gave me a resounding "yes". I am grateful for their permission. So here we are.

Please keep these things in mind!

This book is a notebook, and it reads like it. Pretend you are watching a football game and one person is the play-by-play announcer and one person is the color commentator. In this book, the real story is the book I am quoting and summarizing and that is the New Testament. That is the only story. I hope folks read this book once, and the New Testament 1000 times.

My comments are only the color commentary, and you should know a few things about those comments.

1) In no case did I knowingly change anything. The story is the story and no revised version of it is anywhere close to the real deal. If you find any inaccuracies in my commentary, I would just ask for a little grace and forgiveness. I'm on a journey, too!

2) This book does not include every story in the New Testament, although it includes most. It includes the stories that resonated and touched me as I was reading them.

3) I tried to write "in the spirit". What that means is I wrote whatever was moving me at the time I was writing it. That means that some comments in Luke might feel different than my comments in Hebrews. I can't explain it, it was just what was moving me at the time I wrote it.

4) Very rarely did I knowingly make this about my "opinion". This book is not about my opinion on these stories, nor should it be for anyone. I learned that it is about learning the truth rather than me trying to outthink God.

5) Many of comments are in short words and street talk. Just my "in the moment" translation. You will see a lot of "wow", "amazing" and "incredible" to lead off my comments. Sometimes you might even see an incomplete sentence. That's just because that's how I think, and this is a notebook. So, you get my notes.

6) Sometimes I just ask a question. Other times I said, "I don't know what this story means". I hope that add some authenticity and transparency to your reading.

7) Sometimes I underlined things, sometimes I used bolded font. I had a choice to as to bold the quotes from the Bible or bold my comments and I chose to bold some of my comments. Because the

story is the Bible not my interpretation of it, and you can't bold an entire book!

8) There is definitely some repetition, both in the gospels as well as in my comments. That's because some of the gospel stories repeat, and some of my takeaways from those stories are consistent. This book is designed to connect the dots of those stories to build the case for the impenetrable truth of the story of Jesus.

9) This book is not about religion. It is about faith, and there is a difference. I hope this book is a bridge for those that believe that Jesus was the Son of God, not a wedge to divide us by "church". The Body of Christ and the Kingdom of God are the family of believers and we are more alike than different. And while Jesus encouraged us to bond together in love, he never required anyone to go to any specific Church.

10) The quotations included come from the NIV Bible (New International Version)

This book is a gift to my kids from their Dad. Salvation is a gift from Jesus, and I hope they receive it.

Enjoy.

THE GOSPEL OF MATTHEW

Matthew wrote the story of Jesus for a Jewish audience. Being the first book of the New Testament, it was intended to be a bridge from the books of the Old Testament to the story of Jesus. Matthew focuses his writing on introducing Jesus as the true promised messiah, as well as the describing and explaining Kingdom of Heaven.

Both Matthew and Luke trace Jesus Genealogy. The genealogies are different and there are different theories as to why that is. The important part is that the Old Testament predicted that Jesus would be a descendant of David and both accounts trace Jesus to David.

MATTHEW 2

This is a beautiful account of the angel's visit to Joseph, telling him he need not be afraid, that what was conceived in his wife was from the Holy Spirit and he will save his people from their sins. All of this is fulfillment of what was prophesied in Isaiah 7:14, "The Son will be called Immanuel which means, "God with us". What a great way to start the New Testament! **Matthew tells us immediately that Jesus is God!**

We hear about the visit of the Magi, which is the three kings that went to Jerusalem to try to find Jesus. King Herod was not happy about a new "king" so he asked the chief priests where Jesus was. They quoted what was foretold in Micah 5:2. He is in Bethlehem. **Think about that…..Jesus birth was foretold centuries earlier…..even to the finest detail of him being**

born to a young virgin in a small town called Bethlehem. Herod told the magi to go find Jesus and report back so he could worship him. Herod was lying; he wanted Jesus killed out of jealousy. The magi found Jesus and gave him their gifts. After the magi left, an angel visited Joseph and told him to take Jesus across the border to Egypt where Herod couldn't kill him. When Herod found this out, he ordered the killing of all baby boys under the age two. Because Jesus was already gone, this seems to be out of pure rage. This was foretold in Jeremiah. When Herod died an angel appeared to Joseph and told him he could return to Judah. But Herod's son was now ruling, so Joseph took this family to Nazareth which is where Jesus was raised.

MATTHEW 3

Between chapters two and three, Matthew jumps 30 years in the life of Jesus. This is where he introduces John the Baptist. John the Baptist was a strong man, a warrior-like Preacher. He told people to get their act together, repent and be baptized. He told them that he would baptize them with water, but Jesus was planning to baptize them with the Holy Spirit and fire. John the Baptist then baptizes Jesus, which is a beautiful depiction of our faith as well as the importance of baptism. **We get baptized to show our faith to the world and that's what Jesus was doing.**

MATTHEW 4

Jesus is tempted by Satan in the desert with food and power. I love how Jesus says, "Don't tempt God." **This is a lesson we all need to remember. Jesus also says to worship only him, do not worship any false Gods!** Their society had a lot of false Gods in their culture and so do we. We worship money, power, consumerism, hobbies, clothes, people and the list goes on and on. Jesus says, "there is only one!". Jesus also warns Satan to not put God to the test. **In other words, it is OK to ask God to do big things in our lives. But it is not OK to say, "If you are truly God, you will do x". This challenges God's**

divinity, and it is the opposite of submitting to God's will. It is holding him accountable to our will which is the opposite of placing our faith in God.

John the Baptist gets thrown in jail and Jesus returns to Capernaum, preaching that the kingdom of heaven is near. Jesus also begins to call the first disciples. I love how Jesus demonstrates his leadership conviction when he calls Peter and Andrew to "come follow me", and they do. they drop everything and follow him. Would I be willing to drop everything and follow a man that I did not know? I just don't know. Jesus must have had an amazing presence to gain the disciples alliance and loyalty so quickly. Jesus begins to heal the sick of Galilee.

MATTHEW 5

This is one of my favorite chapters in the Bible: the beatitudes. This is also known as the sermon on the mount. It is a beautiful description of how God views his people.

- Blessed are the poor in spirit
      for theirs is the kingdom of heaven
- Blessed are those who mourn
      for they will be comforted
- Blessed are the meek
      for they will inherit the earth
- Blessed are those who hunger and thirst
      for they will be filled
- Blessed are the merciful
      for they will be shown mercy
- Blessed are the pure in heart
      for they will see God
- Blessed are the peacemakers
      for they will be called sons of God
- Blessed are those who are persecuted because of righteousness
      for theirs is the kingdom of heaven

- Blessed are you when people insult you and persecute you and falsely say all kinds of evil against you because of me
- Rejoice and be glad because great is your reward in heaven for in the same way they persecuted the prophets who were before you.

I love this passage so much. It's what I read at my mom's funeral because it describes her to a tee! We always need to come to the aid of the least, the last and the lost. And we need to remember that our faith will be tested, and we will be persecuted because of it. We need to stand firm, and we will be rewarded. **Our reward may not come while we are on this earth, but we need to be ok with that, because the reward of permanence in paradise transcends any rewards we might receive here.**

Most of the time the reference to the sermon on the mount stops at the Beatitudes. But Jesus goes on to preach about many things including the "law", murder, adultery, divorce, love for your enemy, giving to the needy, prayer, worry and judging. This must be the longest stretch of continual preaching that Jesus ever did. Here are my favorites from this passage:

> **Salt of the earth**: we have saltiness because we know the truth. Don't lose it. Salt make everything around it better.

> **Light of the world:** we have seen the light, so we need to put our lamp out so people can see it.

> **Fulfillment of the law**: Jesus is the fulfillment. <u>Follow his lead</u>.

> **Murder:** it's not just about physical murder, anger can be murder.

> **Settle disagreements quickly.**

> **Adultery**: lust is another kind of adultery.

> **Don't swear**

> **Turn the other cheek.**

Love your enemies: This is a powerful statement by Jesus. He says: "Even pagans love those that love back." **The real thing to do as a follower of Jesus is to love your enemies. There is no greater demonstration of our commitment to Jesus than when we show grace and mercy to those that persecute us.** That is what he did. Plus, when we do it, we attract people to the "peace and love" that we demonstrate. And when we attribute our actions to our faith in Jesus, we give glory to God.

Give to the needy: But don't broadcast your deeds. If you do that, your reward is on earth. Do it quietly and your reward is in heaven. That is so hard! Our human nature is to what to take credit for the good that we do. **Once we truly align ourselves with Jesus, we feel that approval from him, so we don't need earthly approval.**

Prayer: the disciples ask Jesus how they should pray, and Jesus very simply recites the Our Father. Such a simple prayer that says:

"God you are so holy and glorious we ask you to give us just what we need to do your will and please forgive us." So powerful.

Treasures in heaven: This is life altering. Jesus doesn't say you can't have money. He says you can't serve God and money. "Where your treasure is, there your heart will be".

Worry: Jesus encourages us by saying God will take care of us. Don't worry about tomorrow.

Judging others: Jesus says, "Why do you look at the speck in your neighbor's eye and pay no attention to the plank in your eye." Judge yourself first, then help others.

Narrow and wide gates: Wide is the gate to destruction and it's real easy to find. Narrow is the gate to following Jesus to heaven and few find it.

A tree and its fruit: A bad tree can't bear good fruit and vice versa.

"People will recognize by the fruit you bear". This includes your words, your deeds and your children! Bear good fruit!

Wise and foolish builders: if you hear the words of Jesus and don't pay attention, you are building your life on sand. Everything will be washed away. **Listen to his words, apply them in your life, and it's like building your life on a rock. Nothing of this earth can wash it away.**

MATTHEW 8

These are mostly stories of Jesus healing and other miracles. The centurion's servant is a great story in that the man says he has slaves and soldiers that answer to him, but he tells Jesus, "I don't deserve to have you under my roof." That posture of repentance is why Jesus saves his servant. **No matter how "great" we are in man's eyes, we are all the same in Jesus' eyes. He asks us to maintain a posture of repentance.**

The story about the "cost of following Jesus" is a tough one to comprehend. A man said," I will follow you wherever you go, I just need to bury my father first." Jesus said, "Let the dead bury their own, you won't always have me." **His point is that you must be willing to give up everything to follow Jesus.**

Jesus calms the storm while he and his disciples were in the boat. I love when Jesus states, "You of little faith." It's so true. We have such little faith when it comes to the true power of God. The last healing in chapter 8 is a strange one. He heals two demon possessed men and makes the spirits enter a herd of pigs who run into a lake and drown themselves. People were so scared by this and ask Jesus to leave the region. I guess if I didn't know he was Jesus, it would scare me too.

MATTHEW 9

In Chapter 9, the opposite happens. Jesus heals a paralytic, and the crowds were in "awe" and began praising God. I wonder why the difference. The next story is so awesome. Jesus calls the apostle Matthew to follow him. He sees Matthew sitting at his tax collector booth (tax collectors were hated) and Jesus says two words, "follow me". **The first time I really studied the leadership lessons of Jesus, I realized how truly <u>cool</u> this man was. He was a strong, soft-spoken leader who led with love.** Who can walk up to people and say, "let's go, give up everything. You have been chosen." When people ask Jesus why he hangs out with tax collectors and sinners, his answer is world changing and the cornerstone of following Jesus.

"It is not the healthy who need a doctor, but the sick. But go and learn what this means: I desire mercy not sacrifice, for I have not come to call the righteous, but sinners". Jesus is saying, "Not only do I hang out with sinners, that's why I'm here." Jesus then tells the story of putting a new patch on an old garment or pouring new wine into old wineskins. He says, "nobody does that." **His point is that following Jesus is not a patch on your old life, it is a whole new life! We cannot keep our faith in Jesus compartmentalized. It becomes who we are.**

Jesus heals a woman who has been bleeding for 12 years, raises a dead girl to life and heals a blind and mute person. A couple of interesting things happen. First, Jesus tells them, "Don't tell anyone about this." I can't figure out why Jesus would do this. Maybe it's a connection to a future statement of "blessed are those who have not seen and still believe". It could also be that Jesus did not want to be discovered by the authorities yet (because we know how that ends!) Second, they don't listen to him, they spread the world all over the region. Third, the pharisees believed that all his work is by "the prince of demons" Satan.

MATTHEW 10

Starts with a great quote from Jesus: "The harvest is plentiful, but the workers are few". **Jesus is talking about the fact that there are so many people who need to hear the good news but there are so few people to deliver that news. We need to be the deliverers.** Jesus shares with us the names of his 12 disciples and he follows that with the specific instruction on where to go and what to say. These are truly "life words" for all of us to live by and absolute guidance on how to be a disciple of Christ.

This is a summary of Jesus' instruction:

Go to the lost sheep of Israel. Jesus went to the sinners. That's where he wants us to go Heal the sick, raise the dead (confuses me…maybe he means raise the spiritually dead to spiritual life) and cleanse the lepers. Jesus wants us to heal in his name.

Take nothing with you. **This is Jesus' constant message of "I will sustain you". He is enough.**

I love how Jesus said, "Let your peace rest on it." The houses you stay at, Jesus brings peace. Then comes some very important guidance. "If people don't listen to you, shake the dust off your feet and go to the next town". **I think Jesus is referencing what he said in terms of a plentiful harvest and few workers. There are so many souls to save, we can't waste time on folks with no interest.** Jesus also reminds the disciples that they will be persecuted on account of him. He reassures them, "don't worry about what to say, the words will be given to you (by the Holy Spirit)". That is so reassuring. So many times, I have prayed the words, "please put the right words in my heart and mind at this time." There is no question I have felt the power of the Holy Spirit when I am speaking or praying.

Jesus also tells them to keep going through all the cities quickly, essentially telling them that there is not enough time before Jesus returns to judge all. I love how Jesus tells them to not be afraid. again, this is reassurance that they know the truth. The truth will always win. When you know the truth, you never have to shy away from it.

Verse 32 is life changing. Jesus says, "Whoever acknowledges me before men, I will acknowledge him before my Father. whoever disowns me, I will disown them before my Father." **We can never deny our faith in Christ. We need to remember that when we are asked a simple question like "what faith are you?". We cannot deny our alliance to Jesus.**

Jesus says some eye-opening things. He says that he will divide us all. It's scary. Basically, "you are with me or against me". If you love anyone, family included, more than him, you are out! "Whoever finds his life will lose it. whoever loses his life for my sake will find it". **Give up everything for Jesus and you will find life!**

MATTHEW 11

This chapter is a little confusing. It is about Jesus and John the Baptist. It is essentially about the two of them testifying on each other's behalf. Jesus then denounces some of the cities where he performed his miracles because they did not repent. Jesus shares with us that at times he is revealed to children, but not kings. I think this is his way of saying that anyone can be saved. He says, "come to me. all you who are weary, and I will give you rest…learn from me for I am gentle and humble in heart". This is such a comforting statement. It is also a great paradox in that in the chapter before, he says he came to divide the world. That is the beauty of Jesus—powerful and loving. **And we get to choose the team captained by Jesus. Jesus us provides us with comfort and rest.**

MATTHEW 12

Jesus declares himself Lord of the sabbath. The Jews challenge his ability to heal on the Sabbath, but he does it anyway. After he healed a man with a shriveled hand, the pharisees began a plot to kill Jesus. Jesus left that place and a lot of people followed him as he healed. This was fulfillment of the prophet Isaiah:

"Here is my servant, whom I have chosen, the one I love, in whom I delight; I will put my spirit on Him, and he will proclaim justice to the nations. He will not quarrel or cry out. No one will hear His voice in the streets. A bruised reed he will not break, and a smoldering wick he will not snuff out; till he leads justice to victory. In his name the nations will put their hope".

Then some very important things happen. He hears a demon possessed man and the onlookers accuse him of being "of Beelzebub" — Satan. Jesus says, "A kingdom divided amongst itself cannot stand." He goes explains that he just drove out Satan, why would Satan do that to himself. **Another great example of how incredible Jesus was at teaching. "A nation divided against itself cannot stand" is a phrase for all areas of life—church, family, school, work. We need to be uniters not dividers.**

Jesus talks about the fact that we cannot blaspheme about the Holy Spirit. It has always confused me that Jesus says, "I will forgive blasphemy against me, but not against the Holy Spirit." He references the "good tree good fruit" metaphor. It is so simple and yet so powerful. If you are **full of good**, you will leave good behind your actions, deeds, relationships, and children. The opposite is also true,

MATTHEW 13

Begins with the parable of the sower. Such an awesome reminder for all of us. Seeds on a rocky path get eaten by birds, seeds in rocky places with a little soil may spring up quickly but will wither and die because the soil was shallow. Some fell amongst the thorns where other plants choked out the plants. The seed that fell on good soil produced "100, 60 or 30 times what was sown".

He is not talking about seeds to grow plants, he is talking about seeds of the truth of his mission to save the world of its' sins and to deliver us to heaven with his Father. Jesus says, "He who has ears. Let him hear." We must be the **good soil** so that word of God takes root and blossoms in our lives. When we do it will produce "100, 60 or 30 times" by bringing others to Jesus. Then the disciples ask Jesus why he teaches in parables. His answer is that he is giving them the secrets of the kingdom of God. He also tells them how lucky they are to hear that they hear and see what they see. "Many have come before you, wanting to see what you see". **Regarding the sower, Jesus reminds us that if our seeds don't take root, Satan will come and snatch it away. How true.**

Jesus shares a series of parables.

> **Parable of the weeds**. So profound. A farmer plants a crop of wheat, then an enemy (Satan) plants a bunch of weeds to destroy the wheat. The farmer's worker asks if he wants him to go remove the wheat. Jesus says, "No. Let them grow together. At harvest, we will burn the weeds and I'll take my wheat to <u>my</u> barn." This is a beautiful depiction of what it will be like at the end of time. Jesus will take his people home and burn the rest.

> **Parable of the mustard seed**. The smallest of seeds can grow into a large tree where the birds of the air perch on its branches. The kingdom of God is like a mustard seed where we can all take refuge.

> **The parable of the yeast.** The word of God is like yeast that needs to work its way through our entire being for us to become fully enriched by Jesus.

The parable of the hidden treasure. A man finds a treasure in a field. He loves it so much that he buries it and buys the entire field. We need to do whatever we can to get our hands around God's treasure—his love.

The parable of the net. I have personally experienced this when I went to India. The fisherman dragged a net 50 yards wide from 5 feet of water to the beach. When they got to the beach there was a mountain of sea creatures. The woman then proceeded to keep the "good" edible fish and tossed the snakes and sea urchins back into the ocean. **Once again this is what God will do at the end of time.**

Jesus talks about how difficult it is to have honor or be respected in your hometown. It's not impossible, but often the people that have known you for your entire life still see you as the little fifth grader in math class. **Sometimes you need to spread your wings!**

MATTHEW 14

Begins with the powerful story of the beheading of John the Baptist. On Herod's birthday, his granddaughter danced for him, so he offered to give her whatever she wanted. She asked for the head of John the Baptist on a platter and her wish was granted.

Jesus feeds 5000 people—one of the great miracles in the Bible for me. This is one of those moments where Jesus gives confidence to us that if we follow him, he will take care of our needs. Jesus says, "Bring them to me." Same thing happens in the next miracle where Jesus walks on water. Jesus says, "Take courage, it is I. Do not be afraid." I love that. Face the world with courage. Jesus is so strategic in term so when and how he demonstrates his divinity to the world that it is watching him.

MATTHEW 15

The pharisees tell Jesus that his disciples break the law when they don't wash their hands before they eat. Jesus said to not confuse the law of God with tradition. He quotes Isaiah by saying:

"These people honor me with their lips
but their hearts are far from me.
they worship me in vain.
their teachings are but rules taught by men."

With Jesus it is all about our heart! This is a common theme that we see throughout the New Testament. **Jesus is begging us to give him our hearts.**

I love what Jesus says next. **It's not what goes into a man's mouth that makes him unclean, it's what comes out of his mouth that makes him unclean.** To me, that means that our words are important, they mean things. They can be used to effectively communicate our ideas, and they can be used to hurt people or lift them up. We need to not say mean things or gossip. "When a blind man leads a blind man, they both will fall into a pit." **Don't follow people who are uniformed or falsely confident.**

Jesus also tells us that it is all about our heart. If our heart is clean our words will be clean as well. Jesus then proceeds to heal the Canaanite woman's daughter and feed the four thousand.

MATTHEW 16

The pharisees and Sadducees demand a sign from heaven from Jesus. He basically says, "back off, no sign will be given". (Except the sign of Jonah). Jesus is not like a magician…..he doesn't perform for applause from the crowds. **He performs to give to Glory to God.**

Jesus shares an important reminder about "teachings". He tells the disciples to be on their guard against the yeast of the pharisees and Sadducees. They ask him if it is because "they bring no bread". He challenges their faith and reminds them that he fed 4000 people with seven loaves and 5000 people with five loaves. He is talking about their "yeast" which is their teachings. **Don't let <u>any</u> false teachings find their way into your life! Because false teachings spread inside of you and become your new reality.** The next section is when Peter acknowledges that Jesus is "the Christ". Jesus tell Peter that "he is blessed, on his rock he will build his church and the gates of hell will not overcome it." I'm still a bit confused on this passage. The Catholic church basically uses this to justify and establish the position of "pope" for 2000 years and I don't think that is Jesus' intent. The Greek word for Peter is "petro" or "rock". So, Jesus was perhaps using that as a connection with Peter. Clearly Paul had a bigger influence on worldwide Christianity than Peter.

The end of chapter 16 is huge. Jesus predicts his death for the first time. Then when Peter says, "This won't happen to you," and Jesus says, "Get behind me Satan". That is a tough quote to stomach. I think Jesus is saying, "don't get in the way of me accomplishing my Father's will."

Jesus' next piece is worth memorizing. "If anyone would come after me, he must deny himself and take up his cross and <u>follow</u> me. For whoever wants to save his life <u>will lose it</u>, but whoever loses his life for me <u>will find it</u>. What good will it be for a man if he gains the whole world and forfeits his soul? Or what can a man give in exchange for his soul? For the son of man is going to come in his father's glory with his angels, and then he will reward each person according to what he has done. I tell you the truth, some who are standing here will not taste death before they see the Son of man coming in his kingdom". **The key to a fulfilling life is having a willingness to to give up your life for a relationship with Jesus and you will be with him forever!**

MATTHEW 17

This is the story of Jesus' transfiguration before his disciples. His face shined like the sun and his cloak became white as snow. A voice came from the clouds and said, "this is my son whom I love, with him I am well pleased". God is professing his love for Jesus to the whole world. He finishes with "listen to me". Jesus proceeds to heal a young boy but it is not without a few slightly confusing passages. A man brings his son to Jesus and says, "Your disciples could not heal him". Jesus seems to be frustrated and says, "How long do I have to put up with this perverse generation". When the disciples ask Jesus why they were unable to drive out the demon, Jesus says, "because you have such little faith. If you have faith as small as a mustard seed, you can move a mountain from here to there. Nothing is impossible." Such a powerful statement about faith.

MATTHEW 18

Jesus tells his disciples that children "are the greatest in the kingdom of heaven." He tells us to humble ourselves like little children. He also tells us to welcome children and to never lead a child to sin. He says the world is full of sin "but woah to the man through whom they come." Don't be a conduit to sin. We have many opportunities to lead people to sin, and many opportunities to lead people away from sin. Choose the latter! Jesus tells a story about how strong his love is for us when he shares the parable of the lost sheep. He reminds us that a shepherd will abandon 99 of his sheep to find the one that is lost. Jesus will always rescue us when we are lost.

Jesus tells us how to handle conflict with a friend. First try to handle it between the two of you, then bring in a fellow believer to mediate, then tell your conflict to the church. Jesus reminds us that wherever two or three are gathered in his name, he is there with us. He also says, "whatever is bound on earth will be bound in heaven, whatever is loosed on earth will be loosed in heaven." For me, this means bind relationships on earth!

Jesus tells the story of the unmerciful servant. **This is a story about forgiveness.** A servant owes his master a lot of money and Jesus says that the master should forgive him 7 x 70 times. The servant went and tried to collect the debts owed to him, but he did it with threats and violence. The master called him out and said, "I gave you a chance, and you didn't give others the same chance." Jesus says, "This is how God will treat each of us." **Show mercy. Forgive each other.**

MATTHEW 19

Jesus reminds us that divorce is wrong, nearly 100% of the time. That is because at the time of marriage God makes two individuals into one, and if God did it, man can't "undo" it. Jesus makes another plea for children, "Let them come to me…for the kingdom of heaven belongs to them."

Understanding the next story can literally change a person's life. It's the story of the rich young man. He asks Jesus what he needs to do to have eternal life. Jesus tells him to obey the commandments, and the rich young man says, "I have done that." Jesus says, "if you want to be perfect, go sell all your possessions and follow me." The man went away because he had great wealth. Jesus explains that it is easier for a camel to go through the "eye of a needle" (gate of a city) than for a rich man to enter the kingdom of God." The disciples ask, "who then can be saved." Jesus tells them that with God, all things are possible. He also issues his decree that at the end of time, the first shall be last, and the last shall be first. All of this is meant to remind us to humbly follow Jesus. Don't aim for "greatness" in this world at the expense of a relationship with Jesus because greatness will come later. **You can have money and power, but it can't be your goal. Your goal must be Jesus. And it's not just about money. It's about any habit, addiction, obsession, or attraction that you have that supersedes Jesus.**

MATTHEW 20

This chapter starts out with one of Jesus' most compelling parables—the worker in the vineyard. A landowner hires some workers in the morning and promises to pay them a "denarius" ($). A little later he hires more, a little later a few more and then hires more at the end of the day. He promised to pay each of them a denarius. When the workers that worked the full day complained that they should be paid more, he said two things:

1) You got what we agreed upon. (We all need to stop worrying about what others "got". It breeds envy and jealousy

21

2) The first shall be last and the last shall be first. There are two powerful messages in this: This is not about working in the vineyard; it is about salvation. Those that believe they are "first" or "righteous" in God's eyes will not be. They will move to the back of the line. And if you come to Jesus at the end of your life—you will be in heaven. **It is <u>never</u> too late to follow Jesus!**

The last story in this chapter is also very powerful. Jesus tells his disciples, "Whoever wants to be great among you must be your servant." I love this so much. Jesus, the Son of God, is all about being a servant. Serve others. Wash their feet. "Give your life as a ransom for many". **This is such a powerful lesson about what it means to follow Jesus. <u>Be last!</u>**

MATTHEW 21

This is the story of Palm Sunday—Jesus' triumphal entry in Jerusalem. Jesus' riding on a donkey as a "gentle king" was fulfillment of Zechariah 5:9. When Jesus reached the temple, he saw all the vendors and money changers and got very angry. He said, "My house is a house of prayer, you are turning it into a den of robbers."

Jesus reminds his disciples of the power of prayer. "If you believe, you will receive what you ask for in prayer". Sometimes I find this very hard to understand. It doesn't seem like our prayers always get answered the way <u>we</u> want them to be. **Regardless, we need to keep praying because the more we do, the more in tune we become with the voice of Jesus.**

While Jesus is in the temple, the chief priests question Jesus, "By what authority are you doing these things?" (miracles). Jesus brilliantly counters with, "Do you think it's from heaven or men?" They say, "We don't know." Jesus says, "Then I'm not going to tell you." Jesus is challenging them to believe!

The parable of the two sons. A father asks his two sons to work in his vineyard. The first said, "No", but went to work. The second said, "Yes", but didn't. Jesus says the father would favor the first son. His point was to remind the people that John the Baptist showed them the way and they did not follow. Prostitutes and tax collectors will enter heaven before them.

Jesus shares a little history with the parable of the tenants. A farmer had a vineyard and he rented it to some tenants. When harvest time came, he sent multiple servants to collect his fruit, but each time the tenants beat and killed the servants. Finally, the landowner sent his son, thinking, "They will never kill my son!" They kill his son.

Jesus quotes the Old Testament and says, "The stone the builders rejected has become the capstone." **He is speaking of the fact that God sent many before Jesus to try to "right the ship". People didn't listen. In essence, they killed God's word so God sent his only Son and you/we rejected that too, and it has become the capstone.**

The Kingdom of God can be taken away from you and given to a people who will produce fruit.

MATTHEW 22

Begins with Jesus' "many are called few are chosen" parable of the wedding banquet. A king invites a whole bunch of people to his son's wedding, but no one comes. He goes to the street corner and invites strangers. Someone shows up not properly dressed and the king throws him out. **I believe this is all about the fact that God has called us to his Son's "wedding" and we must be prepared in every way to celebrate with him.**

The Pharisees challenge Jesus by asking him if it is right to pay taxes to Caesar. Jesus' answer is once again simple and profound, "Give to Caesar what is Caesar's, give to God what is God's." Jesus is in no way against us "supporting" the governments of this world, but he reminds us that we need to give back to God a small percentage of what he gave us, which is everything. **I remember a story that clarifies why we need to give back to God. If someone handed you a dollar and said, "can I have a dime back for some** food?" Would we give it back? The answer is of course, yes. So, if we believe God gave us everything, we should happily give back to him. We need to be a <u>Joyful giver.</u> Jesus shares with the Pharisees the greatest commandment of all, "love the Lord your God with all your heart, all your soul and all your mind. This is the first and greatest commandment. And love your neighbor as yourself." The Pharisees didn't expect Jesus to say what he said. They thought he was going to pull one of the old Jewish laws out as the greatest. Jesus then says, "all the law and the prophets hang on these two commandments." This is so important. **It's the reason that following Jesus is so simple because all he ever asks us to do is love.**

MATTHEW 23

Details Jesus' "seven woes" speech to the disciples and the crowds. This can be a very complex reading and tough to comprehend. This is what I pull from Jesus' message. Don't be a hypocrite. Always practice what you preach. Don't do things for men to see. Do it because it's right. "Whoever exults himself will be humbled. Whoever humbles himself will be exalted." **Always live humbly. Always show the kingdom of God to others and help them get there. Don't swear. Giving money is important but giving mercy, justice and faithfulness is more important. Clean your insides before cleaning your outsides.**

We need to own up to the sins of our past and repent. Be wise to the messengers that God sends to us. I have read the seven woes speech many times, but never did I understand how profound it is until I summarized it in my own words!

MATTHEW 24

Jesus is telling his disciples about the end of time and what it will be like. The descriptions and metaphors are astounding. Jesus reminds his disciples that many false prophets will come in his name, and we need to be on guard against those people. Nation will rise against nation, there will be wars and famine and earthquakes, families and communities will be separated according to who believes and who does not. He reminds us that we will be persecuted for our belief in him. Jesus says, "heaven and earth will pass away but my words will never pass away." He also tells us that we need to be ready for the end of time because we never know when it will be. People do not want to believe this passage. They create a false narrative of what Christianity is. It's whatever they want to believe at that time to "get" what they want from the faith. Jesus warns us against that posture. **The faith is believing in Jesus, doing what he said to do, not creating our version of it, based on what is convenient for us. We need to be very careful about building our faith around what feels good, or what "makes sense" to us. That doesn't make it true. There is a truth in following Jesus, and to twist that truth to make ourselves comfortable is a big mistake.**

Jesus shares two quick parables about this. He says, "like a thief in the night." In other words, if we knew a thief was going to rob us at night, we could "be" ready by locking our doors, etc. He also says that it's like servants working when the master is away. When the master returns, he will find favor among those servants that were working while he was away. We are God's servants, and we need to work for him until Jesus returns. **We need to be always ready by being great followers of Jesus, regardless of the circumstances.**

MATTHEW 25

Every word in this chapter is Jesus speaking. He shares three parables. The first is the parable of the 10 virgins waiting for their bridegroom. Five were foolish and five were wise. The wise ones put oil in their lamps. The bridegroom came at night and the foolish ones had no oil for their lamps. Jesus says, "Keep watch for you do not know the day or the hour." **Once again, Jesus is reminding us that we need be always ready for his second coming.**

Jesus shares the parable of the talents. This story gets misconstrued by a lot of people. Jesus speaks of a master who gives three different servants five, three and one talent. (talent was money, about $1000.) The servants with five and two doubled their talents. The servant with one buried it and gave it back to his master, thinking it would make him happy. The master was angry and said, "You wicked lazy servant." **Jesus is not talking about money, or worldly talents; he is talking about our knowledge of him, and what we do with that knowledge**. That's why he says, "He who has much, will be given more and he who has little, it will be taken away. He is challenging us to always move closer to him. Clearly, he would not take away the provisions of the poor. **We move closer to God, and he allows us to see him clearer.**

Jesus finishes chapter 25 with a timeless message. He says God will separate us into two groups, sheep, and goats. He will say to one group, I was hungry, and you gave me something to eat, and I was thirsty, and you gave me something to drink, I was a stranger and you invited me in, I needed clothes, and you clothed me." They said back to him, "When did we do these things." Jesus says, "Whatever you did for the least of my brothers, you did for me." Most people neglect the second part of the story. He tells the group that did not help him to "get out", make no mistake, we are to help the poor, the hungry and the broken hearted out of love. **And not everyone will be rewarded by God!**

MATTHEW 26

This is a very full chapter, and it begins with a plot to kill Jesus by the chief priests and the elders. Following that, Jesus is blessed with expensive perfume by a woman, at which point Jesus' disciples challenge the situation by saying she could have sold the expensive perfume and given the money to the poor. Jesus tells them, "You will always have the poor, but you will not always have me…this woman was preparing me for burial." Personally, I struggle a little with this passage. I guess it is simply Jesus reminding his followers that "he is God".

Prior to the disciples dining at the last supper Judas makes the deal with the chief priest to hand Jesus over for 30 silver coins. Jesus kicks off the last supper by telling his disciples that one of them is going to betray him.

Jesus tells them all, "For the person who is about to betray me, it would be better for him to have never been born." Jesus shares with them the bread and wine, "This is my blood of the covenant." these are important words that Jesus utters because he goes on to explain that the covenant is the forgiveness of sins. **That is the covenant that he is speaking about. I think he is telling his disciples that this is his final gift of himself to them, and them eating and drinking the wine with him formalizes the covenant. (an agreement)**

Jesus tells peter that Peter will deny his friendship with Jesus three times, and Peter essentially says, "No way, even if I have to die with you, I will never disown you".

Jesus walks out to Gethsemane to pray, and a few important things happen there. He asks his disciples to keep watch with him, but they fall asleep three times. Jesus tells them, "Your mind is willing, but your body is weak." **Note to self: We must keep our bodies strong to carry out the difficult things that our mind wants us to do.**

Jesus also asks God to "Take this cup way from me". **This is a beautiful depiction of Jesus being human. He simply did not want to die but knew that he had to.**

Judas than approaches Jesus along with a large group of people with clubs and swords. What follows is, in my opinion, some of Jesus' finest moments.

First, he doesn't run. When Judas kisses him as a signal to the captors, Jesus just says, "Do what you came for." In other words, "Let's get on with this."

Second, Peter then cuts off a soldier's ear and Jesus says, "put down your sword. If you live by the sword, you will die by the sword." I think this was Jesus' telling Peter how he wanted the Church to be built.

Third, he acknowledges his Father, basically saying, "I could crush these guys if I wanted to." "Do you not think I could call on my Father and he will at once put at my disposal 12 legions of angels?"

Fourth, he challenges them, "Am I leading a rebellion? Every day I sat in the temple teaching, and you didn't arrest me."

Matthew uses some interesting terminology when he describes Jesus in front of Caiaphas, the high priest, and the whole Sanhedrin, which is basically the church leaders. He said, "They were looking for false evidence against Jesus so they could put him to death." **Who looks for false evidence? That implies that they know Jesus was innocent—perhaps they just didn't like him. I just love how cool and collected Jesus is as they are charging him with these crimes, like blasphemy.**

As per Jesus' prediction, Peter denies knowing Jesus (out of fear for his life) three times. The odd thing is Peter doesn't even realize he's doing it until the rooster crows, as Jesus also predicted. **I wonder how many times i have denied being a follower of Jesus and didn't even realize I was doing it.**

MATTHEW 27

Judas tells the high priests that, "He has betrayed innocent blood." The high priests essentially say, "That's your problem, not ours." Judas throws the 30 pieces of silver into the temple and then hangs himself. In a wild twist, the chief priests realize they can't put the money in the church treasury because it's "blood money". So, they used it to buy land, so they had a place to bury dead foreigners. Interestingly, this was foretold by the prophet Jeremiah. When they bring Jesus before pilot, pilot asks him, "Are you the king of the Jews?" Jesus doesn't hesitate and basically says, "I sure am." It's important we remember that this was Jesus, "original king of the Jews". He was sent by God to create a new covenant with his people (the Jews). This covenant was designed to fulfill the old covenant, which is the hundreds of laws in the first five books of the bible. The new covenant was designed to be so much simpler. Admit that you are a sinner. Commit your life to follow Jesus! Simple. But not easy! Pilate read all the charges against Jesus, and Jesus didn't say a word! I think it's because Jesus knows his time was over and it didn't matter. Then a very wild thing happens. It was customary during Passover to release one prisoner to the people. Pilate gives the people a choice: to offer up Jesus or a convicted murderer, Barabbas. The people asked for Barabbas. Pilate weakly gives in, releases Barabbas, and proceeds to have Jesus flogged. **It's kind of pathetic leadership. He knows Jesus is innocent, but literally "washes his hands" of Jesus and hands him over to be killed. He was afraid to do the right thing, which a leader cannot be.** It is so sad to think about what the soldiers due to Jesus next. They mock him, spat on him, strip him, put a crown of thorns on him and mockingly call him king.

The soldiers take Jesus to Golgotha to be crucified. The way this reads in the bible, one would think it was a long way from where they beat him, or where he was interrogated by Caiaphas or Pilate. All these places are within 100 yards of each other. I saw all of them at the Church of the Holy Sepulcher in Jerusalem. The soldiers made bets to see who would get his clothes and they put a sign over his head that said,

"This is Jesus, the King of the Jews". They all made fun of him by saying, "If you are a king, if you are the Son of God, if you could rebuild the temple in three days, then save yourself. As Jesus was dying, darkness came over the land. (This is why people say the weather is always bad on a good Friday, which is untrue.) When he died, the curtain of the temple split in two, the earth shook, rocks split, and dead were raised to life. Finally, the people that were mocking Jesus believed, "surely this was the son of God."

Jesus dying on the cross is the first cornerstone of our faith. (The second being his resurrection). He died to absorb our sins so we could reconcile our relationship with his father. It is the ultimate act of selflessness. The soldiers had Jesus buried in a tomb, but because Jesus predicted his own resurrection, they had the tomb guarded for three days.

MATTHEW 28

On Sunday morning, Mary and Mary Magdalene went to Jesus' tomb. When they arrived, an angel appeared, and the earth shook and frighten the guards. That angel told Mary and Mary Magdalene to look at the tomb and to see that he was gone and then to go tell the disciples that he has risen and gone ahead into galilee. When they left, they ran into Jesus, and he said the very same thing. The guard at Jesus' tomb went and told the chief priests that Jesus had risen from the dead. **They didn't want anyone to know this because that meant Jesus was telling the truth the whole time.** So, they paid the guards large sums of money to stay silent. To this day the Jews believe that Jesus' body was stolen. Jesus met the disciples and provided what is now known as the great commissions. **As followers of Jesus, this is our responsibility!** "All authority on heaven and earth has been given to me. Therefore, go and make disciples of all nations baptizing them in the name of the father, the son in the holy spirit. And teaching them to obey everything I have commanded you and surely, I am with you always to the end of the age!"

This is Jesus' "Great Commission" for his followers. We need to share the good news!

THE GOSPEL OF MARK

The theme of the book of Mark is to introduce Jesus as the Messiah and the authority over all people. The stories shared are very similar to those in Matthew. Matthew was writing to a Jewish audience and his gospel was meant to be a bridge to the Old Testament for the Jewish people. Mark's Gospel was written to a gentile (non-Jewish audience). While Matthew's story begins with the conception and birth of Jesus, Mark starts with John the Baptist.

MARK 1

Mark begins by quoting what is written in Isaiah, "I will send a messenger for you who will prepare your way. A voice calling in the desert. Prepare the way for the Lord. Make straight paths for him."

John the Baptist was a "tough" man. He spent a lot of time in the desert, wore clothes made of camel's hair and ate locusts and wild honey. He spent his time baptizing people in the Jordan River. He preached repentance and forgiveness of sins. His main goal was to defer praise to Jesus, telling everyone, "One is coming who is more powerful than I, whose thong of his sandal I am not fit to stoop down and untie. I baptize you with water, he will baptize you with the Holy Spirit."

I wonder what or who those people thought the Holy Spirit was.

Mark completely skips over Jesus' childhood. He jumps right to John the Baptist baptizing Jesus in the Jordan River. When Jesus comes out of the river, the skies are torn open and God's voice says, "You are my Son, whom

I love, with you I am well pleased. Jesus goes into the wilderness where he is tempted by Satan. Mark does not write in colorful details. He just tells us that Jesus began to proclaim the good news after John was put in prison. Jesus says, "The time has come, the Kingdom of God has come near. Repent and believe the good news."

I have always believed that Jesus is the greatest leader of people of all time. Billions of people have followed his teachings for 2000 years. One of the best examples of this is how he calls his first disciples. When he saw Simon and Andrew fishing, he said, "Come follow me and I will make you fishers of men." **He is directive, strong and very emphatic while being wise enough to speak the language of his audience. "Fishers of men". Brilliant.** James and John were also fisherman. Mark tells us that Jesus called them, and they left their boats, and they also left their father in the boat with the hired help. Without knowing Jesus, they got up and left their families to follow Jesus. It's amazing how fast Mark gets right into Jesus' work on earth—very little build up. He goes right to Jesus preaching in the temple. He also cured a man of impure spirits. Word of Jesus spread very quickly.

Mark is very clear that early in Jesus' ministry he heals many people, including his disciple Simon's mother. He heals many in the town both physically and mentally. Then Jesus does something worth noting—he prays "in a solitary place". **Praying alone is important.** Jesus continues to heal many people including a leper that begs Jesus to heal him. The leper says, "If you are willing, can you make me clean?" Jesus says, "I am willing." Then, "be clean." This is an interesting story because of what happens next. Jesus tells the leper to not tell anyone what happened. He says, "Go show everyone that you are clean as a testimony." I am not sure exactly why Jesus didn't want him to "tell". The next section explains that because the leper did not listen and ended up telling people, such that Jesus could no longer enter bigger towns. Perhaps he wanted to do his work a bit more secretly early in his ministry, even though he didn't go to big towns, people came from everywhere to see him.

Jesus moves on to Capernaum to continue preaching and healing. Capernaum is on the North Shore of the Sea of Galilee. While he is preaching in the synagogue, people come from all over to hear him. Four people try to get a paralytic to Jesus, but they can't get through the crowds. So, they cut a hole in the roof and lower him to Jesus. Jesus says because of their faith, "Your sins are forgiven". It's all about faith. Next comes the calling of Levi, the tax collector. This is an important story. Jesus tells Levi to follow him. Most tax collectors are very corrupt—they are sinners. Then Jesus goes to Levi's house for dinner. The "teachers of the law" question why Jesus eats with sinners. Jesus makes a timelessly profound statement, "It is not the healthy who needed a doctor, I have not come to call the righteous, but sinners." **Jesus is here to help us. We are all sinners. No matter what we have done. No matter how far we have fallen. Jesus is our safety net. At times, when people are at their lowest, they don't feel worthy of praying, or going to Church. Jesus tells us that's when he welcomes us most.**

MARK 2

Finishes with two great stories. The first is some people question why Jesus' disciples are not fasting. he basically tells them, "Because they are with me." He asserts his own divinity. Then he shares this very important metaphor of what it means to be a follower of Jesus. "No one sews a patch of unshrunk cloth on an old garment. If he does the new piece will pull away from the old, making the tear worse. And no one pours new wine into old wineskins. If he does, the wine will burst the skins and both the wine, and the wineskins will be ruined. "No, he pours new wine into new wineskins". **Following Jesus is not a patchwork job. You must give up your whole life, all of you. If you try to put Jesus into one small bucket of your life, it does not work!**

Jesus' disciples saw workers in the field on the Sabbath and they asked Jesus how they can do what is unlawful (work on the Sabbath). Jesus references a story in the Old Testament where a king shares his food with those that are hungry on the Sabbath. He says, "The Sabbath was made for man, not man for the Sabbath. So, the Son of Man is Lord even of the Sabbath." Once again, Jesus is asserting his own divinity to his disciples.

MARK 3

Begins with Jesus healing a man with a shriveled hand. After the Pharisees witnessed this, they began to plot with the Herodians on how to kill Jesus. Mark gets "right to the point" in all his writings. Here we are in chapter 3, and we are already discussing Jesus' death. Jesus then withdrew "lakeside" which is meant to be the Sea of Galilee. Because of what he had done, massive crowds began to follow Jesus. He had his followers prepare a boat for him in case he needed to "not be crowded". Jesus went to a mountainside and appointed his 12 apostles; Simon (Peter), James, John, Andrew, Philip, Bartholomew, Matthew, Thomas, James, Simon the zealot and Judas, who would betray Jesus.

People were following Jesus everywhere. The "teachers of the law" said that "Jesus was possessed by Beelzebub". As usual, Jesus has a brilliant response. When they say, "By the prince of demons, he drives out demons", Jesus says, "How can Satan drive out Satan?" Such a simple and poignant way to respond. He also says, "A kingdom divided against itself cannot stand, and a house divided against itself cannot stand." This has so many applications in life. A quarrel within a Church can bring it down, a divorce within a family can bring it down. Jesus also tells the crowds to "Never blaspheme against the Holy Spirit." Mark closes the chapter with a short reference when Jesus' "Family" arrives. His "mother and brothers" are outside. Jesus says, "Who are my mother and brothers? Whoever does God's will is my brother and sister and mother." **To be a brother to Jesus—do God's will and his work! Follow Him!**

MARK 4

Contains several parables. The first is the parable of the sower. A farmer sows his seed. Some fell on the path and the birds ate it. Some fell on rocky places. Plants sprung up but the sun scorched them because they did not take root. Others fell among the thorns, so the plants were choked. And "still others fell on good soil, it came up and produced a crop, 30, 60, 100 times". Jesus says, "Whoever has ears to hear, let him hear." He then says, "The secret of the kingdom of God has been given to you. But to those on the outside everything is in parables so they may be ever seeing, but never perceiving; ever hearing, but never understanding; Otherwise, they might turn and be forgiven". Jesus explains what he is talking about. **This is all about the word of God. Listen and learn. The seed is the word. Let it fall on good soil. <u>Be</u> the soil. If it falls on the path, Satan will snatch it away. Don't be a fool and let the opportunity to learn the word of God pass by!**

Jesus tells them to make sure to **share the word.** He does that by using the metaphor of the lamp on the stand. He says, "If you have a lamp, do you put it under a bed or a bowl? No…instead you put it on its stand." **We need to be lamps of the word of God, and we need to shine for all to see.**

The parable of the growing seed is so powerful. "This is what the kingdom of God is like. A man scatters a seed on the ground night and day, whether he sleeps or gets up, the seed sprouts and grows though he does not know how. all by itself the soil produces grain, first the stalk, then the head, then the full kernel in the head. as soon as the grain is ripe. He puts the sickle to it because the harvest has come". I love this story so much. **The word of God, the message of the Grace of Christ is so good, so powerful, that it will spread on its own. The plant is a metaphor for people. The word grows people in faith. and the harvest is when God takes his people to heaven.**

Jesus compares the Kingdom of God to a mustard seed, which is the very smallest of seeds that becomes "the largest of all of garden plants". The word of God, the kingdom of God, will grow because of **truth**. Jesus and his disciples left the crowd and went across the Sea of Galilee. A huge wave came on the boat and almost swamped them. The disciples woke Jesus and they said, "Don't you care if we drown." Jesus stood up and said, "Quiet, be still" and the wind died down. Then he said to his disciples, "Why are you so afraid? Do you still have no faith?" The disciples were petrified, and I am perplexed by the next line as they say to each other, "who is this, even the wind and the waves obey him." It's as if they still don't know who Jesus is; maybe they don't.

MARK 5

Begins with a strange story. A wild, demon possessed man, whom they cannot even restrain with chains, approaches Jesus. Jesus says, "come out of that man." The strange part is that Jesus then sends the evil spirits of the group (there were several) into a herd of 2000 pigs. The pigs then ran down the hill into a lake and drowned themselves. The demon possessed man wanted to travel with Jesus, but Jesus told him to go home "and tell your family how much the Lord has done for you, and how he had mercy on you." He did that and the people were amazed. **I love how Jesus wanted to be known for his mercy.**

Mark talks a lot about the large crowds that follow Jesus. A man approached Jesus and told him that his little girl was dying. While they were going to the man's house, another woman approached Jesus from behind. She had been bleeding for 12 years. She simply wanted to get close enough to Jesus to touch his clothes, which she did. Jesus said to her, "daughter, your faith has healed you." He said to the Synagogue ruler, "don't be afraid just believe." I love the combination of these two parts of the story. **1) Just Believe. 2) Just 'come to Jesus'. We need to lay our lives at the feet of Jesus.** Jesus told the girl (who they thought was dead) to get up, and she did. Jesus gave strict orders to the crowd to not tell anyone what they had seen. I think that is because if word got out too quickly, he couldn't finish his work and his teachings.

Jesus and the disciples went back to Nazareth. All the people were questioning what he was doing. They knew he was just a carpenter, but they couldn't believe the wisdom he showed in his teachings. And they couldn't believe the miracles he was doing. and "they laughed at him". Jesus says, "Only in his hometown, among his relatives, and in his own house is a profit without honor. This can be very true in life as well. People who knew you when you were 10, often have a tough time seeing you at 30, especially if you have become successful. Jesus proceeds to go from village to village teaching. He also sends his 12 disciples and gives them power to teach and gives them very specific instruction, "Take nothing for the journey except a staff. No bread, no bag, no money in your belts. Wear sandals, but not an extra tunic. Whenever you enter a house stay there until you leave that town. And if the place does not welcome you, shake the dust off your feet when you leave as testimony against them."

This is a <u>powerful</u> message from Jesus. This is a message about the fact that all we really need is him and his message—take nothing with you. It's a message about the importance of us sharing the good news, and a message about what to do if we are rejected. Move On! Too many souls to be saved!

King Herod heard about all the good works that John the Baptist was doing so he had him arrested. John told Herod that it was unlawful for him to marry his brother Philip's wife, Herodias. So, Herodias held a grudge against John. Herod, on the other hand, feared and protected John. On his birthday, Herod had a banquet at which the daughter of Herodias danced for him, and it pleased him so much that he told her he would give her whatever she wanted. So, she asked her mother Herodias. Her mother said, "the head of John the Baptist." While he did not want to do this, His promise to the girl caused him to carry out this terrible act and he had John beheaded, and the head was presented on a platter.

Remember that Jesus had sent the 12 disciples into the villages to teach. Afterwards, Jesus called the disciples together to rest and eat. They had taught so many people that all of them followed the disciples to their solitary place. The disciples wanted to send the people away to get something to eat in the villages, but Jesus said, "You give them something to eat." They realized that it would cost eight months wages to feed that many people. So, the disciples gathered all the food they could from the crowd—five loaves of bread and two fish. All 5000 people ate until they were satisfied, and the remaining leftovers filled 12 baskets because of the miracle Jesus just performed.

Jesus disbursed the crowd and sent the disciples in a boat across the Sea of Galilee. The Sea of Galilee is not as big as most people think—only 8 miles x 13 miles. I saw this with my own eyes when I stood on the shore of the Sean on my trip to Israel. In the middle of the night, Jesus saw them straining at the oars because it was windy, So he walked on the water to reach them. The disciples were terrified. **He said, "Take courage, it is I. Do not be afraid." Jesus consistently encouraged his disciples to not be afraid. The number of times he said, or referenced "don't be afraid" is enormous. We need to remember to say that when we see Jesus working in our lives. He's got us.**

They landed their boat in Gennesaret, and the people there recognized Jesus. They ran throughout their villages and carried their sick on mats to wherever he was. They begged him to heal their sick and all who touched him were healed.

MARK 7

The Pharisees saw Jesus' disciples eating food with "unclean hands". This kicked off a powerful exchange with them. He tells them that Isaiah was right when he wrote in 29:13, "These people honor me with their lips, but their hearts are far from me. They worship me in vain. Their teachings are but rules taught by men". Then he says, "you have let go of the commands of God and are holding on to the traditions of men." He explains, "Listen to me, everyone, and understand this. Nothing outside a man can make him unclean by going into him. RATHER, IT IS WHAT COMES OUT OF A MAN THAT MAKES HIM UNCLEAN…FOR FROM WITHIN, OUT OF MEN'S HEARTS, COME EVIL THOUGHTS, SEXUAL IMMORTALITY, THEFT, MURDER, ADULTERY, GREED, MALICE, DECEIT, LEWDNESS, ENVY, SLANDER, ARROGANCE, AND FOLLY."

Jesus' main message is so clear. Keep your heart clean!!

7:24-30, Mark relays a story that I do not understand. A woman begs Jesus to rid her daughter of a demon. Jesus says, "first let the children eat. It's not right to toss the children's bread to the dogs. The woman responds, "But even the dogs under the table eat the children's crumbs." Jesus says, "For such a reply, you may go, the demon has left your daughter." This is one of those stories that I cannot find meaning.

MARK 8

Begins with a crowd of 4000 people following Jesus for three days with no food. He was concerned that if he sent them home to eat, they would collapse on the way. He told his disciples to gather up the seven loaves they had along with "a few small fish". After they all ate, the disciples gathered up seven baskets of broken pieces of bread. The pharisees questioned Jesus and tested him by asking him for a sign from heaven. Jesus said, "Why does this generation ask for a sign? I tell you the truth, no sign will be given." **I love the fact that he says, "this generation". This story could be written <u>today</u>.**

As they got to the other side of the Sea of Galilee, the disciples got out the one loaf of bread. Jesus says, "be careful—watch out for the yeast of the pharisees and that of Herod." The disciples were confused and thought it was because "they had no bread". Jesus says, "why are you talking about having no bread? Do you still not see or understand? Are your hearts hardened? Do you have eyes but fail to see? And ears but fail to hear?" He challenges them to remember feeding 4000 and 5000 people.

"Do you still not understand?" I love how Jesus speaks in parables and challenges them to understand, but more importantly, always challenges them to <u>think</u>. The <u>yeast</u> of the pharisees is false teaching. If it gets in your mind and your heart, you will be contaminated. Do not let false teachings into you. **Only the yeast of Jesus can feed 9000 people.**

The next two passages end the same way—with Jesus telling people to not tell anyone about him. The first one is after Jesus heals a blind man; he tells the man to "not go into the village". Jesus and his disciples were traveling through the villages, and he asks them, "Who do people say I am?" They replied, "Some say john the Baptist, others say Elijah, and still others say one of the prophets." Jesus asks, "But what about you, who do you say I am?" Peter answered, "You are the Christ." Jesus warned them not to tell anyone about him. I think this is all about Jesus knowing that the sooner the leaders started hearing the things that Jesus was doing, the sooner they would put a stop to it. Which is exactly what is about to happen as the next passage describes Jesus predicting his own death.

Jesus tells his disciples that he is going to have to suffer many things by the elders, chief priests and teachers of the law. He will be killed and three days later he will rise again. Peter pulls him aside and "rebukes him" and is basically saying these things cannot and will not happen. Jesus' response is harsh, but important. He says, "Get behind me Satan. You <u>do not</u> have in mind the things of God, but the things of men." This is important because Jesus <u>knows</u> he needs to go through this death and resurrection to fulfill God's promise and to establish the covenant. His disciples don't understand that…yet. He is warning Peter to not question him. Then Jesus utters some of the most important words in the bible:

"If anyone would come after me, he must deny himself and take up his cross and follow me. Whoever wants to save his life will lose it. But whoever loses his life for me and for the gospel will save it. What good is it for a man to gain the whole world yet forfeit his soul? Or what can a man give in exchange for his soul. If anyone is ashamed of me and my words in this adulterous and sinful generation, the Son of Man will be ashamed of him when he comes in his father's glory with the holy angels."

This is just so important. If we chase only earthly riches, we will lose our soul which is only found in Jesus. We need to seek him in every part of

our life. We need to be willing to give it all up for him and to follow him with total confidence that he is the way to salvation! Is Jesus' name on the jersey that I wear every day? Am I proud of that jersey?

MARK 9

Begins with the story of Jesus' transfiguration. Jesus took Peter, James, and John high on a mountain. At that moment, his clothes became "dazzling white" and he was there with Moses and Elijah. They heard God's voice say, "This is my Son whom I love. Listen to him." Such powerful words! Suddenly they only saw Jesus, they could no longer see the other two. When they came down the mountain, Jesus told them not to tell anyone what they saw until he had risen from the dead. Peter, James, and John did keep the matter to themselves, but they did not understand what rising from the dead meant.

Jesus came upon a large crowd that was arguing about the fact that Jesus' disciples could not drive out an evil spirit from a man's son. Jesus says a few poignant things before he heals the boy. "Oh, unbelieving generation. How long shall I stay with you. How long shall I put up with you. Bring the boy to me." The father says, "...if you can do anything..." Jesus quickly rebuts him by saying, "If you can? Everything is possible for him who believes."

The boy was healed, and the disciples asked Jesus, "Why couldn't we drive it out?" Jesus' response is so thought-provoking. He says, "This kind can only be driven out with prayer." Wow, the power of prayer. Once again Jesus did not want anyone to know where they were. He tells them, "The son of man is going to be betrayed into the hands of men. They will kill him and after three days he will rise." The disciples were afraid to ask him to explain it.

I love the story about what happens on the way to Capernaum. The disciples are arguing about "who is the greatest". I assume this means "the greatest disciple". Because Jesus explains it like this, "If anyone wants to be first, he must be the very last. And the servant of all." He took a little child in his arms and said, "whoever welcomes one of these little children in my name, welcomes me. And whoever welcomes me does not welcome me, but the one who sent to me." **This is so beautiful because Jesus is both describing being a servant leader—serve others, and the importance of serving of the young, the weak, the small and the poor.**

John informs Jesus that someone is driving out demons, but he is "not one of us". Jesus tells him to "let him do it, no one who does a miracle in my name can in the next moment say anything bad about me. For whoever is not against us, Is for us. I tell you the truth, anyone who gives you a cup of water in my name, will not lose his reward." **Do things in Jesus' name!**

Jesus continues in his discussion of little children, "If anyone causes one of these little ones to sin it is better for him to be thrown into the sea with a large millstone tied around his neck. If your hand causes you to sin, cut it off. It is better for you to enter life maimed than with two hands to go into hell where the fire never goes out." Jesus says the same thing about your eyes and feet. Then he says something <u>so important,</u> "Salt is good, but if it loses saltiness, how can you make it salty again? Have salt in yourselves and be at peace with each other." Jesus is talking about "living with the spirit". **When it gets <u>in you</u> don't lose it. Keep the saltiness in every fiber of your being. The saltiness is the Holy Spirit!**

MARK 10

Jesus gives us some very clear direction about divorce. The Pharisees asked him if it's legal for man to divorce his wife. He asked them what Moses said, to which they replied," Moses permitted a man to write a certificate of divorce and send her away." Jesus said, "It's because your hearts were hard that he wrote that law. At the beginning of creation God made the male and female. For this reason, a man will leave his father and mother and be united to his wife and the two will become one flesh. So, they are no longer two, but one. Therefore, what God has joined together let man not separate." Jesus explains that those who divorce and remarry commit adultery. This is one of those things Jesus says that is crystal clear. God makes you <u>one</u>—so it cannot be separated. (**Remember: What God has joined, man cannot separate**)

Jesus is surrounded by a bunch of children and the disciples prevented them from touching Jesus. He rebuked them and said, "Let the Little children come to me...the kingdom of heaven belongs to such as these." Jesus took the kids in his arms and blessed them. This is such a beautiful picture of who Jesus is!

The rich young man is such a powerful story. A man asks Jesus what he needs to do to inherit eternal life. Jesus recites some of the commandments to him and the man says, "Teacher, all of these I have kept since I was a boy." Jesus "looked at him and loved him", then he said, "one thing you lack—go sell everything and give to the poor. Then you will have treasure in heaven. Then come follow me." The man looked down and went away because he was wealthy and could not give it all up for Jesus. Can't you just see Jesus "looking at him and loving him" in a fatherly way. **He's looking at the man knowing he is about to tell him something that he is not ready to hear. Am I ready to hear this message? Would I sell everything to follow Jesus?**

Jesus asks the children, "How hard is it for the rich to enter the kingdom of God?" Jesus says, "it is easier for the camel to go through the eye of the needle then for a rich man to enter the kingdom of heaven." The eye of the needle is not literal, it refers to the gate into the city. These two passages are related. It's not because a man is rich that makes it difficult to get into heaven, it's because he may not be willing to give it up. We need to sacrifice everything for God.

The disciples remind Jesus that they have left everything to follow him, and he tells them that anyone who is willing to sacrifice all, will inherit eternal life. He says, "Many who are first will be last, and the last first." **This is Jesus telling us, once again, to not seek earthly riches or accolades because they mean nothing at the throne.**

Be a servant, subjugate to yourself to people to share the good news. Jesus also says, "with man this is impossible…all things are possible with God."

This theme of "being last" continues when James and John ask Jesus, "to be at your right and your left in the glory." This was right after Jesus again predicted his death to them. Jesus tells them, "Those places are not for me to grant." Then he gathers them altogether and says, "whoever wants to become great among you must be your servant. And whoever wants to be first must be a slave to all. For even the son of man did not come to be served, but to serve, and to give his life as a ransom for many."

This passage is <u>so important</u>. This is why I follow Jesus. Because he tells us to <u>serve</u> each other. And he reminds us that his whole existence is an act of service by giving his life for our salvation! He is God, but he is also the greatest servant who ever lived.

Mark 10 ends with Jesus and his disciples on their way to Jericho and they are approached by a blind man. Jesus heals his blindness and says, "Your faith has healed you!"

MARK 11

The story of Jesus' triumphal entry into Jerusalem is the story of "Palm Sunday". Jesus instructed his disciples to go ahead of him and retrieve a specific "Colt" for him to ride into the city. As he did so, people laid cloaks on the ground for the Colt to walk on and shouted, "blessed is he who comes in the name of the Lord." It's a beautiful picture of them welcoming him into the city. The next day, Jesus got to the temple area and saw all the vendors and moneychangers. (To this day the streets of "the old city" are full of street vendors.) This is the one story where it appears Jesus lost his temper. He overturned their tables and forbade them from carrying merchandise through the temple. He said, "Is it not written my house will be called a house of prayer for all nations. But you have made it a den of robbers." When the chief priests heard this, they looked for a way to kill him, because the whole crowd was amazed by him. In the morning, as they were walking, they came upon a fig tree that they had seen the day before. When Jesus saw it again prior, he cursed it because he was hungry, and it had no fruit. This day, the tree had withered, and the disciples were amazed. Jesus uses this as an opportunity to teach about prayer. "Whatever you ask for in prayer, believe that you have received it and it will be yours. And when you stand praying, if you hold anything against anyone, forgive him, so that your Father in heaven may forgive your sins".

The power of prayer is incredible. I think Jesus is telling us to make sure our posture before God is right when we pray—our mental/heart posture. God doesn't seem to always give us what we want, but he does give us what we need. That's why we must always submit to his grace and his will. The power of forgiveness is life changing. While it is good for the person we forgive, the magic of forgiveness is that the forgiver wins, because his heart gets changed and he/she can love again. And that is what Jesus asked us to do.

When they arrive in Jerusalem, the chief Priests approached Jesus and asked him, "By what authority are you doing these things? And who gave you the authority to do these things?" Jesus says to them, "Answer me one question. John's baptism…was it from heaven or men?" They said, "We don't know." Jesus said, "Neither will I tell you by what authority I'm doing these things!"

I think what Jesus is telling them, or thinking is, "The fact that you don't know/believe that I'm from heaven prevents me from telling you the rest of the story." He wanted to see their faith!"

MARK 12

Begins with the same story that it is in Matthew 21—the story of the master who had planted a vineyard and rented it to some tenants. at harvest time, the owner sent a servant to collect from them, but they beat him up and killed him. This happened multiple times. The farmer thought that if he sent his only son, they surely would not beat and kill him, but they did. Jesus is telling this story to the chief priests, Etc. Then he says to them, as it is written (psalm 118:22):

The stone the builders rejected
has become the cornerstone.
the lord has done this
and it is marvelous in our eyes.

Jesus is telling them: my Father sent prophet after prophet, and you rejected them. Then he sent me, his one and only Son, and you are rejecting me. I am the cornerstone. The chief priests and elders knew he was talking about them, so they looked for a way to arrest him. They were afraid of the crowds following Jesus, so they went away.

The next story is another repeat from Matthew— the story of paying taxes to Caesar. The Pharisees and Herodians said, "teacher we know that you are a man of integrity. You aren't swayed by others because you pay no attention to who they are: But you teach the way of God in accordance with the truth. Is it right to pay the Imperial tax to Caesar or not? Should we pay, or shouldn't we?" This was all a scam, a lie. They were trying to trick Jesus into saying, "Don't pay tax to Caesar" Because they wanted to arrest him for rebelling against the Roman Empire. Jesus stopped them in their tracks. He said, "why are you trying to trick me? Whose picture is on the denarius (coin)…pay to Caesar what is Caesar's, pay to God what is God's." The Bible says, "They were amazed at him." I think they were mainly amazed that he caught them in their trickery.

The Sadducees question Jesus about what will happen when we die— who will be with whom (marriage). Once again, he calls them out for their lack of knowledge of Scripture (exodus)—He says everyone will be angels in heaven. Then one of the <u>all-important</u> scripture passages occurs. One of the teachers says to Jesus, "of all the Commandments, which is the most import-ant one?" **Jesus says, "Love the Lord your God with all your heart, with all your soul, with all your mind and with all your strength. The second is this: Love your neighbor as yourself. There is no greater commandment than these." Think about those words! This is why I say that following Jesus is so simple. That is all he asks us to do. Those are his laws. Love. It covers everything.**

Jesus says to them, "Watch out for teachers of the law. They like to walk around in flowing robes and be greeted with respect in the marketplace. And they have the most important seats in the synagogue and places of honor at banquets. They devour widows houses (think about that) and for a show, make lengthy prayers. These men will be punished most severely." This is an important passage. What he was saying was true 2000 years ago, and it is even more true now. The damage that has been done by false prophets and criminal clergy is horrific. **Watch closely what leaders say and do, because not all of them are real.**

I love the last story of Mark 12. Jesus was in the temple where people were giving their offerings. While the rich people gave large amounts, a poor widow put it in a few cents. Jesus tells his disciples, "Truly I tell you; this poor woman has put more money in the treasury then all the others. They gave out of their wealth but she, out of her poverty, put in everything, all she had to live on." **What we give back to God (it's all his to start) is a measurement of our heart for him. And he sees it. He doesn't need our money. He needs the heart of our best self.**

MARK 13

A short but extremely powerful chapter—it is Jesus telling his disci-ples about the end of time. It begins when they're leaving the temple and the disciples are marveling about all the "Great buildings". Jesus says, "Not one stone will be left on another. Everyone will be thrown down." Peter, James, John, and Andrew asked him, "When will these things happen? And what will be the sign that they are about to be fulfilled?" These are the things that Jesus said about the end of time:

1) Watch out that no one deceives you. Many will come in my name claiming, "I am he" and will deceive many.

2) When you hear of wars and rumors of wars do not be alarmed. Such things must happen, but the end is still to come.

3) Nation will rise against nation, and kingdom against kingdom.

4) There will be earthquakes in various places. these are the beginnings of birth pains.

5) You must be on your guard. You will be handed over to the local councils and flogged in the synagogues.

6) On account of me you will stand before governors and kings as witnesses to them.

7) The gospel must be preached to all nations.

8) Whenever you are arrested and brought to trial do not worry about what to say. Just say whatever is given to you at the time, for it is not you speaking, but the Holy Spirit.

9) Brother will betray brother to death, and a father, his child. Children will rebel against their parents and have them put to death.

10) Everyone will hate you because of me but the one who stands firm to the end will be saved.

11) When you see "the abomination" that causes desolation, standing where it does not belong, let the reader understand—then let those who are in Judea flee to the mountains.

12) Let no one on the house top go down or enter the house to take anything out. Let no one in the field go back for their cloak.

13) How dreadful this will be for nursing mothers.

14) Pray this will not take place in winter. Because those will be days of distress equaled from the beginning when God created the world, until now, and never will be equaled again.

15) If the Lord had not cut short those days no one would survive, but for the sake of the elect whom he has chosen, he has alas shortened them. At that time if anyone says to you, "here is the Messiah" or look "here he is", do not believe him. For false messiahs and false prophets Will appear and perform signs and wonders to deceive.

16) Be on your guard. **I told you everything ahead of time.**

17) But in those days, the sun will be darkened, and the moon will not give its light. The stars will fall from the sky and the heavenly bodies Will be shaken.

18) At that time people will see the son of man coming in clouds with Great power and glory. And he will send his angels and gather his elect from the four winds from the ends of the earth to the end of the heavens.

Jesus tells them, "Heaven will pass away, but my words will never pass away. He tells them to keep Watch because you just don't know when this will happen.

I essentially rewrote chapter 13 verbatim because almost the entire chapter is Jesus' words. **This is why I say following Jesus is <u>simple but not easy</u>! It is costly, and we need to be willing to sacrifice everything and everyone to follow him! And while it sounds like a sacrifice (it is), the payoff is enormous. We get peace on earth and eternity in heaven for our faith.**

MARK 14

Jesus was in Bethany two days before the Passover celebration. The chief priests were scheming to arrest Jesus and kill him. They didn't want to do it during Passover because they felt people would riot. Jesus was eating at Simon the leper's house when a woman approached him and poured expensive perfume on his head. Some of the people there were upset because they felt the perfume could be sold to give the money to the poor. Jesus says, "Why are you bothering her. She has done a beautiful thing. The poor you will always have with you, and you can help them anytime you want, but you will not always have me. She did what she could, she poured perfume on my body beforehand to prepare for my burial. Truly I tell you, whenever the gospel is preached throughout the world, what she has done will also be told, in memory of her." And Jesus was right. This is the story of "Jesus anointed at Bethany" that has stood the test of time.

Mark does not go into as much detail about Judas' betrayal of Jesus. He just says, "Judas went to the chief priests to betray Jesus. They were delighted to give him money."

The Last Supper

Jesus sends two of his disciples ahead of the group and tells them that they will find a man carrying a jar of water and instructs them to ask that man to prepare a place for them to celebrate Passover.

How did Jesus know that man would be there? Jesus begins the dinner by telling the disciples that one of them will betray him and they all say, "Surely not!" He continues, "Woe to the man who betrays the Son of Man. It would be better for him if he had never been born." Jesus took bread and said, "take it; this is my body." Then he took a cup and gave thanks. He gave it to them and said," this is my blood of the covenant which is poured out for many. Truly I tell you I will not drink again from the fruit of the vine until that day when I drink it new in the Kingdom of God."

What strikes me about Jesus' words here is the depth he goes into to explain the wine and not the bread. **Everything Jesus did was about establishing a new covenant (agreement) between God and his people. He reconciled us to God by dying and proved his divinity by rising from** the dead. If he didn't rise, he could have just been a man who was a good teacher. Jesus' comments about his blood explain everything. C.S. Lewis brilliantly wrote that Jesus was either a liar, a lunatic or Lord. Jesus said he was God. Which means if he wasn't he wasn't lying. Or he was crazy. Or he really was. He was much more than a great teacher.

MARK 15

Mark's version of Jesus going on trial in front of Pilate. As is typical for Mark (in my opinion), his version is less colorful, just very fact-based. Pilate asks Jesus, "Are you king of the Jews?" Jesus responds, "You have said so." Pilate continues to ask Jesus questions such as, "Do you know how many things they are accusing you of?" Just as Matthew, Jesus does not reply; he just stands there quietly and confidently. I think he did that because he knew what was going to happen and because I think he wanted to demonstrate that **HIS SPIRIT is impenetrable**—you can't get to him. "Pilate was amazed". It is customary at the time of the festival to release one prisoner at people's request. They asked for Barabbas to be released. Pilate asked if they wanted Jesus "the King of the Jews" and then Mark inserts a very interesting commentary. He says, "Knowing it was out of self- interest that the chief priests had handed Jesus over to him." This is all about the fact that Jesus was teaching a "new covenant of love". **Jesus taught following him vs. the traditional Jewish law that the chief priests were teaching and that was very threatening to them.**

Jesus was flogged and was handed over to be crucified. One of the most moving travel experiences I have ever had was walking through the Church of the Holy Sepulcher in Jerusalem. That is where Jesus stood trial, was beaten, crucified, and buried. It was beyond moving to stand where all of that occurred. This is what happened to Jesus: They put a robe on him to mock his Kingship, they put a crown of thorns on his head, they hit him on the head with a staff to make sure the crown "stuck", they spit on him, then they "fake worshiped him" and lead him off to be crucified. **It really happened.**

Surprisingly, where Jesus is crucified is very close (100-200 feet) from where he was beaten. And his burial was also about the same distance. They put a sign on his cross that read "King of the Jews". They hung "two rebels" along with Jesus, but Mark's version does not tell the story of the one rebel being saved because of his faith in Jesus before dying, which is a beautiful depiction of the fact that it is never to be saved by faith in Jesus.

The crowd said to Jesus, "So! You who are going to destroy the temple and rebuild it in three days, come down from that cross and save yourself." "He saved others, but he can't save himself". **Little do they know that he was saving everyone.**

Mark says, "At noon, darkness came over the whole land." Jesus cried out, "Eloi eloi lama Sabachthani" which means "my God, my God. Why have you forsaken me". With a loud cry "Jesus breathed his last".

When he died the curtain of the temple was torn in two from top to bottom and a centurion said, "surely this man was the Son of God."

Joseph of Arimathea, a prominent member of the council, asked Pilate for Jesus' body. Pilate was surprised that Jesus was already dead. Joseph wrapped Jesus' body in linen cloth, placed it in a tomb "cut of rock" and then he rolled a stone against the entrance of the Tomb.

MARK 16

Mary Magdalene, Mary the mother of James and Salome, (Salome was the wife of Zebedee and Mother of James and John) went to the tomb to anoint Jesus' body. When they got there, the stone had already been rolled away. A young man was dressed in a white robe and was sitting on the right side. They were alarmed. "don't be alarmed, you are looking for Jesus the Nazarene. He is risen. He is not here. See the place where they laid him. But go, tell his disciples and Peter, "he is going ahead of you into Galilee. There you will see him, just as he told you." Trembling, the women left and told no one because they were afraid.

Footnote: the earliest manuscripts end at the sentence above. This is obviously a very anticlimactic version of Jesus' resurrection. It is very abrupt and awkward. The consensus among biblical scholars is that versus 9-20 were added by scribes after Mark's original gospel was written by him. The writing style is very different. The transition from 8-9 does not flow, and there are 18 words in 9-20 that Mark does not use anywhere else in his gospel. In chapter 19, Jesus is referred to as "Lord God". Mark never referred to Jesus as such. Also, in 17 and 18 there is a reference to "sons" and that does not appear anywhere else in the four gospels.

I will summarize 19-20 below and perhaps I will be able to show some inconsistencies.

Verse 9 is almost a repeat of verse 1 only it is disconnected. It says that Jesus appeared to Mary Magdalene, and she went and told Jesus' friends. (In verse eight, it says they told no one) chapter 12 says he appeared in a "different form to two of them. They were returned and told the 'Rest'. Jesus found the 11 disciples eating and he got mad at them for their lack of faith and stubbornness and refusal to believe those who had seen him after he had risen. This is what Jesus said, "go to all the world and preach the gospel to all creation. Whoever believes and is baptized will be saved but whoever does not believe will be condemned and these signs will accompany those who believe: In my name they will drive out demons, they will speak in new tongues, they will pick up snakes with their hands and when they drink deadly poison it will not hurt them at all, they will place their hands on sick people and they will get well. After he said that, he was taken up to heaven and he sat at the right hand of God. The disciples went out and preached everywhere.

Every person has a different view of their favorite gospel. Mine is not Mark. I find his delivery of the story of Jesus far less colorful and not inspiring as the others. It is very clear (after studying 9-20) that those verses were written by someone else. To me, those don't sound like words that Jesus would say. **However, learning that was inspiring in <ins>itself</ins>!**

THE GOSPEL OF LUKE

I love Luke's version of the story of Jesus. He is a very visual writer and paints vivid pictures of Jesus' Ministry. The theme of his gospel is to ensure everyone knows that **Jesus is the Savior of the world.**

LUKE 1

Luke begins by telling us that many people have "undertaken to draw up an account of the things that have happened and have been fulfilled among us". He assures us that he has personally investigated everything. Luke dedicated and/or wrote his gospel to a man named Theophilus, who was probably a Roman officer.

A man named Zechariah was married to a woman named Elizabeth. They had no children because Elizabeth could not conceive. Zechariah was in the temple and an angel of the Lord appeared to him. The angel said, "Do not be afraid, Zechariah, your prayer has been heard. Your wife Elizabeth will bear you a son, and you are to call him John." The angel tells him what a joy John will be, and he will "be Great in the sight of the Lord." He lets them know that he will be filled with the spirit, will bring people to God, and will go on before the Lord. This was the beginning of the story of John the Baptist.

In the sixth month of Elizabeth's pregnancy God sent the same angel Gabriel to a virgin named Mary who was pledged to marry a man named Joseph. Gabriel said to her, "do not be afraid Mary, you have found favor with God. you will conceive and give birth to a son. And you are to call him Jesus.

He will be great, and he will be called son of the most high. The Lord will give him the throne of his father David and will reign over Jacob's descendants forever. His kingdom will never end." These are important words to describe everything that will happen in Jesus' Life. Mary was confused because she was a virgin. Gabriel tells her, "The Holy Spirit will come upon you." He says, "No word from God will ever fail." Mary responded beautifully, "I am the Lord's servant, may your word to me be filled." For me, this is a beautiful depiction of who Mary was. She was not God, not divine, but a very Godly person.

Mary visits Elizabeth. Upon greeting her, the baby leaped in Elizabeth's womb. Mary then said to Elizabeth (this is commonly referred to as "Mary's song".):

"My soul glorifies the Lord, and my spirit rejoices in God my Savior, for he has been mindful of the humble state of his servant. From now on all generations will call me blessed, for the Mighty one has done great things for me. (This is a very important verse. Mary is calling herself blessed because of what God has done for her, not because of what she has done.) Holy is his name. His mercy extends to those who fear him, from generation to generation. He has performed Mighty deeds with his arm.

He has scattered those who are proud in their innermost thoughts. He has brought down rulers from their thrones but has lifted up the humble. He has filled the hungry with good things but has send the rich away empty. He has helped his servant Israel, remembering to be merciful to Abraham and his descendants forever, even as he said to our fathers".

After Mary had been with Elizabeth for about three months she returned home. Then Elizabeth gave birth to a son. The neighbors wanted to name the baby boy Zechariah. Elizabeth spoke up and said, "His name is John." They asked Zechariah what he thought the boy's name should be. To their surprises, he wrote on a tablet, "His name is John". Zechariah was filled with the Holy Spirit and prophesied beautifully about his son. The final words of the prophecy were "and you, my child, will be called a prophet of the most high; for you will go on before the Lord to prepare the way for him, to give his people THE <u>knowledge of salvation</u> through the forgiveness of their sins, because of the tender mercy of our God, by which the rising sun will come to us from heaven to shine on those living in darkness and in the shadow of death to guide our feet into the path of peace".

This prophecy by John the Baptist's father is an important statement about his son's role in Jesus' beautiful story.

LUKE 2

This is one of <u>the</u> most recognizable chapters in the Bible. It is a story of the birth of Jesus. Matthew and Luke are the only ones that begin with the birth of Jesus and Luke provides a much more detailed and vivid picture of the occurrence of events. This is the version that is most often read in churches on Christmas.

"In those days Caesar Augustus issued a decree that a Census should be taken of the entire Roman world. This was the first census that took place while Quirinius was governor of Syria, and everyone went to his town to register. So, Joseph also went up from the town of Nazareth in Galilee to Judea, to Bethlehem, because he belonged to the house of David. He went there to register with Mary who was pledged to be married to him and was expecting a child. While they were there the time came for the baby to be born and she gave birth to her firstborn, a son she wrapped in clothes and placed him in a manger because there was no room for them in the inn.

And then there were shepherds living out in the fields nearby keeping watch over their flocks at night. An angel of the Lord appeared to them in the glory of the Lord shone around them, and they were terrified. But the angel said to them, 'do not be afraid, I bring you good news of great joy that will be for <u>all</u> people. Today, in the town of David, a Savior has been born to you. He is the Christ, the Lord. This will be a sign to you: You will find a baby wrapped in cloths, lying in a manger". Suddenly a great company of the heavenly host appeared with the angel, Praising God and saying,

> "Glory to God in the highest heaven,
> and on earth peace to men on whom
> his favor rests".

The story of Jesus' birth is so beautiful it is almost reminiscent of a song or poem. I love to read it on Christmas morning. As Luke says, "This is good news for <u>all</u> people."

When the angels left, the shepherds agreed they needed to go to Bethlehem to "see this thing that has happened". Eight days after Jesus was born, Mary and Joseph took him to Jerusalem to "be presented to the Lord" and be circumcised.

A man named Simeon, who was a good man, was told by the Holy Spirit that he would not die before he had seen "the Lord Christ". Simeon took Jesus in his arms and said:

> "Sovereign Lord, as you have promised,
> you now dismiss your servant in peace.
> for my eyes have seen your salvation,
> which you have prepared in the sight of all
> people: A light for revelation to
> the Gentiles, and for glory to
> your people Israel".

Mary and Joseph marveled at what he said. Then Simeon said, "This child is destined to cause the falling and rising of many in Israel, and to be a sign that will be spoken against, so that the thoughts of many hearts will be revealed. And a sword will pierce your own soul too."

He had to be referring to when the soldiers stab Jesus on the cross. That must be like a "soul piercing" for a parent.

Luke's story jumps to Jesus when he was 12 years old. Mary and Joseph went to Jerusalem to celebrate Passover. When they left to return home, they did not realize that Jesus had stayed behind. They had traveled a full day before they realized he was not with them. After three days of searching, they found him in the temple courts. He was listening to the teachers and asking them questions. The people were amazed at his understanding. Mary told him how worried they were. Jesus said, "Why were you searching for me? Didn't you know I had to be in my Father's house?" They didn't understand. They returned to Nazareth and "Jesus grew in wisdom and in favor with God and men".

John the Baptist prepares the way

LUKE 3

John the Baptist was in the desert and the Word of God came to him. He traveled in the areas that were all around the Jordan River. He was preaching "a baptism of repentance for the forgiveness of sins". He was quoting Isaiah:

"A voice of one calling in the desert,
Prepare the way for the Lord,
make straight paths for him.
every valley shall be filled in,
Every mountain and hill made low.
The crooked roads shall become straight,
and all mankind will seek God's salvation".

Crowds of people came to be baptized by him. John scolded them, telling them that they need to behave properly and act in accordance with God's will. He tells them, "The man with two tunics should share with the man who has none, and the one who has food should do the same". He tells the tax collectors to not collect more money than they should (this was very common) and he told the soldiers to not extort money or accuse them falsely. "Be content with your pay".

Because of how powerfully John the Baptist was preaching, many thought he could be the Christ. John basically told him, "No way". "I baptize you with water. But one more powerful than I will come, the thongs of whose sandals I am not worthy to untie. He will baptize you with the Holy Spirit and with fire. His winnowing fork is in his hand to clear his threshing floor and to gather the wheat into his barn, and he will burn up the chaff with unquenchable fire."

John is illustrating how God/ Jesus will select their believers when that time comes. A winnowing fork is a pitchfork, and the process of winnowing is raising the wheat up in the air with a fork. The "chaff" is a lighter and blows away in the wind and the wheat (for food) falls to the ground. John is using this analogy because the crowds Understand it. The chaff will blow away in the wind and be burned. **The wheat will be gathered up by God and taken home with him and that is the followers of Jesus. Unfortunately, this is the flip side of the grace of God. If we choose not to accept his grace, we will most certainly end up in a very bad place. But he gave us the answer. We've all heard the question "Why would a kind and merciful God send people to hell". The best answer I have heard is "God doesn't send anyone to hell. We are going there because of our sinful nature. God gave us a way out".**

Jesus was baptized by John with all the people. When this occurred "the Holy Spirit descended on him in body form like a Dove. And a voice came from heaven: 'You are my Son, whom I love; with you I am well pleased'".

Luke tells us that Jesus begins his ministry at age 30. It also then traces his genealogy all the way back to Adam.

Interestingly, the genealogy that is traced in this version it Is different than the one in Matthew. The lists differ in many ways. Matthew starts with Abraham and continues to Jesus. Luke starts with Jesus and goes back to Adam. Matthew has 27 generation from David to Joseph. Luke has 42. Importantly they disagree on who Joseph's father was. Matthew says it was Jacob, Luke says Heli. There are many "theories" that try to explain the differences in the two genealogies....those theories are beyond the purpose of this book!

LUKE 4

Jesus spent 40 days in the desert, and he ate nothing. At the end of the 40 days, he was hungry. the devil tempted him by saying "If you are the Son of God, tell this stone to become bread." Jesus said, "Man does not live by bread alone". Then the devil took him to a high place and said Jesus could "have it all" if he worshiped him (Satan). Jesus said, "Worship the Lord your God and serve him only". Then the devil took him to the highest point of the temple and told Jesus that he should throw himself down and his angels will catch him. (As it is written in psalm 91:11,12), Jesus said, "Do not put the Lord your God to the test."

This last statement by Jesus is so important. We need to be careful to not put God to the test by saying conditional prayers, "If you are God, you can do this for me." He is God. And he can do whatever he wants. We need to humbly ask for things if they are in accordance with his will. When we tie the outcome of our prayer to God's divinity (or lack thereof) that's where we run into problems. Jesus went to Galilee and preached in all the synagogues. Then he returned to his hometown of Nazareth. He ran into some resistance and said, "No prophet is accepted in his hometown." This statement seems to be very true in many areas, not just faith, even in business. People who knew someone when they were 10 years old, sometimes always see them as being 10. Jesus went to the home of Simon, and he healed Simon's mother of a fever. He healed all the people that were brought to him. At daybreak, he went to be by himself, and the people begged him to stay. Jesus said, "I must preach the good news of the kingdom of God to other towns also because that is why I was sent."

LUKE 5

The calling of the first disciples is such an excellent depiction of two things. First, Jesus' leadership is on full display. Second, it demonstrates people's willingness to give up everything to follow Jesus.

Jesus is teaching on the shore of a lake, and he saw two empty boats that were left by the fishermen who were washing their nets. Jesus got in the boat and asked Simon to put the boat a little offshore. He taught the people while sitting in the boat. after he finished, he told Simon to go to deeper water and put his nets down for a catch. Simon told Jesus that they had been working all day and night and had not caught anything, "But because you say so, I will let down the nets". They caught so many fish their nets began to break. They signaled their partners to bring the other boat to help and there were so many fish, both boats almost sank.

Simon Peter realized what just happened, so he fell at Jesus' knees and said, "Go away from me Lord, I am a sinful man." Jesus said to Simon, "Don't be afraid, from now on you will catch men." Luke says, "So they pulled their boats up on the shore, left everything and followed him." **Think about that one! It was a demonstration of Jesus' greatness, his forgiveness, and his leadership in about five minutes.** And for that, people were willing to give up everything. After that, Jesus was in one of the towns nearby and he healed a leper. He told the man not to tell anyone and he instructed him to show himself to the priest and suggest to him that he sacrificed the way Moses commanded as his testimony. I believe the reason Jesus did this was he still wanted to stay "off the radar" of the priests and soldiers until he could establish a bigger legion of followers/ believers.

One day, Jesus was teaching Pharisees in teachers of the law, people were bringing the sick to be healed. The crowds were too big to get to Jesus, so they cut a hole in the roof and lowered their friend to Jesus. When Jesus saw their faith he says, "Your sins have been forgiven." I find it interesting when Jesus tells sick people their sins are forgiven. Almost as if their sins are the same reason they are sick. That must have been the thinking of 2000 years ago…. same way they explain lepers being sinners. The Pharisees are confused because Jesus is forgiving sins and only God can do that. Jesus says, "Why are you thinking these things in your hearts? Which is easier, to say, 'Your sins are forgiven,' or 'Get up and walk'? But I want you know that the Son of Man has authority on earth to forgive sins." He then said to the paralyzed man, "I tell you, get up, take your mat and go home." Everyone was amazed and gave praise to God. They were filled with awe and said, "we have seen remarkable things today." **God's remarkable things are on display every day. I just need to recognize them.**

A very important thing happens next. Jesus walks up to a tax collector named Levi and says, "Follow me." Tax collectors were hated in the time of Jesus because they were corrupt. The way it worked was tax collectors essentially bought the right to collect taxes for the Roman empire. It was like a franchise, and they could collect as much as they wanted. So people hated them. Jesus went to Levi's house to have a big banquet and the Pharisees said to Jesus, "Why do you eat with tax collectors and sinners." Jesus' response is so timeless and powerful, "It is not the healthy who need a doctor, but the sick. **I have not come to call the righteous, but sinners to repentance." This is it! This is Jesus' mission. No person is "too far gone". Most religious leaders hung out with the "good people". Not Jesus. He wanted the sinners. He was showing them a new way. A new life. And that has not changed in 2000 years.**

The next story is so very profound. Jesus tells the crowd, "No one tears a patch from a new garment and sews it on an old one. If he does, he will have torn a new garment and the patch from new one will not match the old. And no one pours new wine into old wineskins. If he does, the new wine will burst the skins, the wine will run out and the wineskins will be ruined. No, new wine must be poured into new wineskins. And no one after drinking the old wine wants the new, the old is better."

Jesus is saying that we are a totally new person when we except his calling. We are made totally new. We cannot hold no to old patches of our life and truly follow Jesus. It's an all or nothing thing. Following Jesus is not a patchwork job.

LUKE 6

Begins with Jesus declaring himself Lord of the Sabbath and demonstrating it as well. In Jewish culture, the Sabbath (Saturday) is a day of total rest. I witnessed this when I was in Israel. Everything; Bars, restaurants, etc., are closed until sunset on Saturday. Then everyone emerges from their homes. The Pharisees saw Jesus' disciples picking grain to eat. The Pharisees felt as if picking up the grain was unlawful, so they challenged Jesus. Jesus reminded them of how David treated those that were hungry on the sabbath. He gave them food. Jesus said, "I am a Lord of the Sabbath." On another Sabbath, he was teaching in the synagogue and there was a man with a shriveled hand. Jesus healed him and said, "which is lawful on the Sabbath: to do good or to do evil? To save life or destroy it?" The Pharisees were furious with Jesus and began to discuss what to do with him.

The rest of chapter 6 is incredible. Jesus goes up to a mountainside to pray. When he returns, he chooses his 12 disciples: Simon (Peter) and his brother Andrew, James, John, Philip, Bartholomew, Matthew, Thomas, James, Simon, Judas (son of James) and Judas Iscariot.

After he healed many people, he said to them:

'Blessed are you who are poor,
For yours is the kingdom of God.
Blessed are you who hunger now,
For you will be satisfied.
Blessed are you who will weep now,
For you will laugh.
Blessed are you when men hate you,
When they exclude you and insult you

And reject your name as evil,
Because of the son of man".

"Rejoice in the day and leap for joy because great is your reward in heaven. For that is how their fathers treated the prophets".

This passage is Luke's version of "Sermon on the Mount" or "the Beatitudes" that is in Matthew 5. Matthew's version is quoted more often. Jesus goes on to instruct them:

"But woe to you who are rich,
For you have already received your comfort.
Woe to you who are well fed now.
For you will go hungry.
Woe to you who laugh now,
for you will mourn and weep.
Woe to you when all men speak
well of you. For that is how their
fathers treated the prophets".

Jesus tells his disciples to love our enemies, do good to those who hate you, Bless those who curse you, and to pray for those who mistreat you. **This is the <u>real magic</u> of following Jesus. Jesus teaches love. Love—all the time. When we can find love in our hearts for someone who has mistreated us, there we will find Jesus.**

Jesus also challenges his disciples by saying, "If you love those who Love you, what credit is that to you? Even sinners love those who love them." He's challenging us to love when it is difficult to love, not just when it is easy. "Love your enemies, do good to them, and lend to them without expecting to get anything back…be merciful, just as your father is merciful". Jesus delivers a message that has stuck with me in a big way, "Do not judge, and you will not be judged. Do not condemn and you will not be condemned. Forgive, and you will be forgiven…for with the Measure you use, it will be measured to you."

All of us can be so judgmental. Jesus is saying, "Just don't do it!" We don't know people's stories. Whatever lens we look at people through, they will look at us through. Let that be a very gracious lens. He uses a great metaphor, "Why do you look at the speck of sawdust in your brother's eye and pay no attention to the plank in your own eye? You hypocrite, first take the plank out of your eye and then you will see clearly to remove the speck from your brother's eye". **Take a hard look at ourselves first.**

Jesus talks about what we can do by being good people. He does this by talking about a tree. "No good tree bears bad fruit. Each tree is recognized by its fruit…the good man brings good things out of the good stored up in his heart, and the evil man brings evil things out of the evil stored up in his heart. for out of the overflow of his heart his mouth speaks".

It's all about our heart. Fill our hearts with Jesus and it will be filled with good things. And we will project good things.

Jesus challenges the disciples to not only hear his words but do what he says. He says when we hear him and put his words into practice, it's like a man who builds his house on a foundation of <u>rock</u> where floods and "Torrents" can't shake it. But the one who hears his words and doesn't put them into practice is like building your house without a foundation. "The moment the torrent struck that house, it collapsed and it's destruction was complete".

This is real. This happens to people. It happens to families. Do not dismiss the message of Jesus. He tells us in advance, what will happen if we do. Build your house on solid ground. <u>Him.</u>

The faith of the centurion reminds us that no matter how "important" we are, we must always remind ourselves of our reliance on Jesus. The centurion had a servant who was about to die. The elders told Jesus that "The man deserves to have you do this because he loves our nation and has built your synagogue". So, Jesus went. The centurion sent friends to say to Jesus, "Lord don't trouble yourself; I do not deserve to have you come under my roof." He says that he has many soldiers under his command, and they do what he says. But he does not feel worthy of Jesus. When he heard all this, he was amazed and said, "I tell you I have not found such great faith even in Israel." The men returned to the house and found the servant well.

Jesus went to a small town called Nain. A group of people were carrying out a dead person. It was the only son of a widow. Jesus approached the coffin and said, "Young man, I say to you, get up." The dead man got up and began to talk. The people were amazed and praised God. "A great prophet has appeared among us. God has come to help his people". The news about Jesus spread throughout Judea and the surrounding country.

The next section about John the Baptist is a little confusing. The disciples of John's heard about the things Jesus was doing. He sent them to Jesus to ask, "Are you the one who was to come or should we ask someone else." This confuses me because my assumption has always been that John the Baptist knew all along who Jesus was. Jesus tells the men, "Go back and report to John what you have seen and heard." And then he lists all the miracles. He finishes with "blessed is the man who does not fall away an account of me." Jesus turns to the crowd that is with him and essentially validates everything positive about John.

Since John baptized so many of the people, Jesus says, "What did you go out of the desert to see?" And then he reminds them John was not a rich man in fancy clothes, living in the palace. He says John was more than a prophet. As it is written in Malachi 3:1," I will send my messenger ahead of you, who will prepare your way before you". He also tells them there is no one on earth greater than John, but John is less than the "least" in the kingdom of heaven. **That's not a slam on John, it's a vision of how great heaven is.**

Everyone who was baptized by John was excited, but those that were not (Pharisees) rejected this message. Jesus stands shares a great quote that is timeless:

"Wisdom is proved right
by all her children."

JESUS: HIS LIFE, HIS LOVE, HIS PROMISE

In my own words, "The greatest teller of truth is time".

One of the Pharisees invited Jesus to have dinner with him. A woman who lived a sinful life came and poured perfume on Jesus' feet and washed them with her tears. The Pharisee said, "If Jesus were a prophet, he would know what kind of person she was." Jesus then goes "Full on Jesus" on the Pharisee.

Jesus says that two men owe someone money. One owes 50, and the other owes 500. Neither has the money to pay the man back, so he canceled both debts. He asks the Pharisee, "Who will love the lender more?" The man says it will be the man who owed 500. Jesus tells him, "You have judged correctly." He tells Simon that he came into his house, and he didn't serve Jesus anywhere near as intentionally as this woman did. He says, "her sins have been forgiven for she has loved much but he who has forgiven, loves little." He tells the woman, "Your sins are forgiven. Go in peace."

We are never beyond God's grace. He will <u>always</u> forgive our sins. His grace came along with our love for him. And our forgiveness of other people is our reflection of love for our God.

LUKE 8

Begins with the parable of the sower. Jesus tells a crowd of people that a farmer was scattering his seed. Some fell on the path, and it was trampled on, and the birds ate it up. Some fell on the rocks and when the plants came up, they withered because they had no moisture. Other fell amongst the thorns which grew up with it and choked the plants. Still other seed fell on good soil. It yielded a crop 100 times more than what was sown.

Jesus says, "The seed is the word of God." The seeds on the path are the ones that the devil takes away from their homes so they can't be saved. The seeds on the rock are the ones that receive the word, but when they are tested, they fall away. The seeds on the thorns are like those who hear it but as they go on their way they are choked by life's worries, riches, and pleasures, and they don't mature. But the seed on the good soil stands for those with a noble and good heart who hear the word, retain it and by persevering, produce a crop.

For me, this story could have been written <u>today</u>. The lesson is that it's up to us to choose which seed we will be.

Once we receive Jesus' message, what will we do with it? Jesus told the crowds that, "No one hides a lamp in a jar or puts it under a bed. He puts it on a stand so that those that come in can see the light. For nothing that is hidden that will not be disclosed…consider carefully how you will listen. whoever has less will be given more, whoever does not have, what he thinks he has Will be taken away from him."

This verse gets taken out of context very often. People think Jesus is talking about money and possessions. It is clearly building off the previous parables, referring to the word of God. **Listen to the word of God, apply it in your life, and you will hear God and more. Ignore it and you will eventually stop hearing it. And people will see God through you and be inspired to find God in their lives. That is the Kingdom**

Jesus and his disciples got into a boat and proceeded to the other side of the lake. A big storm came in and almost swamped the boat and the disciples were afraid they were going to drown. Jesus stood up, rebuked the wind, and calmed the storm and simply said to the disciples, "Where is your faith?" The disciples were blown away and said, "Who is this? He commands even the winds and the water, and they obey him."

Seems to me that Jesus enjoyed reminding them of who he was every once in a while.

After that we hear the story of Jesus healing a demon possessed man. He drives the demons out of the man and into a herd of pigs who run down a hill and into a lake drown themselves. In Luke's version, the people were so afraid at this point that they asked Jesus to leave town. The man who was healed wanted to go with Jesus, but Jesus told him to go into town and tell the people what God has done for him.

A man named Jairus came to Jesus and asked him to come heal his 12-year- old daughter. On their way to his house, a woman who had been bleeding for 12 years came up behind Jesus and touched him. Jesus "felt the power go out from me". She had been instantly healed by touching Jesus and he said, "daughter your faith has healed you." Jesus then proceeded to Jairus' House where they thought his daughter had died. Jesus told them that she was sleeping and told her to get up. Her parents were astonished. Jesus told them not to tell anyone what had happened. Why did Jesus tell the demon possessed man to tell everyone and told the girl not to tell anyone?

LUKE 9

Jesus sends the 12 disciples out to drive out demons, cure diseases and to preach the kingdom of God. He says, "take nothing for the journey— no staff, no bag, no bread, no money, no extra tunic." this is such a strong reminder of the fact that Jesus asks us to be willing to give up everything to follow him. God will provide. He also tells them if they go on to a town where they are not welcome, they need to "shake the dust off their feet" And move on. I think Jesus is telling us to find those who are willing to listen. **Too many people need to hear the good news for us to waste time with those who don't want to hear it.**

At that time, Herod had been hearing all the things that Jesus was doing but he couldn't figure out who he was. He had beheaded John the Baptist, and some thought some prophets had come back to life. He wanted to meet Jesus.

The apostles returned from their mission, and they reported to Jesus what they had done. He took them to a town called Bethsaida to be by themselves. The crowds found out where they were, so they followed Jesus there. Jesus welcomed them and healed those that needed to be healed. Late in the day the disciples told Jesus that they thought the crowd should be sent home to get something to eat and to rest. Jesus told the disciples to feed the crowd. They only had five loaves of bread and two fish. They put the people in groups of 50. Jesus gave thanks to Heaven and distributed the food to the 5000 people. Afterwards they had 12 basketfuls of leftovers.

Jesus asked his disciples who the crowds thought he was. They said, "Some say Elijah, some say John the Baptist, or one of the prophets." He asked them what they believed. Peter said, " The Christ of God."

For the first time, Jesus tells him what is going to happen. "The Son of Man must suffer many things and be rejected by elders, chief priests, and teachers of the law. And he must be killed and on the third day he must be killed and be raised to life." And then we hear Jesus tell us what it means to truly follow him, "If anyone would come after me, he must deny himself and take up his cross and follow me. For whoever wants to save his life will lose it, but whoever loses his life for me will save it. What good is it for a man to gain the whole world and forfeit his very self? If anyone is ashamed of me and my words, The Son of Man will be ashamed of him when he comes in glory..."

It is so important that we understand what Jesus is saying. The earthly cost of following Jesus can be heavy, but the eternal gain is enormous. The gain of following Jesus is Jesus, His peace while we are on Earth, and eternity in heaven. Once we realize how incredible those two things are, it makes it easier to let go of the things that we are offered by the world. Jesus took Peter, James, and John with him and went up onto a mountain to pray. As he was praying his face changed, and his clothes became bright as lightning. Elijah and Moses appeared with him. They were talking about Jesus' departure and what was going to be fulfilled. Then a voice came from heaven and said, "This is my son whom I have chosen. Listen to him."

The next day a man told Jesus that his son was possessed by demons and that the disciples were unable to drive them out. While the boy was approaching Jesus, the demon threw him to the ground. Jesus "rebuked the evil spirit, healed the boy and gave him back to his father".

The disciples began arguing amongst themselves who was the greatest of them. Jesus took a little child and said, "Whoever welcomes this little child in my name, welcomes me...for whoever is least among you—he is the greatest." This is Jesus reminding us not to seek greatness on earth. Seek humility, seek servanthood.

As they were walking along a road, a man said, "I will follow you wherever you go." Jesus told him that he had no place to sleep, and the man said, "first let me go bury my father." Jesus says something that is difficult for us to hear, "Let the dead bury their own dead, but you go and proclaim the kingdom of God." Another person says, "I will follow you Lord, but first let me go back and say goodbye to my family." Jesus says, "No one who puts his hand to the plow and looks back is fit for service in the kingdom of God."

This may seem arrogant of Jesus—like he is being "disrespectful of our families". That is not the case. He is reminding us that He is the key to us being with his Father. Following him is first, all else is second.

LUKE 10

Jesus sent 72 disciples into neighboring towns. He says, "The harvest is plentiful. But the workers are few...do not take a purse, or bag, or sandals." He tells them to stay where they are welcomed, but don't stay if they are not. He told them to go into the streets and says, "Even the dust of your streets that sticks to our feet we wipe off against you. Yet be sure of this, the kingdom of God is near. I tell you; it will be more bearable on that day for Sodom (burned to the ground) than for that town". We cannot force people to listen, but we do have a responsibility to try to tell them. He then tells them, "He who listens to you listens to me; He who rejects you, rejects me; but he who rejects me, rejects the one who sent to me."

To me, this reminds us that we cannot separate Jesus from God. <u>Jesus is the only path to the Father!</u>

The seventy-two later returned and rejoiced, saying to Jesus, "Lord, even the demons submit to us in your name." Jesus tells them that happened because he gave all the power to them. But he also reminded them to not rejoice in that, "but rejoice that your names are written in heaven.". Jesus then prays with joy and says to God, "…You have hidden these things from the wise and learned and revealed them to little children."

This tells me that the good news is available to everyone, and we all have a responsibility to spread it. It also reminds me to not care what others think of me. It only matters what God thinks of me.

On one occasion, an expert in the law stood up to test Jesus. he asks what he needs to do to inherit eternal life. And Jesus shares what, in my opinion, are two of the most important things in the entire Bible. This is the cornerstone of Jesus. "Love the Lord your God with all your heart and with all your soul and with all your strength and all your mind; And love your neighbor as yourself". **Plain and simple, Jesus asked us to love.**

The man asked Jesus, "Who is my neighbor?" Jesus goes on to share the parable of the good Samaritan. The story is that a man gets beaten, robbed, and left for dead. A priest passes by and does nothing, as does a Levite. But a Samaritan bandages his wounds, and takes him to an inn to take care of him. He leaves two silver coins to the innkeeper and assures him that he will cover any additional expenses. He asked the man, "Which of the three were his neighbor?" The man says, "The one who had mercy on him."

We are called to have mercy on all people.

The end of chapter 10 is a great little story about Mary Magdalene and her sister Martha. Jesus and his disciples went to their home and Martha was upset because Mary wasn't helping her with preparations. She said to Jesus, "Tell her to help me." Jesus says, "Martha, Martha, you are worried about many things but only one thing is needed, Mary has chosen what is better, and it will not be taken away from her."

Jesus is saying, stop worrying. Stop stressing over unimportant things. Focus on him. Focus on the good news! When you look at the world through the lens of Jesus, it's like wearing the best sunglasses that

you have ever worn as you look at a bright sun. The filter makes everything more beautiful.

LUKE 11

One of Jesus' disciples asked him to teach him to teach them how to pray. Jesus responds with what is most likely the very first reciting of the Our Father. That prayer is so simple and so beautiful. I will summarize it below in very simple words:

> **"God, you are holy,**
> **May your kingdom be here.**
> **Give us only what we need.**
> **Forgive our sins and help us forgive others.**
> **Deliver us from Satan".**

Jesus tells a story and uses it to show the power of prayer. He tells a story about a man who goes to a friend at midnight, and it asks for a loaf of bread to share with a visiting friend. Though The man is sleeping, he gets up and gives him the bread because of the man's "boldness". Then Jesus says this about prayer, "ask and it will be given to you; seek and you will find; knock and the door will be opened to you. For everyone who asks receives; He who seeks finds; and to him who knocks the door will be opened."

These are powerful words from Jesus. We need to be careful not to let them confuse us. It doesn't mean that if we ask for a million dollars, we will get it. We need to take it within the context of the verses that precede it, the Our Father. **If we pray to God, and ask him for "daily bread", in his will, he will deliver. It's all about staying aligned to his will.**

Jesus drives out some demons in a man and the onlookers claim that he is doing it by Satan. Jesus says, "Any kingdom divided against itself will not stand, and a house divided against itself will fall." He is basically saying, "Why would Satan drive out Satan?" (Just as he said in previous versions of stories like this). He assures that he is doing it by the finger of God. He says,

"When a strong man fully armed guards his own house, his possessions are safe. But when someone stronger attacks and overpowers him, he takes away the armor in which the man trusted and divides up the spoils." **He is telling us to protect our house by standing with him, so no one stronger can overtake us (your house, your life, your family).**

A woman spoke up and said, "Blessed is the mother who gave you birth and nursed you." He replied, "Blessed rather are those who hear Word of God and obey it."

Jesus shares his "lamp of the body" lesson. "No one lights a lamp and puts it in a place where it will be hidden, he puts it on a stand so that those who come may see the light. When your eyes are good, your whole body also is full of light. But when they are bad, your body is full of darkness. See to it see to it that the light within you is not darkness. Therefore, if your whole body is full of light, and no part of it is dark, it will be completely lighted as when the light of a lamp shines on you".

The fuel that creates the light is the message of Jesus. Peace, love, kindness, joy, compassion. We need to fill our eyes with that message, and we will be a "lamp of light" that others will be attracted to.

After Jesus finished speaking, a Pharisee invited him to eat with him, which Jesus did. The Pharisee noticed that Jesus didn't wash before the meal. Jesus then delivered the "seven woes" and he began by saying, "You Pharisees clean the outside of the cup, but inside you are full of wickedness."

His other warnings:

— You give to God 1/10 of your "harvest", but you neglect justice and the love of God

— You love the most important seats in the marketplace

— You are like unmarked graves which men walk over without knowing it (I don't understand this)

— You load people down with burdens they can hardly carry and you don't lift a finger to help them

— You have persecuted the prophets

— You have taken away the key to knowledge you have not yet entered, but you have hindered those who are entering

My takeaway from Jesus' message in the "seven woes"—don't be a hypocrite. Walk the walk. Don't say one thing and do another. And he told us what to do.

After this speech, one in which Jesus "called out" the Pharisees, they began to oppose him fiercely. Jesus' message to the Pharisees continues. As he speaks to a crowd of the many thousands, he tells him to be on guard against the yeast of the Pharisees, which is hypocrisy. There is nothing concealed that will not be disclosed or hidden that will not be made known.

Jesus' reference to yeast is an important one. A very small amount of yeast affects the entire loaf of bread. Similarly, false teaching, even a small amount can take over your mind and lead to hypocrisy. Stay on guard because misrepresentations of what Jesus said are everywhere! And some of them can sound "easier" or "more attractive" on the surface. They make us feel better, and that's what makes them so dangerous.

Jesus also famously says, "Indeed the very hairs of your head are all numbered." that tells us that God has a plan for each of us and always has. He finishes with "do not be afraid". **That is so reassuring that Jesus is telling us that despite the struggles we may face in our life, as long as we stand with Jesus, we need not be afraid.**

LUKE 12

This chapter is so powerful. Much of it is worth quoting from beginning to end. "I tell you, whoever acknowledges me before men, the Son of Man will also acknowledge him before the angels of God. But he who disowns me before men will be disowned before the angels of God. And everybody who speaks a word against the Son of Man will be forgiven but anyone who blasphemes against the Holy Spirit Will not be forgiven". This is a little confusing to me. I believe Jesus is saying that when he leaves, he is entrusting our Counsel to the Holy Spirit so we can't blaspheme against him.

The Parable of the Rich Fool

Jesus is crystal clear on this topic. A man asks Jesus to tell his brother to divide his inheritance with him. Jesus said, "Who appointed me to be a judge or arbiter between you? Watch out. Be on your guard against all kinds of greed. A man's life does not consist in the abundance of possessions." Then he tells the short parable that is so impactful. A man's land produces a large crop so much that he has nowhere to store the surplus. He decides to tear down his barns and build bigger ones. He thinks, 'I will have many good things laid up for many years. Take life easy; eat, Drink and be merry!' God says to him, "you fool. This very night your life will be demanded from you. then who will get what you have prepared for yourself." This is how it will be with anyone who stores up things for himself but is not rich toward God."

This passage is life changing. Jesus is telling us once again that things in this life will pass by, but God will not. He is clear. It's not bad to "have things" but getting things at the expense of the relationship with Jesus is <u>tragic</u>!

What follows is another life-changing passage. Jesus tells us <u>not to worry</u>. "Do not worry about your life, what you will eat; or about your body, what you will wear. Your life is more than food, and the body more than clothes…who of you by worrying can add a single hour to your life? Since you cannot do this very little thing, why do you worry about the rest"? He goes on to say, "Seek his kingdom, and these things will be given to you as well."

This is a tough one. As people, we worry. I know I do. But Jesus' last line is the most important line. Focus on Jesus and the Kingdom. And

what happens is the things that satisfy you change. And not only does God satisfy those needs, but your life also becomes more fulfilling.

Jesus says, "Do not be afraid, little flock, for your Father has been pleased to give you the kingdom. Sell your possessions and give to the poor. Provide purses for yourself that will not wear out, a treasure in heaven that will never fail, where no thief comes near, and no moth destroys. For where your treasure is, there your heart will be also.

I do not know how literal Jesus is being when he says to sell all your possessions, but I do know that his last line has proven true every time. It's not having possessions that is dangerous, it's loving them. **It's not having money that is dangerous, it's loving money that traps people. <u>Love God first</u>! And your perspective on the joy that money brings you will change.**

Jesus says, "Be dressed and ready for service and keep your lamps burning, like servants waiting for their master to return from a wedding banquet, so that when he comes and knocks they can immediately open the door for him".

The important word for me is "be". Jesus doesn't say, "get ready". He says, "be ready". He is clear—you won't have time. Prepare yourself because it (his return) could happen anytime.

"The servant who knows the master's will and does not do what the master wants will be beaten with many blows. But the one who does not know and does things deserving punishment will be beaten with a few blows. (Think about a child you've had to worn multiple times versus a first-time offense.) From everyone who has been given much, much will be demanded; and from the one who has been entrusted with much, much more will be asked."

This quote gets misused often. People apply it to the concept of money. Not that it is not true in that context, but Jesus is talking about the "gifts" (spiritual) that he gives us, as well as the depth of our knowledge

of him. **Example: if we have a deep knowledge of Jesus, we have a responsibility to share it.**

Jesus shares some tough news. He says, "Do you think I came to bring
peace on earth? No, I tell you, but division." He goes on to tell them what
will divide families—basically those that believe and those that don't. We
need to follow him first. That is a very difficult passage to grasp. **People want
to believe that "all good people go to heaven". This is 100% not true and
Jesus said it repeatedly. Sometimes people even think "bad" people go to
heaven because God loves us all and he is merciful. That is not true either.
Jesus is saying in no uncertain terms, "I will divide the believers from the
nonbelievers. My mercy is that I told you the rules of the game before we
started." (My quote, not Jesus'!) When we think about it, this stands to the
reason of Jesus coming in the first place. Why did Jesus come? Because we
were separated from God, and God sent his Son to reconcile us back to
him. So, if Jesus is the key to reconciling ourselves back to God, then one
must follow Jesus to get to God. If you can get to God without following
Jesus, then why did God sacrifice his only Son?**

LUKE 13

Jesus reminds us of all about the power and importance of repentance.
He once again uses a parable to make his point—a man had a fig tree growing
in the vineyard and he went to look for fruit but did not find any. The man
told his caretaker, "For three years now I've been coming to look for fruit
on this fig tree and haven't found any. Cut it down! Why should it use up
the soil?" The caretaker replied, "Sir, leave it alone for one more year, And
I'll dig around it and fertilize it. If it bears fruit next year, fine. If not, cut it
down." I think Jesus is the caretaker here. he is willing to be patient and he
will "fertilize us", but he is not going to wait forever. **Remember, he told us
that as we are sharing the gospel, and people reject us, "shake the dust off
your feet" and move on!**

Jesus healed a woman on the Sabbath who was crippled for 18 years. The synagogue leader was angry with Jesus at the fact that "he worked" on the Sabbath. Jesus used a great analogy to make his point. He says to them, "you hypocrites." Then he challenges by reminding them that they untie their donkeys on the Sabbath so they can get water. Jesus "untied a woman" who had been crippled for 18 years. **Such a brilliant challenge! Jesus is such a great teacher!**

Jesus describes the kingdom of God by comparing it to a mustard seed and to yeast. The mustard seed grows into a tree that birds perch on its branches, and the yeast works its way through the entire loaf of bread. **The kingdom is all-encompassing. It offers a haven of peace for all of us (like the birds). And it can and should take over our whole lives (like the yeast).**

When someone asked Jesus who would be saved, he said, "Make every effort to enter through the narrow door, because many will try to enter and will not be able to. Once the owner of the house gets up and closes the door you will stand outside knocking and pleading, 'Sir open the door for us.' but he will say, "I don't know you or where you came from.'"

Jesus is reminding us that he, and he alone is the narrow door, and that is the only door to salvation. He finishes with, "Indeed there are those who are last who will be first, and first who will be last."

Being first in the kingdom of the earth is no guarantee you will be first in the kingdom of God. You will probably be last.

Some Pharisees came to Jesus and told him that Herod wants to kill him. Jesus' response is epic, "go tell that fox, I will keep driving out demons and healing people…and on the third day I will reach my goal. In any case, I must press on…."

He says," Jerusalem, Jerusalem you who kill the prophets and stone those sent to you, how often I have a longed to gather your children together as a hen gathers her chicks under her wings, and you were not willing. Look, your house is left to you desolate. I tell you; you will not see me again until you say, 'blessed is he who comes in the name of the Lord.'"

Jesus is expressing deep sorrow for Israel. He is telling them they are doomed until they accept him.

LUKE 14

This chapter begins with another story about working (healing) on the Sabbath. There was a man who was suffering from dropsy (excessive swelling) and Jesus asked them if it is legal to heal on the Sabbath. Like his story about untying a donkey when he healed the woman, he says, "If you had a son or an ox that fell into a well, who of you would not pull it out?" They had nothing to say.

As they were sitting down to eat, Jesus noticed how they all picked their places at the table. He tells them, when invited to a wedding banquet, don't pick the place of honor at the table, because it might be reserved for someone else. He says to pick the lowest place, so your friend will have the opportunity to grant you a higher place. **This is terrific advice for life. Stay humble!**

Jesus also tells them, when they have a banquet, don't invite friends or relatives because they can repay you. Instead "invite the lame, the blind, the crippled, and you will be blessed. Although they cannot repay you, you will be repaid at the resurrection of the righteous".

Jesus shares the parable of "the great banquet". A man was preparing a great banquet. When it came time, his friends made up a bunch of excuses as to why they couldn't attend. He told his servant to go into the streets and invite the lame, the blind and the crippled. The servant did so.

Jesus then proclaims, "None of those men who were invited will get a taste of my banquet." Message: Jesus is inviting us, we better accept!

The Cost of being a Disciple

This is a difficult passage to read because it is a wake-up call. Jesus turns to the large crowds following him and says, "if anyone comes to me and does not hate his father and mother, wife and children, brothers, and sisters—yes even their own life—such a person cannot be my disciple. And whoever does not carry their cross and follow me cannot be my disciple."

Wow. That's a very tough challenge from Jesus. I have found this entire statement to be true. One must love Jesus, first last and always. And I have found that when we do that, the other relationships in our life blossom! When you look at people through the eyes of Jesus, you can't help but become more accepting and less judgmental.

"Suppose one of you wants to build a tower. Won't you first sit down and estimate the cost to see if you have enough money to complete it? For if you lay the foundation and are not able to finish it, everyone who sees it will ridicule you, saying, 'this person began to build and wasn't able to finish'".

Jesus says, "Salt is good, but if it loses its saltiness, how can it be made salty again?"

"Whoever has ears to hear let him hear."

The salt metaphor is <u>so</u> good. When we get enlightened by the story of Jesus, we can't lose our commitment to stay sharp and enlightened. We must stay focused on continuing to live in the word—study it, learn it and apply it. That's how we stay salty.

LUKE 15

The tax collectors and "sinners" were listening to Jesus, but the Pharisees mocked Jesus because he was welcoming and eating with "sinners". **(How ironic is that—Jesus was clear that sinners were the reason he was here.)** He uses the parable of the lost sheep to make his point. He says that anyone who was a shepherd of 100 sheep, and one got lost, he would go and find that one sheep. He says it will be just like that in heaven, "There will be more rejoicing in heaven with one sinner who repents than

99 righteous people." Jesus also uses a lost coin to make the same point. If you have 10 coins in your pocket and you lose one, you still look for the lost coin. (My translation)

The Parable of the Lost (prodigal) Son

This is a timeless parable that Jesus uses to demonstrate his love for us and for anyone who comes to him or returns to him.

A father had two sons. The younger one asked for his share of his inheritance early. He took the money and set off for a distant country and squandered everything, and then there was a famine where he was, and he couldn't get anything to eat. He realized what a fool He was because even his father's servants were well fed. He decided to go home and apologize to his father. Before he arrived home, his father saw him and ran to him, hugged him, and gave him a kiss. He ordered his servants to bring the best robe. He put a ring on his finger and sandals on his feet and ordered that the best calf be killed for a celebration. He said, "For this son of mine was dead and is now alive; was lost and is now found." The older son was upset because he had been so loyal to his father, and his brother squandered all his father's money, and yet his brother received the celebration. The father's response is <u>so</u> good, "my son, you are always with me, and everything I have is yours. But we had to celebrate and be glad, because this brother of yours was dead and is alive again; He was lost and is found."

Most of us can identify with the loyal brother, why should the disloyal brother receive better treatment then the loyal one? **It is about celebrating the repentant heart of the younger brother and Jesus is talking about what it will be like in the Kingdom of God. As believers, when a sinful thief or drug addict gets baptized, we celebrate. It would be foolish for us to be jealous of their baptism because we already have what did they just got. As Jesus says, "Everything I have is yours!" Other's "getting" Jesus, doesn't take away from us already having him.**

JESUS: HIS LIFE, HIS LOVE, HIS PROMISE

LUKE 16

This chapter talks a lot about money. Jesus' primary message in this passage is that no servant can serve two masters. Either he will hate the one and love the other or he will be devoted to the one and despise the other. You cannot serve both God and money and I have found this to be very true in my own life. Note: it does not say you can't *have* both, it says you can't *serve* both. **In times where I'm very focused on God, I find myself realizing how unimportant money really is, when you compare it to the unending love of God. Unfortunately, in times where I was money centric, I found myself more distant from God.** Jesus said to the Pharisees, you are the ones who justify yourselves in the eyes of men, but God knows your hearts. What is highly valued among men is detestable in God's sight."

Don't try to please men. Please God.

The story of the rich man and the Lazarus is about the vast difference between Heaven and Hell. Lazarus was a leper and a beggar. He sat at the gate of the rich man begging for food. When he died "Angels carried him to Abraham's side". The rich man also died but he was buried "in hell". As he looked up and saw the beggar at Abraham's side, the rich man called to Lazarus asking him to, "Dip his finger in water to cool his tongue because he was in agony in this fire." Abraham replied to him, "son, remember in your lifetime you received your good things, while Lazarus received bad things, but now he is comforted here, and you are in agony. And besides all this, between us and you a great chasm has been fixed so that those who want to go from here to you cannot, nor can anyone go from there to us."

LUKE 17

Begins with Jesus teaching about sin, repentance, and forgiveness. He tells us that "things that cause people to stumble" are bound to come. But he instructs us to not cause others to stumble and he says if a brother or sister sins against you, rebuke them. I think he is saying to let them know that they sinned against you. He says if they repent, we are to forgive them. Even if they sin against you seven times, if they repent seven times, you must forgive them.

We must remember that at the heart of this teaching is love—Jesus' first commitment. None of us can truly forgive sins—only God can. Forgiving other people's transgressions against us allows us to love— which is what Jesus asks us to do. It is another example of the beauty of forgiveness, because both the forgiver and the forgiven benefits and relationship is restored. God's forgiveness of our sins through the death and resurrection of Jesus is what restored our relationship with God himself.

Jesus was on the way to Jerusalem when ten men who had leprosy approached him. Jesus said, "Go show yourselves to the priests." As they walked away, they were cleansed. One man came back and threw himself at Jesus' feet to thank him. He was a Samaritan. Jesus said, "Were not all ten cleansed? Where were the other nine? Rise and go; your faith has made you well." The message to me is that God wants us to acknowledge the things that he does in our lives. **Doing so will bring glory to him and draw others to him.**

A very important message on the Kingdom of God follows. The Pharisees asked Jesus when the Kingdom of God would come. Jesus replied, "The coming of the Kingdom of God is not something that can be observed, nor will people say, 'here it is' or 'there it is' because the kingdom of God is in your midst." **The message for me is that the Kingdom of God just "is". It is everywhere because everything is God's. And because it is his, we cannot build it. We can only accept God's invitation to partake in it. We cannot build things that we do not control. But we can attract others to receive God's invitation to it.**

Jesus says the same thing about himself. He said people will claim they have seen Him, and they will go running, saying, "here he is, or "there he is." He said his day will be like lightning flashing in the sky, but first he must suffer many things and be rejected by this generation. He compared it to

JESUS: HIS LIFE, HIS LOVE, HIS PROMISE

Noah and Lot. People were eating and drinking and celebrating when Noah entered the Ark, then the flood destroyed it all. In the days of lot, they were doing the same and fire destroyed it all. He recalls that Lot's wife returned and looked at the fire. Don't do that! "Whoever tries to keep their life Will lose it, and whoever loses their life Will preserve it".

We need to realize that God created us. He wants us to be with him forever, and we need to do whatever it takes to make sure that is where we end up.

LUKE 18

Jesus encourages us to never give up on our prayers. He says God will grant justice to those who cry out his name. We need to pray faithfully.

The parable of the Pharisee and tax collector. This man went up to a temple to pray and the Pharisee essentially said, "God, I thank you for I am not like other sinners. I fast two times per week and give 1/10 of all I get." The tax collector stood in the back because he knew that he was a sinner. Jesus said, "I tell you that this man, rather than the other, went home justified before God. For all those who a exalt themselves will be humbled, and all those who humble themselves will be exalted."

God loves us. But we can never brag to God. Because when we brag, we are in front of God, giving credit to ourselves. We pale in comparison to greatness of God.

People were bringing little babies to Jesus, but the disciples were not allowing them to get close. Jesus said, "Let the little children come to me and do not hinder them, For the kingdom of God belongs to such as these. Truly I tell you anyone who will not receive the kingdom of God like a little child will never enter it."

This is such an important passage because it once again explains what the Kingdom of God is. We don't create it or build it—it just _is_ and

always has been. God built it and he has dominion over it. He just wants us to join his club.

A rich man approached Jesus and said, "Good teacher, what must I do to inherit eternal life?" Jesus' response is both shocking and enlightening. He says, "Why do you call me good? No one is good except God."

Wow, at this moment, Jesus doesn't even consider himself good. He defers to his Father.

First Jesus tells him to follow the Commandments and the man assures Jesus that he has done that since he was a boy. Jesus tells him that he lacks one thing, "Sell everything you have and give to the poor, and you will have treasure in heaven. Then come, follow me." (**I find the order of this sentence to be fascinating.**) The man became sad because he was wealthy. Jesus said, "how hard it is for the rich to enter the kingdom of God! It is indeed easier for a camel to go through the eye of the needle than for a rich man to enter the kingdom of God." (The eye of the needle is the gate to the city.)

This teaching scared the crowd and they asked, "Who then can be saved?" Jesus said, "What is impossible with men is possible with God."—**He is essentially saying that anyone can be saved.** No matter where you are in your life, following Jesus can deliver you to eternity with God in Heaven.

Peter said, "Truly I tell you, no one who has left home or wife or brothers or sisters or parents or children for the sake of the kingdom of God will fail to receive many times as much in this age, and in the age of eternal life." **If we give it up for God, we will regain it in heaven.**

Luke 18 finishes with Jesus predicting his death for a third time—but the disciples were still confused.

Finally, Jesus heals a blind beggar, and he began to follow Jesus and praise God. The people who saw it also praised God.

Zacchaeus the Tax Collector

LUKE 19

As Jesus entered Jericho, a tax collector name Zacchaeus wanted to see him. But Zacchaeus was too short to see over the crowd so he climbed a fig tree so he could see Jesus. When Jesus saw him, he called him by name and told him to come down so he could stay at his home. The people didn't understand Jesus' motivation because Zacchaeus was a sinner. Zacchaeus said, "look, Lord. here and now, I give half of my possessions to the poor, and if I cheated anybody out of anything I will pay back four times the amount." Jesus said, "today salvation has come to this house, because this man, too, is a son of Abraham. For the Son of Man came to seek and save the lost."

Jesus is so consistent in his message. If we repent of our sins and follow him, we will find salvation!

Parable of ten minas (money—1 = 50 shekels)

A nobleman went to a distant country to have himself appointed king. He gave 10 servants 10 minas each to put to work while he was gone. when he returned home the first servant told him that his 10 minas were now worth 20, so the man put him in charge of 10 cities. The second servant earned five more minas, so he put him in charge of five cities. The last servant came back with only the original 10 minas. He said, "I was afraid of you, because you are a hard man. You take out what you did not put it in, and you reap what you did not sow." The rich man gave his money to the other servants and said, "Everyone who has, more will be given, but as far as the one who has nothing, even what they have will be taken away."

This is an important parable that needs to be researched to understand. This occurs while Jesus is approaching Jerusalem. The crowds think he is coming to establish his kingdom immediately, but he is going to Jerusalem to die. But he will return. In this parable, Jesus is the noble man that goes to heaven to be king. **When he returns, he will assess what we have done with the word of God while we are on earth. If we "grew" it, we will be rewarded.**

If we did not, we won't. In the parable, the nobleman asks for all his "detractors" to be killed. I don't want to be a detractor of the good news!

After this, Jesus entered Jerusalem on a colt. The whole crowd chanted, "Blessed is the king who comes in the name of the Lord. Peace in heaven and glory in the highest." The Pharisees told Jesus to "rebuff your disciples" But Jesus said, "I tell you, if they keep quiet, the stones will cry out!" I love this statement by Jesus. He is telling he Pharisees that this message is so powerful, that if you silence my Disciples, even the stones will find a way to share it. Wow!

I love this. He is saying, "no matter what you do, the story will not be silenced!"

As he entered the city, he cried, and said, "If you, even you, had only known on this day what would bring you peace, but now is hidden from your eyes. The days will come upon you when your enemies will build an embankment against you and encircle and hem you in on all sides. They will dash you to the ground you, and the children within your walls. They will not leave one stone on another because you did not recognize the time of God's coming to you."

This is such a profound statement. This is Jesus saying, "what have you been waiting for is right in front of your eyes. It's me!"

Jesus rebuked those that were selling in the temple, reminding them that it is a house of prayer. The chief priests wanted to kill him, but they couldn't figure out how because the people hung on his every word!

LUKE 20

The chief priests and elders approached Jesus and asked him, "by what authority are you doing these things?" Jesus basically tells them, "I'm not telling." I think he did that because they were nonbelievers.

Parable of the Tenants

A man planted a vineyard and rented it to some tenant farmers. At harvest, he sent a servant to get some of the fruit of the harvest. The tenants beat the man and sent him away. The owner sent two more servants and they did the same thing. The owner thought that if he sent his son, surely they would respect him. The tenants thought if they killed the son, the inheritance would be theirs. Jesus said, "what then will the owner do to them? He will come and kill those tenants and give the vineyard to others." When the people heard this, they said, "God forbid!" At which point, Jesus famously said:

> "The stone the builders rejected
> has become the cornerstone."

And he says, "everyone who falls on that stone will be broken to pieces; anyone on whom it falls will be crushed."

In this parable, Jesus is the son who is killed. The servants that were beaten were the prophets. **Jesus is telling them that the one you rejected is the one that will crush you.**

All along the Pharisees thought the Jesus was leading a rebellion. So, they asked him about paying taxes to Caesar. Jesus calmly said, "Pay to Caesar what is Caesar's. Pay to God what is God's." Timeless, simple message.

The Sadducees ask Jesus what will happen to marriages in heaven. Jesus basically tells them that marriages are for this age on earth, in heaven, we are all angels, and we all belong to each other.

Jesus issues a stern warning about the teachers of the law. He says, "beware of the teachers of the law. They like to walk around in flowing robes and love to be greeted in the marketplaces and have the most important seats in the synagogues and the places of honor at banquets. They devour Widows' houses and for a show make lengthy prayers. These men will be punished most severely."

This is a harsh message. Note: Jesus is not saying all religious leaders are bad. He is saying <u>beware</u>. Be on your guard for leaders who say

one thing and do another. And beware of teachers that change the messages that Jesus himself delivered to the people. Read what HE said. Don't let anyone change it. Follow one man: Jesus. Follow one book: The Bible. What is the logic of following another book that was taken directly from the Bible and rewritten by people to suit their own needs. Read the original.

LUKE 21

Jesus was in the temple watching the rich putting their gifts into the offering. An old widow gave two small copper coins. Jesus said, "This poor widow has put in more than all the others. All these people gave out of their wealth; and she out of poverty, gave all she had to live on." **This is what it means to give our hearts to Jesus. It is total submission to his will. Sacrificial giving says that Jesus is first in our lives.**

As the disciples were remarking about beautiful the temple was, Jesus tells them that eventually every stone will be turned down. He says people will come and claim to be Jesus, but do not follow them. He also said not to be afraid of wars and uprisings because those things must happen before the end. I appreciate the heads up, the warning, from Jesus!

"Nation will rise against nation, and kingdom against kingdom". He also says, "before all this, they will seize you and persecute you. They will hand you over to synagogues and put you in prison…on account of my name. And so, you will bear testimony to me. But make up your mind not to worry beforehand how you will defend yourselves. For I will give you words and wisdom that none of your adversaries will be able to resist or contradict. You will be betrayed even by parents…relatives and friends, and they will put some of you to death. Everyone will hate you because of me. But not a hair on your head will perish. Stand firm and you will win life!"

Jesus explains all the things that will occur at the end of time. **Imagine the strength of his leadership—to tell people how hard it will be to follow**

him, and then to build an army of billions of followers. He says, "Heaven and earth will pass away, but my words will never pass away." He tells them to, "Be careful, or your hearts will be weighed down with carousing, Drunkenness and the anxieties of life, and that Day will close on you suddenly like a trap. …be always on the watch and pray that you may be able to escape all that is about to happen and that you may be able to stand before the Son of Man."

We need to <u>BE</u> ready. Not <u>GET</u> ready.

LUKE 22

As Passover approached, the chief priests were looking for a way to get rid of Jesus. (They thought he was threat and was rebelling against him. He was not!). Judas went to them and offered them a deal. They were delighted and agreed to pay Judas the money for handing over Jesus.

The Last Supper

Jesus told his disciples where to prepare Passover. They did so, and at the right time they sat down to eat. Jesus told them that he was excited for this meal because he knew it would be his last. He took some bread and said, "This is my body given for you; do this in remembrance of me." Then he took the cup and said, "This cup is the new covenant in my blood, which is poured out for you." These are important words that we need to remember. We take communion to remember Jesus and the new covenant. **It's a covenant built on love rather than the random laws of the past or random laws and traditions imposed by religions.**

Jesus informs them all that one of them is about to betray him and they try to figure out who it is. While they were discussing it, they also try to figure out "who was the greatest". Jesus' message is so profound and timeless. "The greatest among you should like the youngest, and the one who rules like the one who serves. For who is greater, the one who is at the table or the one who serves? Is it not the one who is at the table? But I am among you as one who serves. You are those who have stood by me in my trials. And I confer on you a kingdom just as my father conferred one on me, so that you may eat and drink at my table in my kingdom and sit on thrones, judging the 12 tribes of Israel". **This is such a beautiful testament to who Jesus was and what makes him different. Rather than putting himself above others, he calls himself "a servant". Jesus was the greatest servant leader in the history of the world.**

Jesus tells Peter to "strengthen your brothers". Peter tells Jesus that he is ready to go to prison and death for Jesus and Jesus basically says, "you will deny that you know me, three times!" Peter was shocked and said, "that will never happen." Jesus retreated to the Mount of Olives to pray. He asked the disciples to pray so that they would not fall into temptation. Jesus prayed very earnestly and asked God, "Father, if you are willing, take this cup from me; yet not my will, but yours be done." According to Luke, Jesus was in anguish, and his sweat was like drops of blood falling to the ground. It is truly amazing when Jesus displays his own humanity.

While Jesus was speaking, a crowd came up to him, led by Judas, who tried to kiss Jesus. Jesus called him out right on the spot. "Are you betraying the Son of Man with a kiss"? His comments are almost "how dare you"?!

One of the disciples drew a sword and cut off the ear of the high priest's servant. Jesus said," No more of this." Then he touched and healed the man's ear. He even cared for his enemies.

I love what Jesus says next, "Am I leading the rebellion, that you have come with clubs and swords? Every day I was with you in the temple courts, and you did not lay a hand on me. But this is your hour—when darkness reigns."

It's important to recognize that all the persecution of Jesus is because they thought he was rebelling against Rome—which he was not. He was actually telling them that their old covenant was a good thing.

They have been waiting for that covenant to be fulfilled and he is here to fulfill it. He was welcoming them.

The soldiers seized Jesus and led him away. Peter followed at a distance. Three different times people ask Peter if he knew Jesus and three different times Peter denied it, as Jesus predicted. Luke depicts a very strong visual. The guards blindfolded Jesus and began to beat him. Then they challenged him to "prophesy" as to who hit him when he couldn't see them.

Jesus is led before Pontius Pilot and King Herod and they ask him, "If you are the Christ, tell us." Jesus responds, "If I tell you, you will not believe me…from now on, the Son of Man will be seated at the right hand of the mighty God." they all asked, "Are you then the Son of the Mighty God?" He replied, "You are right in saying that I am."

I would have loved to see their faces when Jesus said this!

Then they said, "Why do we need any more testimony? We have heard it from his own lips." They tried him for calling himself God, but we were worried about his "rebellion". His rebellion would take away their power.

LUKE 23

This is the often quoted and recited trial, crucifixion, death, and burial of Jesus.

They led him off to Pontius Pilate and told him Jesus was "subverting our nation, opposed to paying taxes to Caesar (both are lies) and claimed to be Christ, a King." Pilate asked Jesus if he is king of the Jews and Jesus said, "Yes, it is as you say." I find it interesting that he didn't ask Jesus about the other two charges that were lies. When Pilate heard that Jesus was a Galilean, he sent him to Herod, because he was under Herod's jurisdiction. Herod was excited because for a long time he wanted to see Jesus perform miracles. He grilled Jesus with questions, but Jesus did not answer. Then Herod and his soldiers ridiculed and mocked Jesus.

Three times Pilate (Herod sent him back to Pilate) asked the people what crime Jesus committed. It's obvious that Pilate did not want Jesus punished. **Pilate was a <u>weak</u> leader. He knew the right thing to do, and he didn't do it.**

They led Jesus away and made Simon of Cyrene Carry his cross. As Jesus was placed on his cross, Jesus says, "Father forgive them for they know not what they are doing." This is such a strong message about the power of forgiveness. Forgive even those that may put you to death.

Two criminals were hung with Jesus. One of them insulted Jesus by saying, "Aren't you the Christ, save yourself and us." The other criminal said, "Jesus remember me when you come into your kingdom." Jesus answered him, "...today you will be with me in Paradise." This man was promised salvation on his "deathbed". By following Jesus, it is never too late!! When you run to Jesus, he will always accept you. **People struggle with understanding how criminals can live a life a crime and ultimately be saved by Jesus and end up in heaven with him. This is the answer. It is Jesus acknowledging that once you admit that Jesus is your savior, God's grace takes over and you will be with him in paradise for eternity.**

Darkness came over the land from 6 PM to 9 PM, and Jesus called out to God, "Father, into your hands, I commit my spirit." Then he "breathed his last".

A man named Joseph asked Pilate if he could have Jesus' body. He took his body off the cross, wrapped it in linen cloth and placed it in a tomb. It was right before the Sabbath (nothing happens in Israel on the Sabbath) so it was <u>all quiet</u> until Sunday morning.

LUKE 24

On the first day of the week, a group of women (Mary Magdalene, Mary mother of James) went to the tomb to apply spices to Jesus' body. But when they got there, they did not find his body. Two men whose clothes "beamed like lightning" said to the women, "Why do you look for the living among the dead?" Remember how he told you while he was still with you in Galilee," The Son of Man must be delivered into the hands of sinful men, be crucified on the third day and be raised again." Then they remembered his words. When they got back to the tomb, they told all these things to the eleven. But they didn't believe the women because their "words were like nonsense". (Raised from the dead?). Peter wanted to see for himself, so he ran to the tomb and saw the strips of cloth (from Jesus' wrap) lying on the ground. He went away, wondering what had happened.

Two of the group were going to a village named Emmaus, about 7 miles from Jerusalem. While they were talking about everything that had happened, Jesus himself walked up along with them. They didn't recognize him. Jesus asked them what they were talking about. One of them, Cleopus, basically said, "Are you a visitor, haven't you heard what has happened around here?" They then explained to Jesus all the details of Jesus' life, death, and resurrection. Jesus challenged them and essentially said to them that they are "foolish" because all of what happened was foretold by the prophets and by Scripture concerning himself. Almost like, why are you surprised? They convinced Jesus to stay with them. At this point they still didn't even recognize him.

When they were eating Jesus took some bread and broke it and gave it to them. The group then recognized Jesus, who promptly disappeared from their sight. This group immediately went to Jerusalem and found the 11 apostles and said, "it is true the Lord has risen and appeared to Simon." While they were still talking, Jesus appeared among them and said, "Peace be with you." Jesus said to them, "Why are you troubled, and why do doubts rise in your mind? Look at my hands and my feet, it is I, myself. Touch me and see me. A ghost does not have flesh and bones, as you see I have." They were overjoyed and amazed but still didn't really believe it was him. I love what Jesus does next. He says, "Do you have anything to eat?" (I think he did this to prove his humanity.) While eating he said, "This is what I told you while

I was still with you. Everything must be fulfilled that is written about me in the law of Moses, the prophets, and the psalms."

He told them, "This is what is written. The Christ will suffer and rise from the dead on the third day, and repentance and forgiveness of sins will be preached in his name to all nations beginning at Jerusalem. you are witnesses of these things. I am going to send you what my Father has promised (Holy Spirit); but stay in the city until you have been clothed with power from on high."

Jesus led them out to Bethany, lifted his hands and blessed them, then he left them and was taken up to heaven. Then they worshiped him with great joy.

The word "fulfill" is so important. This was all planned in advance by God. It was his plan to reconcile us back to him! Jesus came to reconcile us back to his Father. So, it makes sense that our acknowledgement of him, as our Savior, is the key to us being with God forever.

THE GOSPEL OF JOHN

This gospel is incredible. It is thought-provoking, uplifting and speaks to the depth and richness of Jesus. It is divided into two major sections. Chapters 1-12 include a few public miracles which are expressly meant as signs pointing to Jesus' identity. Chapters 13-21, Jesus is basically alone with his disciples teaching them about his mission, the Holy Spirit and brilliant passages on his **command to love!**

JOHN 1

The beginning of John is so powerful. "In the beginning was the Word and the Word was God. He was with God in the beginning. Through him all things were made; without him nothing was made that has been made. In him was life, and that life was the light of men. The light shines in the darkness but the darkness has not understood it!"

The last line is so compelling. Darkness is the absence of light. People who live in darkness do not see light. If they understood the love of Jesus, they would live in the light. Jesus consistently begs us to see his light and to live in it.

John the Baptist came to tell everyone that true light was coming into the world. John goes on to explain Jesus' role. "He was in the world, and though the world was made through him, the world did not recognize him. He came to that which was his own, but his own did not receive him. Yet to all who received him, to those who believed his name, he gave them the right to be children of God—children not born of natural descent, nor of human

to be children of God—children not born of natural descent, nor of human decision or a husband's will, but <u>born of God</u>. The Word became flesh and made his dwelling among us. We have seen his glory. The glory of the one and only who came from the father. Full of grace and truth".

Wow. Read that again. How can anyone read the first page of John and not want to read the rest of the story?! John is explaining to us that Jesus was not conceived by man; he was "of God" from the very beginning. He is also explaining the fact that "his own" (the Jews) did not receive him. But to those he did, he gave them his inheritance.

John the Baptist cries out, "From the fullness of his grace we have all received one blessing after another. For the law was given through Moses; grace and truth came through Jesus Christ. No one has ever seen God, but God the one and only who is at the father's Side has made him known."

John the Baptist's teaching was so compelling that church leaders thought he was Christ, or a prophet, or Elijah. John denied it saying, "I baptize you in water, but among you stands one you do not know. He is the one that comes after me, the thongs of whose sandals I am not worthy to untie,"

John the Baptist's role is so important. He literally "prepared the way", "paving the road" and set up Jesus' audience.

The next day John saw Jesus coming toward him and said, "Look, the Lamb of God, who takes away the sin of the world." And John gave his testimony, "I saw the Spirit come down from heaven as a dove and remain on him. I would not have known him, except the one 'who sent me to baptize with water' told me the man on whom you see the Spirit come down and remain is who will baptize you with the Holy Spirit. I have seen and I testify that this is the Son of God."

The next section of John 1 is filled with stories of Jesus calling his first disciples. It's a great story of the disciple's excitement when they first see Jesus ("Look, the lamb of God!") And very strong leadership in the way Jesus gave direction to these men. For most, he simply said, "follow me". Nathaniel said,

"Rabbi how do you know me?" Jesus responded, "I saw you while you were still under the fig tree before Philip called you." He immediately showed them his wisdom and divinity.

Nathaniel said, "Rabbi, you are the son of God; you are the king of Israel." Jesus said, "You believe because I told you I saw you under the fig tree. you shall see greater things than that…I tell you the truth you shall see Heaven open and the angels of God ascending and descending on the son of man."

This is Jesus saying, " You ain't seen nothing yet!"

JOHN 2

The story of Jesus turning water into wine only appears in John. Jesus, his disciples, and Mary were at a wedding, and they ran out of wine. Mary tells Jesus this, and Jesus says, "Dear woman, why do you involve me?" Almost like, right now? Really? Mary said to the servants, "Do whatever he tells you."

Jesus told them to fill some jars with water and then draw some water out of one jar and take it to the master. The water was turned into wine. Everyone realized what had happened and the master said that this was the best wine. **Typically, the best wine is served first, but not when Jesus is involved. Once again, he "flips the script".**

The significance of the story was this was Jesus' first miracle, the first time he revealed his glory to those around him. John says, "His disciples put their faith in him." Maybe that's the reason he did it.

The next story of John is Jesus clearing the temple of the merchants and moneychangers. John's version is much more detailed, and it occurs at the beginning of the gospel and the others are at the end. John's Gospel is not a chronological account of Jesus' Life so this could be the same event that is reported at the end of the other gospels. In John's version, he not only turns over tables and throws the money on the floor. He said, "get these out of here. How dare you turn my father's house into a market!"

We need to imagine this scene. The merchants don't know that Jesus is God. To them he is just another guy, and he starts flipping over tables. They say to him, " What miraculous signs can you show us to prove your authority to do all this?" Jesus responded prophetically, "Destroy this temple and I will rebuild it in three days." Jesus was talking about his own body, not the building he was in. He meant "I am your temple". When Jesus rose from the dead, his disciples remembered that he had said this. Jesus continued to work many miraculous signs at Passover and people started to believe him.

JOHN 3

A man named Nicodemus, who is a member of the Jewish ruling council, came to Jesus and said, "Rabbi, we know you are a teacher who has come from God. For no one could perform the miraculous signs you are doing If God were not with him." Jesus declares to him, "I tell you the truth, no one can see the kingdom of God unless he is born again." Jesus' words continue (after Nicodemus wonders how someone can be born twice), "No one can enter the kingdom of God unless he is born of water and the spirit. Flesh gives birth to flesh, but the Spirit gives birth to the spirit. You should not be surprised at My saying, 'you must be born again'. The wind blows wherever it pleases. You hear its sound, but you cannot tell where it comes from or where it is going. So, it is with everyone born of the spirit." **Then Jesus introduces the most important words in the entire Bible:**

"For God so loved the world
that he gave his one and only son,
that whoever believes in him
shall not perish but have eternal life.
For God did not send his son into
the world to condemn the world,
but to save the world through him.
Whoever believes in him is not condemned,

but whoever does not believe stands condemned
already because he has not believed
in the name of God's one and only Son.
This is the verdict: Light has come
into the world, but men loved darkness
instead of light because their deeds were evil.
Everyone who does evil hates the light,
and will not come into the light for
fear that his deeds will be exposed.
But whoever lives by the truth comes
into the light, so that it may be seen
plainly that what he has done,
Has been done through God"!

If you follow Jesus, you will have eternal life with God. That is the story of his life, death, and resurrection. If you want to summarize the story of Jesus, and why we should follow him, there it is in John 3:16.

Jesus and his disciples went out into the countryside and were baptizing people. John was also baptizing people and the people with John were questioning the validity of Jesus baptizing people. John said, "A person can only receive what is given them from heaven. You yourselves can testify that I said, 'I am not the Messiah but am sent ahead of him.' The bride belongs to the bridegroom. The friend who attends the bridegroom waits and listens for him and is full of joy when he hears the bridegroom's voice. That joy is mine, and it is now complete. He must become greater; I must become less." **John is saying "Jesus is the bridegroom; I am his friend".**

This is John's greatest testimony. It's important to realize that John had built up a large group of followers. That's why they were challenging Jesus. This is a beautiful pledge of loyalty by John and acknowledgment that Jesus "is the one"! John continues, "The one who comes from above is above all; The one who is from the earth belongs to the earth and speaks as one from the earth. The one that comes from heaven is above all. He testifies to what he has seen and heard but no one accepts his testimony. Whoever has accepted it has certified that God is truthful. For the one whom God has sent speaks the words of God, for God gives the spirit without limit. The Father loves the son and has placed everything in his hands. Whoever believes in the Son has eternal life, but whoever rejects the Son will not see life, for God's wrath remains on them."

Read that last sentence again! It's important because it not only reiterates the promise of eternal life. It explains what happens if you don't grasp that gift. People ignore that part of the story because it's uncomfortable. No one wants to talk about the price of not following Jesus. The answer is right here in front of us. The price is God's wrath and God's wrath is hell.

JOHN 4

Jesus was on his way back to Galilee, and because he was tired, he sat down by a well. A Samaritan woman came by to draw water and Jesus asked her for a drink. The woman responded, "You are a Jew, and I am a Samaritan woman, how can you ask me for a drink?" (Jews and Samaritans do not associate.) Jesus said, "If you knew the gift of God and who it is that asks you for a drink, you would have asked him, and he would have given you living water." **The woman basically says to him, "You don't have anything to draw water and the well is deep...what are you thinking about?" (my translation) Jesus says, "Everyone who drinks this water will be thirsty again, but whoever drinks the water I give him will never thirst. Indeed, the water I give him will become in him a spring of water welling up to eternal life." Beautiful!**

The woman says that she wants some of Jesus' water. He tells her to go get her husband and the woman says, "I have no husband." Jesus seems to be testing her because he says, "You are right. You have had five husbands." And the guy she is with now is not her husband. Because he knew so much about her, she now believes that Jesus was a prophet. Jesus continued to challenge some of the Samaritan beliefs and the woman says, "When the Messiah comes, he will explain everything to us." Jesus says, "I who speak to you—am he."

The Samaritan woman went back to the town and told everyone about Jesus. The people went to see Jesus. The disciples knew that Jesus was hungry and were surprised no one brought him food. Jesus said, "My food is to do the will of him who sent me and to finish his work...open your eyes and look at the fields. They are ripe for harvest." Jesus is saying to his disciples, "Look at all these people who need to hear the good news and be saved!" Many of the Samaritans from that town Believed in Jesus because of all this. "We no longer believe because of what you said, now we have heard for ourselves, and we know that this man really is the savior of the <u>world</u>". **I love how Jesus describes his food......What nourishes him is doing his Father's work. That's true for us too. Once we experience God's love, doing things FOR God nourishes our hearts, minds, body, and soul.**

Jesus left for Galilee. Jesus had always said that "a prophet has no honor in his hometown." But now the people have seen all the miracles he had done.

Jesus arrived in Cana where a royal official whose son was sick, asked Jesus to come and heal him. Jesus called his bluff by saying, "Unless you people see the miraculous signs and wonders, you will never believe." Jesus tells him that his son will live while the man was on his way home. His servants ran to meet him to let him know that his son was alive and the "fever left him in the seventh hour." This is the exact hour that Jesus said, "your son will live." So everyone in his house believed!

JOHN 5

There is a pool in Jerusalem were a great many disabled people go to be healed. There was a man who had been an invalid for 38 years. Jesus asked him, "Do you want to get well?" The invalid replied, "Sir I have no one to help me into the pool...when I try to get in, someone else goes down ahead of me." Jesus said to him, "Go pick up your mat and walk." At once the man was cured. The Jews told him it was against the law to carry his mat on the Sabbath. The man said that Jesus instructed him to do so. The Jews tried to find Jesus, but they couldn't. Later Jesus saw the invalid at the Temple and said, "See you are well again. Stop sinning or something worse may happened to you."

The Jews continued to persecute Jesus for doing work on the Sabbath. Jesus said, "My Father is always at work to this very day, And I too am working." The Jews were upset at Jesus for working on the sabbath, but even more for calling God his Father, making himself equal to God. Jesus goes on to tell them that he can do nothing by himself; He can only do what he sees his father doing. **All this "work on the Sabbath" debate is at the root of the resistance against Jesus. They believe is attacking Judaism and its traditions and he is not.**

"Whoever hears my word and believes him who sent me has eternal life and will not be condemned. He has crossed over from death to life. I tell you the truth, a time is coming and has now come when the dead will hear the voice of the Son of God and those who hear will live. For as the Father has life in himself, so he has granted the Son to have life in himself. And he has given him the authority to judge because he is the Son of Man".

Jesus addresses John the Baptist's testimony. He says that John testified to the truth, but Jesus' testimony is, "weightier than John's." Jesus says, "… you diligently study Scriptures because you think that by them you possess eternal life. These are the scriptures that testify about me, yet you refuse to come to me to have life." He is saying 'you have been preparing for me, I'm here now, and you are rejecting me'. **This is an important concept. The Jews always have believed there will be a Messiah, but they just didn't believe Jesus was him. Even though his precise conception, birth, birthplace were foretold by the prophets in Isaiah and Micah.**

104

"I do not accept praise from men, but I know you. I know that you do not have the love of God in your hearts. I have come in my Father's name, and you do not accept me; But if someone else comes in our own name, you will except him. How can you believe if you accept praise from one another, yet make no effort to obtain the praise from the one and only God"? Wow, what a challenge!

We spend a lot of time seeking the approval of other people which is such a waste of time!!

JOHN 6

Jesus and his disciples crossed the far shore of the Sea of Galilee. A great crowd of people were following them because they saw the miraculous signs Jesus had performed on the sick. Jesus saw a great crowd approaching so he said to Philip, "Where shall we buy bread for these people to eat?" John says in his gospel, "he asked this only to test him, for he already had in mind what he was going to do." Philip told Jesus it would take eight month's wages to feed the 5000 people. Andrew (disciple) found a boy with five loaves of bread and two small fish. Jesus told his disciples to have people sit on the grass and he blessed the bread and the fish. Everyone ate as much as they wanted, and afterward they collected 12 baskets of leftovers. John tells us that the people were amazed, but because, "Jesus, knowing they intended to come and make him king by force, withdrew again to a mountain by himself."

At night, Jesus' disciples got into a boat and set off for Capernaum. Jesus had not joined them. They rowed about 3 1/2 miles and the waters grew rough. They were terrified. Then they saw Jesus approaching the boat, walking on water. "It is I; don't be afraid". They let Jesus into the boat, and it reached shore.

When they found Jesus on the other side of the lake, they asked him when he arrived. Jesus said, "I tell you the truth. You are looking for me, not because you saw miraculous signs, but because you ate the loaves and had your fill. Do not work for food that spoils, but for food that endures to eternal life, which the Son of Man will give you. For on him God the Father has placed his seal of approval." (I love that picture—seal of approval.) The disciples asked him, "What must we do to do the works God requires?" Jesus answered, "The work of God is this: to believe in the one he has sent."

How simple are those instructions? Work for food that endures to eternal life!!!

Verse 30 begins a very important series of statements. The crowd essentially asks Jesus what miraculous signs he will give them so they can believe him. "Our forefathers ate the manna in the desert. 'He gave them bread from Heaven to eat'".

Jesus said, "It is not Moses who has given you the bread from heaven, it is my Father…for the bread of God is he who comes down from heaven and gives life to the world." "Sir," they said, "From now on give us this bread." Then Jesus declared, "I am the bread of life. he who comes to me will never go hungry and he who believes in me will never go thirsty. All that the Father gives me will come to me, and whoever comes to me I will never drive away. For I have come down from heaven but not to do my will but to do the will of him who sent me. And this is the will of him who sent me, that I shall lose none of all that he has given me but raise them up at the last day. For my Father's will is that everyone who looks to the Son and believes in him shall have eternal life and I will raise him up at the last day."

These words from Jesus are just as powerful as what he said to Nicodemus in 3:16. He is crystal clear! He wants to bring us all home with him.

The Jews challenged Jesus by reminding Jesus that he is the Son of Mary and Joseph, so how can he be the Son of God. Actually, this is an insightful challenge from the Jews. What happens next, I believe, is the origin of communion, along with the last supper.

Jesus: "Your forefathers ate the manna in the desert, and they died…I am the living bread from heaven which a man may eat and not die…if anyone eats of this bread he will live forever"!

Clearly Jesus is not saying, "eat my body!" Also, I doubt that he is inferring if you eat bread that is representing his body, you will live forever. He is saying, "Listen to what I'm saying, and believe." The disciples were confused so Jesus clarified, "The Spirit gives life; the flesh counts for nothing. The words I have spoken to you—are spirits and they are life."

These teachings were so direct and unusual, that some disciples stopped following Jesus. Jesus asked the 12 if they were leaving too. Peter assured Jesus they were staying at this time. Jesus told them that one of them would betray him.

JOHN 7

Jesus was in Galilee and was purposely staying away from Judea because he knew the Jews wanted to take his life. His disciples wanted to see him go there so they could see him perform miracles. (to a degree, they were still skeptical.) Jesus told him that the time was not right yet for him to do things publicly. Jesus told them, "The world cannot hate you, but it hates me because I testify that what it does is evil." So, the disciples went on to the feast of the Tabernacle by themselves. They did not know that Jesus went also, alone and in secret. The crowds spoke about Jesus. Some said good things, others said bad things. But no one spoke publicly about him for the fear of the Jews.

This is so true in that people don't like to be told they are evil (or wrong). Think again about what Jesus said in John 3:16. People don't like to live in the light because it shows their sins. They like the darkness because it hides their sins.

Halfway through the feast, Jesus went up into the temple courts and began to teach. The Jews were amazed at Jesus' teaching essentially since he had not "studied". Jesus said, "My teaching is not my own. It comes from him who sent me." Jesus asks them directly why they are trying to kill him, and they tell him because they believe he is demon possessed. Jesus responds, "I did one miracle, and you are all astonished...why are you angry at me for healing the whole man on the Sabbath. Stop judging by mere appearances and make a right judgment."

The crowd was confused because Jesus was speaking publicly, and they knew that people were trying to kill him, but no one was saying a word to him. Jesus assured them that he is "the Christ". "I am not here on my own, but he who sent me is true. You do not know Him, but I know him because I am from him, and he sent me."

From reading John, it sounds like now is when the crowds started getting restless. The Pharisees sent temple guards to arrest him. Jesus said to them, "I am with you only for a short time and then I go to the one who sent to me. You will look for me, but you will not find me; and where I am you cannot come." This totally confused them. They assumed if they wanted to find Jesus, they could. They didn't realize Jesus was talking about heaven. On the last day of the feast, Jesus stood and spoke loudly, "If anyone is thirsty, let him come to me and drink. Whoever believes in me, as the Scripture has said, streams of living water will flow from within him." Jesus was referring to the Holy Spirit who had not yet come. When Jesus said this, many believed he was a prophet or the Christ. Others did not believe him, but no one laid a hand on him.

I love that word picture from Jesus. "Whoever believes in me... streams of living water will flow from within". That is what happens when people embrace Jesus. They understand who he was, what he did, why he did it and they understand what he said to the world, not just what others said about him. The words from the Bible flow like living water from within.

John 7:53-8:11 is not included in the earliest manuscripts.

JOHN 8

This is a story about the forgiving heart of Jesus. A woman was caught in the act of adultery. While Jesus was teaching in the temple courts, they brought the woman before Jesus. They said the law of Moses says we should stone this woman, "Now what do you say?" Jesus said, "If anyone of you is without sin, let him throw the first stone at her." When he said this, those that had condemned the woman went away one at a time. Jesus asked the woman, "where are they? Has no one condemned you?" "No one sir," she said. "Then neither do I condemn you. Go now and leave your life of sin".

The last sentence of Jesus often gets left out of people's recollection of the story. Jesus forgives, but he calls us to stop sinning. Later Jesus said to the people, "I am the light of the world. Whoever follows me will never walk in darkness but will have the light of life." **Again, Jesus' depiction of "light vs darkness" is so compelling. We need to live in the light which is him!**

The Pharisees said, "Here you are appearing as your own witness; your testimony is not valid." Jesus responded to them, "Even if I testify on my own behalf, my testimony is valid, for I know where I come from and where I am going. You judge by human standards; I pass judgment on no one. But with the Father who sent me, in your law it is written that the testimony of two men is valid. I am the one who testifies for myself; My other witness is the father who sent me."

The Pharisees asked him where his Father was, and Jesus told them they did not know his father nor him. He said, "If you knew me you would know my Father." One more time Jesus said to them, "I am going away, and you will look for me, and you will die in your sins. Where I go, you cannot come." He continued, "You are from below; I am from above. You are of this world; I am not of this world. I told you that you would die in your sins; if you do not believe that I am the one I claim to be, you will indeed die in your sins."

Read that again. 'If you do not believe that I am the one I claim to be, you will indeed die in your sins'. I wish people could see the simplicity

in what Jesus was saying. Jesus is not shying away from the consequences of not following him. He is crystal clear.

To the Jews that believed him, Jesus said, "If you hold on to my teaching you are really my disciples. Then you will know the truth, and the truth will set you free."

This is so true about following Jesus. once you understand the content and depth of his message you <u>know</u> it is the truth. And the freedom it provides is so peaceful. Think about a long drive where you have your route planned out on a map, and you know where you are going, you what it takes to get there, and you just enjoy the drive. Compare that to a trip where there is no map, closed routes, and loads of construction. That results in a very stressful trip (aka life). Jesus handed us the map.

Jesus tells the Jews that anyone who sins is a slave to sin and that has no place in his family. He says, "If the son sets you free, you will be free indeed."

Jesus is truly "preaching hard" in these passages. He tells him that if God is their Father (they just told Jesus he was) you would "Love me". He says, "I came from God, and now I am here." He continues to tell them that they are from the devil because they do not believe him. "The reason you do not hear is because you do not belong to God".

The Jews asked Jesus a ridiculous question, "Are we right in saying you are a Samaritan (Jews and Samaritans did not associate with each other) and demon possessed?" Jesus refutes their statement strongly. He says, "if anyone keeps my word, he will never see death."

This confused and frustrated the crowds, and they told Jesus that this confirms that Jesus is demon possessed. They tell Jesus that even Abraham died, as did the prophets." They ask him, "Are you saying you are greater than our father Abraham?" Jesus' response is so awesome. He humbly says, "If I glorify myself, My glory means nothing. My Father, whom you claim as your God is the one who glorifies me...your father Abraham rejoiced at the thought of seeing my day." **Jesus is calling their bluff. He is saying, "You**

worship God, and Abraham is your Father, and both are in my corner."
Jesus told them, "Before Abraham was born, 'I am.'" At that point they picked
up stones to stone Jesus, but he slipped away. Jesus makes an interesting point
here. The Jews acknowledge and worship his Father, just not Him.

JOHN 9

Jesus saw a man who had been blind since birth. His disciples won-
dered, "who sinned, him or his parents", that he would be born blind. Jesus
assured them neither sinned, but this happened, "so that the work of God
could be shown in his life." Jesus spit on the ground and made some mud
and put it on the man's eyes. The man's neighbors asked who allowed him to
see and the man told him it was Jesus. They brought the man who was blind
to the Pharisees, so the Pharisees asked the same question, "Who did this to
you?" When they were told it was Jesus, they said that he could not be from
God, because Jesus does not "keep the sabbath". The man told the Pharisees
that he believes Jesus is a prophet. The Pharisees then asked the man's parents
what they thought. They were afraid of the Pharisees, and because their son
was old enough, they said, "Ask him!"

The man said, "I don't know whether he is a sinner or not. One thing I
do know is that I was blind but now I see." They asked him where they thought
Jesus came from. He replied, "That's remarkable. You don't even know where
he came, yet he opened my eyes. We know God doesn't listen to sinners. He
listens to the Godly man who does his will…if this man were not from God,
he could do nothing." The crowds threw the man out and said, "you were
steeped in sin since birth."

Jesus found the man and asked him, "Do you believe in the Son of
Man?" The man said, "Who is he?" Jesus said, "He is the one speaking to you."
The man said, "Lord, I believe." Jesus said, "For judgment I have come into
this world, so that the blind will see and those who see will become blind."

JOHN 10

The first part of this chapter is a beautiful depiction of Jesus' relationship with his followers.

Jesus: The man who does not enter the sheep pen by the gate but climbs in by some other way is a thief and a robber. The man who enters by the gate is the shepherd of the sheep. The watchman opens the gate for him, and the sheep listen to his voice. He calls the sheep by name and leads them out.

Jesus clarifies: "I am the gate for the sheep. All who have ever come before me are thieves and robbers. The hired hand is not the shepherd who owns the sheep so when he sees the wolf coming, he abandons the sheep and runs away. Then the wolf attacks the flock and scatters it. The man runs away because he is a hired hand and cares nothing for the sheep.

I am the good Shepherd; I know my sheep and mine know me—Just as the father knows me and I know the father—I lay down my life for the sheep."

For me this is an important fact about following Jesus. There is only one. One person to follow. One person to worship. He is the way. No pastor, priest, elder, "saint", or speaker can take his place. This belief is not a translation from somewhere else. It is precisely what Jesus said. Furthermore, anyone who claims to be a follower of Jesus, and then says "follow me" (like a pastor might) run away as fast as you can. We need leaders who say, "don't follow me, follow Jesus".

The Jews continued to 'not believe' that Jesus is who he says he is. "If you are the Christ, tell us plainly". Jesus answered, "I did tell you, but you do not believe."

He tells them they did not believe it because they are not his sheep. "My sheep listen to my voice. I know them, and they follow me. I give them eternal life, and they shall never perish; No one can snatch them out of my hand. My Father, who has given them to me, is greater than all; no one can snatch them out of my Father's hand. I and the Father are one".

Can you imagine the look on the Jews faces when he said this?

They were going to stone Jesus, so he said, "I have shown you many great miracles from the Father. For which of these do you stone me?"

I love how he challenges them with a simple question. They explained that they wanted to stone him for blasphemy. Jesus said, "Do not believe me unless I do what my Father does. But if I do it, even though you don't believe me, believe the miracles, that you may know and understand that the Father is in me, and I in the Father." **This is beautiful. Everything that Jesus is saying and doing in these moments is to glorify God. In our lives, if we are living a life of following Jesus, and we get challenged, our answer is to defer to our devotion to God.**

JOHN 11

This is the story of the death of Lazarus and Jesus raising him from the dead. Lazarus was the brother of Mary and Martha Magdalene. They lived in Bethany, so they sent word to Jesus that he was sick. He told his disciples that he wanted to go see his friends. They cautioned him that the last time he was there, the Jews tried to stone him. Jesus said, "are there not 12 hours of daylight? A man who walks by the day will not stumble, for he sees the world's light. It is when he walks by night that he stumbles, for he has no light."

I think Jesus has two points in this statement.

1) let's go! Don't be lazy!

2) walk in the light of <u>Him</u>.

When Jesus arrived, the sisters told Jesus that he had been dead for four days. Martha said to Jesus, "If you would have been here my brother would not have died. But I know that even now God will give you whatever you ask."

Jesus said, "Your brother will rise again." then he said, "I am the resurrection and the life. He who believes in me will live even though he dies. And whoever lives and believes in me will never die. Do you believe this?"

Martha told Jesus that she believed him and that he was the Christ. Everyone was very sad. Mary and Martha were crying. when they took Jesus to the place where Lazarus lay, "Jesus wept". This is a beautiful reminder of Jesus' humanity. Some of the Jews said, "could not he who opened the eyes of a blind man have kept this man from dying?" Almost like challenging Jesus! "Jesus wept" (John 11:35) is the shortest verse in the bible. 2 words.

They all went to Lazarus' tomb and Jesus told them to take away the stone. Martha was concerned that there would be a bad odor. Jesus said, "Did I not tell you that if you believe, you would see the glory of God?" Jesus looked up to the sky and uttered this beautiful prayer:

"Father, I thank you that you have heard me. I knew that you always hear me, but I said this was for the benefit of the people standing here, that they may believe you sent me".

Jesus calls out, "Lazarus, come out!" "And he did, with his hands and feet wrapped in cloth." (John's Gospel offers no further details on the reaction of the people that were watching, which I find odd.)

Some of the Jews that saw what Jesus did believe in him. Others went to the Pharisees and told them what happened. The Pharisees called a meeting of the Sanhedrin. What is said next is a very telling verse in the plight of Jesus. "Here is this man performing many miraculous signs. If we let him go on like this everyone will believe in him and then the Romans will come and take away both our place and our nation".

The plot to kill Jesus is all about people's belief that Jesus was leading a rebellion against the Roman Empire. And think about the faults in their logic. 'He is hurting no one, he is healing people, he is spreading love, but he is a threat to our power. Let's kill him.' It is a telling statement as to how important power is to people who crave power.

The High Priest Caiaphas spoke up and said, "You know nothing at all. You do not know that it is better for one man to die for the people than that the whole nation perish." Earlier that year Caiaphas had prophesied that

Jesus would die for the Jewish nation, and not only for the nation, but for the scattered children of God, to bring them together and make them one. From that day on, they plotted to take Jesus' Life.

Therefore, Jesus no longer moved about publicly. He went to a village named Ephraim with his disciples. When it was almost time for Passover people went from the villages to Jerusalem. They kept looking for Jesus, as the chief priests had given orders to report back if they had seen him so they can arrest him.

JOHN 12

Jesus went to Bethany, where Lazarus lived. His sister Martha served the dinner, and his sister Mary poured some expensive perfume on Jesus' feet and washed it with her hair. Judas Iscariot objected to this because he thought that the perfume should be sold, and the money be given to the poor. He just wanted to steal the money from the bag as he had done before. Jesus told Judas to leave her alone because, "You will always have the poor, but you will not always have me." A large crowd found out that Jesus was in the area, and they came to see him but also to see Lazarus who had been risen from the dead by Jesus. The chief priests now wanted to kill Lazarus as well because on account of him. Many were putting their faith in Jesus.

The Triumphal Entry

The next day a great crowd of people heard that Jesus was on his way to Jerusalem. They waved palm branches at him and praised him in the streets. The Pharisees were astounded at the attention given to Jesus. "Look how the whole world has gone after him".

There were some Greeks that went to Jerusalem and wanted to see Jesus. Jesus said, "The hour has come for the Son of Man to be glorified… whoever serves me must follow me; and where I am, my servant will also be. My father will honor the one who serves me. Unless a kernel of wheat falls to the ground and dies, it remains only a single seed. But if it dies, it produces many seeds. The man who loves his life will lose it while the man who hates his life in the world will keep it for eternal life! **Wow! This is truly an incredible depiction of how Jesus explained his death. First, he calls his own death (and pending resurrection) 'the hour for the Son of Man to be glorified'. That's Jesus saying, 'I told you it was coming, and now it's here'. Second, he is saying, 'when this happens as I said it would, you can't believe how many believers will follow'. And billions have followed him since that happened.**

Jesus shares his heart. "Now my heart is troubled and what shall I say, 'Father, save me from this hour'? No, it was for this very reason I came to this hour. Father, glorify your name". A voice came down from heaven and said, "I have glorified it, and will glorify it again." Jesus said, "The voice was for your benefit, not mine." As if to say, "I already know that voice!"

Jesus then says, "You are going to have the light just a little while longer. Walk while you have light, before darkness overtakes you. The man who walks in the dark does not know where he is going. Put your trust in the light while you have it, so that you may become sons of the light."

Jesus could not be any clearer to all of us. "Walk in his light".

Many still do not believe what Jesus was saying, and still others did believe because of what they had seen. But they were afraid "They would be put out of the synagogue for they loved praise from men more than praise from God".

Jesus then tells them, "When a man believes in me, he does not believe in me only, he sees the one who sent me. (**In his toughest moments, he continues to glorify God. Do I?**) I have come into the world so that no one who believes in me should stay in darkness. As for the person who hears my words but does not keep them, I do not judge him. For I do not come into this world to judge it, but to save it. There is a judge for the one who rejects me and does not accept my words. That very word which I spoke will condemn him at the last day."

The price of not following Jesus is very costly!

JOHN 13

Just before Passover, Jesus knew that his time to leave the world was coming and he wanted to show the disciples how much he loved them. he poured water into a basin and began to wash his disciple's feet. When he approached Peter, Peter said, "Lord are you going to wash my feet?" Jesus replied, "you do not realize now what I am doing but later you will understand." "No," Peter said, "You shall never wash my feet." Jesus answered, "Unless I wash you, you have no part with me." "Then Lord," Simon Peter replied, "Not just my feet but my hands and my head as well." **This is such a great picture of Jesus' Love and Peter's response is saying, "If getting washed by you is the ticket, I'm all in!"**

We must be willing to bow down, serve others and wash their feet— just like Jesus did!

Jesus said, "Now that I, your Lord, and teacher have washed Your feet you also should wash one another's feet. I have set you an example that you should do as I have done for you. I tell you the truth, no servant is greater than his master nor is a messenger greater than the one who sent him. Now that you know these things, you will be blessed if you do them."

After washing their feet, Jesus informs his disciples that one of them is going to betray him. The disciples were confused, and Peter asked him, "Who is it?" Jesus said that it is the person that, "I will give this piece of bread to." He gave it to Judas; Satan entered him, and Judas left the room.

Jesus proceeds to tell the disciples that he will only be with them for a little while longer. He also tells them, "Where I am going, you cannot come." And then he utters some of the most important words in the Bible,

"A new command I give you:
love one another. As I have loved
you, so you must love one another.

> By this all men will know that
> you are my disciples if you love
> one another."

I am amazed that people refute the teachings of Jesus Christ. All he ever did was encourage us to love each other. Peter asked Jesus where he was going and Jesus said, "Where I am going you cannot follow now, but you will follow later." Peter tells Jesus that he would lay down his life for him. Jesus responds by telling Peter that, "before the rooster crows, you will disown me three times."

How often do we deny our faith in Jesus? Lack of acknowledgment is denial as much as lack of willingness to profess.

JOHN 14

Jesus is preparing a place for all of us. Jesus tries to comfort his disciples because they are worried about him and what will happen next. "Do not let your hearts be troubled. Trust in God; Trust also in me. In my Father's house there are many rooms; If it were not so, I would have told you I am going there to prepare a place for you. And if I go and prepare a place for you, I will come back and take you to be with me that you may also be where I am. You know the way to the place where I am going".

Thomas asked Jesus, "Lord, we don't know where you are going, how can we know the way?" Jesus utters these important words, "I <u>am the way</u>, the truth, and the life. No one comes to the Father except through me."

Jesus could not be clearer for us. If we want to go where he is, the only road is through Jesus. And we have our own room in his house. That's a comforting thought! He goes on to say, "Anyone who has faith in me will do what I have been doing. He will do even greater things than these because I am going to the Father. And I will do whatever you ask in my name, so that the son may bring glory to the Father."

Jesus makes it very important promise, and that is that he is going to send the Holy Spirit.

"If you love me, you will obey what I command. And I will ask the father and he will give you another counselor to be with you forever—the Spirit of Truth. The world cannot accept him because it neither sees him nor knows him. But you know him, for he lives with you and will be in you. I will not leave you as orphans; I will come to you…whoever has my commands and obeys them, he is the one who loves me. He who loves me will be loved by my father, and I too will love him and show myself to him".

"All this I have spoken while I am with you. But the counselor, The Holy Spirit, whom the Father will send in my name, will teach you all things and will remind you of everything I have said. Peace I leave with you; My peace I give you. I do not give as the world gives you. Do not let your hearts be troubled and do not be afraid".

Jesus sends the Holy Spirit, and the Holy Spirit is <u>peace</u>. Not peace as the world understands it (free from conflict/ wars) but peace in our hearts, peace in our minds and peace in our souls." Jesus gives us the only recipe to achieve that! He specifically said, "I do not give as the world gives". Which means "my peace is different". His peace is total lack of fear.

JOHN 15

"I am the true Vine, and my Father is the gardener. He cuts off every branch in me that bears no fruit, while every branch that does bear fruit, he prunes so that it will be even more fruitful…remain in me and I will remain and you. No branch can bear fruit by itself; it must remain in the vine. Neither can you bear fruit unless you remain in me".

This appears to be harsh words from Jesus, That God will "cut us off". But the beauty is he gives us the precise recipe to bear fruit! To characterize God as vengeful is unjust because he tells us how not to get "cut off"!

"As the Father has loved me, so I have loved you. If you obey my commands, you will remain in my love…I have told you this so that my joy may be in you and that your joy may be complete. My command is this: Love each other as I have loved you. Greater love has no one than this: That he lay down his life for his friends…you did not choose me, I chose you and appointed you to go and bear fruit—fruit that will last".

Wow. This is a profound summary of what it means to follow Jesus. He loves us. He asks us to love each other like he did, and the reward we get on earth is complete joy in the peace that only the Holy Spirit can provide. Our reward in heaven is that we get to spend eternity with him.

Jesus warns the disciples that the world hated Jesus so they will hate the disciples as well. "If you belonged to the world, it would love you as its own. But I have chosen you out of the world, that is why the world hates you". **We need to know that sometimes following Jesus comes with a price and we must be willing to pay it, because the reward is enormous!**

JOHN 16

Jesus explains to the disciples that the only way the Holy Spirit can come is if he goes away. The Holy Spirit will "convict the world of guilt in regard to sin, righteousness and judgment; sin, because men do not believe in me; righteousness, because I am going to the father; and judgment, because the prince of this world now stands condemned". **'Convict the world of guilt' is such an incredible word picture.**

He tells them that the Holy Spirit will guide them in all truth. "He will bring glory to me by taking from what is mine and making it known to you. All that belongs to the Father is mine". He also says, "In a little while you will see me no more, and then after a little while, you will see me."

The disciples were totally confused. Jesus knew they were confused so he explained, "…You will weep and mourn while the world rejoices. You will grieve but your grief will turn to joy. A woman giving birth to a child has pain because her time has come; but when the baby comes, she forgets her anguish because of her joy that a child has been born into the world." Jesus is clearly talking about the grief we will feel when he dies and joy we will feel when we see his resurrection.

"I tell you the truth, my Father will give you whatever you ask in my name. Until now you have not asked for anything in my name. Ask and you shall receive, and your joy will be complete".

JOHN 17

Knowing that his death is near, Jesus prays for himself. He knows he is going home. This is a beautiful, profound prayer.

"Father the time has come.
Glorify your Son, that your Son
may glorify you. For you
granted him authority over all
your people that he might give eternal
life to all those you have given him.
Now this is eternal life:
That they may know you, the only one true
God, and Jesus Christ, whom
you have sent. I have brought
you glory on earth by completing
the work you gave me to do.
and now, Father, glorify me in
your presence with the glory I
had with you before the world began"

It's almost like Jesus is saying, "Dad, I'm coming home."

Jesus continues to pray for his disciples. His prayer is in some ways a thank you to his Father for sending the disciples to him. "I will remain in the world no longer, but they are still in the world...Holy Father, protect them by the power of your name...While I was with them, I protected them and kept them safe by the name you gave me…my prayer is not that you take them out of this world but that you protect them from the evil one. Sanctify them by the truth; and your word is truth". **This sounds exactly how we pray for our children when they are not with us.**

The last group that Jesus prays for is all believers. "…that all of them maybe one, Father, just as you are in me and I in you…may they be brought to complete unity to let the world know that you sent me and I have loved them even as you have loved me…righteous Father, though the world does not know you, I know you, and they know you have sent me. I have made you known to them, and will continue to make you known in order that the love you have for me may be in them".

This prayer is so beautiful. Jesus is always deferring to his Father. "Let them see me so they can know you!"

Jesus' composure under pressure

JOHN 18

Jesus and his disciples went into an olive garden. Judas knew he went there, so he led a group of soldiers and officials who were carrying torches and weapons.

Jesus asked them who they were looking for and twice they said, "Jesus of Nazareth". Jesus said, "I am he" and he also requested that they let his disciples go. At that moment, Peter drew his sword and cut off the right ear of a soldier. Jesus scolded him and told him to put his sword away. "Shall I not drink the cup the Father has given me"?

Jesus knew that he needed to go through this to fulfill his mission for coming to earth. The soldiers found Jesus and brought him to Annas (father-in-law of Caiaphas) and then to Caiaphas, who was the high priest that year. Caiaphas was the one who said it would be good if one man would die for the people.

When they led Jesus into the courtyard they said to Peter, "You are not one of this man's disciples are you?" Peter replied, "I am not."

Meanwhile, Caiaphas questioned Jesus and Jesus said, "I have spoken openly to the world. I always taught in synagogues or at the temple, where all the Jews come together. I said nothing in secret. Why question me? Ask those who heard me. Surely, they know what I said." One of the soldiers hit Jesus in the face and said, "Is this the way you answer the high priest?" "If I said something wrong, testify as to what is wrong. If I spoke the truth, why did you strike me"?

I just love the way Jesus handles himself under pressure.

Then another person asked Peter if he was one of Jesus' disciples, and he said no. Finally, a servant asked him the same question and he denied it a third time. As Jesus predicted, a rooster crowed three times, signaling peter's denial three times.

The Jews led Jesus to the Palace of the Roman governor, Pontius Pilate. He asked them what charges were being placed on Jesus. They said if he wasn't a criminal, they wouldn't be bringing Jesus to him. Pilate said, "take him yourselves and judge him by your own standards!" Then Jesus told Pilate that they didn't have the right to execute anyone. Pilate asked Jesus, "Are you the king of the Jews?" Jesus retorted, "Is that your own idea or did others talk you into it?" Pilate said, "Am I a Jew? It was your people and your chief priests who handed you over to me. What is it you have done?"

I'm guessing because Pilate is a Roman and he is saying, "I don't have anything to do with this—your people did this." Jesus said, "my kingdom is not of this world. If it were, my servants would fight to prevent my arrest by the Jews. But now my kingdom is from another place." "You are a king then!" Said Pilate. Jesus said, "You are right in saying I am a king. In fact, for this reason I was born, and for this I came into the world to testify to the truth. Everyone on the side of the truth listens to me!"

Jesus is clearly drawing a line in the sand!

Pontius found no basis for charges against Jesus, so he gave the Jews a choice to have Jesus released, or Barabbas. The Jews shouted that they wanted Barabbas.

JOHN 19

Jesus was sentenced to be crucified. Pilate had Jesus flogged and they twisted together a crown of thorns and put it on his head. They clothed him in a purple robe, mocking him by saying, "All hail King of the Jews."

Pilate repeatedly told them that he found no charges against Jesus. (Amazing then that he had Jesus flogged and that he allowed him to be killed—what a weak leader!)

The Jews told Pilate that the main charge against Jesus was that he claimed to be the Son of God. Pilate interrogated Jesus and said, "Don't you realize I have the power to crucify or free you?" Jesus said, "You would have no power over me unless it was given to you from above." From then on, Pilate tried to continually release Jesus, but the crowds insisted that if he did, "he is no friend of Caesar". (Recall that all this was fear that Jesus was leading a rebellion against the Roman empire.) **Jesus is calmly saying "you have zero power". That's how you stand up to a bully!**

Pilate handed Jesus over to the crowds and said, "Here is your king", and the Jews shouted, "Take him away. Crucify him, we have no king but Caesar." So, Pilate handed him over to be crucified.

The soldiers took charge of Jesus, and they led him out to Golgotha, the place of the skull, to be crucified with two other criminals. They put a sign on his cross that said, "Jesus of Nazareth, the king of the Jews". Many of the Jews protested to change the sign to say that he "claimed" to be the King of the Jews. The soldiers gambled to see who got Jesus' robe. While he was on the cross, Jesus told his mother to treat his disciples as a son and asked his disciple to take care of his mother. From then on, they took her into his home.

Jesus was thirsty so they took a sponge and soaked it in the white vinegar and gave it to Jesus on a stick. Jesus said, "it is finished." Then he "bowed his head and gave up his spirit".

They did not want Jesus hanging on a cross on the Sabbath so they asked Pilate if they could break Jesus' legs. (They broke people's legs so they could not support their body weight and they would die faster.) But they realized Jesus was already dead, so they pierced his side with a spear, bringing sudden flow of blood and water. This is a fulfillment of what is written in Exodus, Numbers, and Psalms, "not one of his bones will be broken".

Joseph of Arimathea and Nicodemus (John 3:16) went to retrieve the body of Jesus. They brought myrrh and aloes to protect the body. They wrapped it in cloth and laid Jesus into a tomb that was in a garden. It was a new tomb where no one had ever been laid.

JOHN 20

Mary Magdalene went to the tomb in the morning and saw that the stone had been removed, so she ran to Peter and said that they have taken Jesus out of the tomb, and they don't know where he is. Simon and the other disciples ran to the tomb and saw the cloth laying on the ground. They saw and believed. Mary Magdalene stayed at the tomb crying. There were two angels in white there that asked her, "Why are you crying?" And she replied, "They have taken my Lord away and I don't know where they have put him." At that moment she turned around and saw Jesus, but she did not know it was him. Then she recognized him. Jesus told Mary to let the disciples know that he was returning to his father. She went to them and said, "I have seen the Lord!"

The disciples were all together, locked in a room, for fear of the Jews. Jesus came in the room and said, "peace be with you." He showed him his hands and his side, and they believed him. "As the Father has sent me, so I send you".

Peter was not with the disciples when Jesus appeared. Peter told them that unless he could see the nail marks in Jesus' hands and put his hands in Jesus' side, "I will not believe it." A week later the disciples were in the same room and Jesus came and said to Peter, "put your finger here, see my hands. Reach out your hand and put it in my side. Stop doubting and believe." Thomas said, "My Lord and my God." Jesus told him, "Because you have seen me you have believed. Blessed are those who have not seen and yet have believed."

That is what is so challenging for people—they have not seen!

John says, "Jesus did many other miraculous signs in the presence of his disciples which are not recorded in this book. But these are written that you may believe that Jesus is the Christ, the Son of God, and that by believing you will have life in his name."

Have life in his name!

Feed the world with this message of Jesus

JOHN 21

A few of the disciples were together and they decided to go fishing but unfortunately, they did not catch any fish. Jesus was on the shore, although they did not realize it was him. He told them to throw their nets on the right side of the boat. They did and caught so many fish they were unable to haul in the nets. They then realized it was Jesus. They went ashore and saw some coal burning so Jesus summoned them to join him for breakfast. This was the third time they had seen him since his resurrection.

Jesus then said to Peter, "Do you truly love me more than these?" "Yes Lord, you know I love you". Jesus said, "Feed my lambs." Jesus said a second time, "Do you truly love me?" after asking him a third time, Peter said, "Lord you know all things, you know that I love you." Jesus then instructed Peter to feed the sheep (followers) and to be ready to withstand the same type of persecution that Jesus suffered.

John's final words are so inspiring.

"Jesus did so many other things as well. If every one of them were written down, I suppose that even the whole world would not have room for the books that would be written"!

HALFTIME THOUGHTS

Summarizing the stories of Jesus, and sharing his exact words was such an uplifting experience. My hope was that God's word would immerse itself deeper into my soul. After reading the New Testament 12 times, I learned that writing the New Testament allowed me to slow down and absorb messages that I had never received before. Even though I may have read the stories many times, this project gave me the opportunity to capture "what it meant to me". Which is tricky, because it is important to read the words as they are written and resist the temptation to alter stories to fit our own narrative or belief system. That said, to articulate how one can apply the principle in any story is a very valuable exercise.

I tried very hard to just "follow the spirit" when I was writing. Sometimes I felt like I was supposed to transcribe a section literally, other times I felt the need to share my perspective, and occasionally I would just write "read that again", because the story itself was so impactful. In no case did I ever change the words that were written, and any time I shared a "perspective" I tried my very best to make sure that what I was saying was biblically accurate. I did that by researching what biblical scholars said about the story and I let my perspective evolve from there. This book is much more a "summary of stories" and "lessons from Jesus" than my perspective. One might wonder why anyone would read a book like this when they could just read the Bible. They are right! The New Testament is much better than my version of it. If my version of it leads a person to read it, then this effort was worth every minute.

As a follower of Jesus, this book was an attempt by me to learn even more about the man I have chosen to follow. The four Gospels are full of stories about Jesus' teachings on a multitude of topics: how to pray, how to treat nonbelievers, how to forgive those who wrong you, how to lead others, how to give glory to God; I could go on forever. Perhaps the "one thing" that was driven deeper in my soul was the ultimate simplicity of the message of Jesus Christ.

LOVE

Everything that Jesus ever talked about was rooted in this one very simple and all-encompassing word.

The key to friendship is love.
> because when you love someone,
> you only want the best for them.

The key to marriage is love.
> Active love. It will make the good times
> great, tough times bearable, and
> every act of love strengthens
> the foundation.

The key to being a parent is love.
> Because when you truly love
> you protect, discipline, give, respect,
> listen and care with a loving heart.

The key to forgiveness is love.
> If you don't love, you can't
> rebuild a broken relationship.
> When you do love, it allows
> you to see the best in others and
> to free yourself from anger.

The key to a joyful spiritual life is love.
Because when you love God
with all your mind, all your
heart, all your strength, and
all your soul, you will know
that God is with you always and
he will bring you joy.

The key to salvation is love. If we love Jesus, and follow Him and believe in Him, He promises that we will spend eternity in heaven with Him.

Gospel stories by chapter

Matthew	Mark	Luke	John
1) The genealogy of Jesus The birth of Jesus Christ 2) The visit of the Magi The escape to Egypt The return to Nazareth 3) John the Baptist prepares the way The Baptism of Jesus 4) The Temptation of Jesus Jesus begins to preach The calling of the first disciples Jesus heals the sick 5) The Beatitudes Salt and light The fulfillment of the law Murder Adultery Divorce	1) John the Baptist prepares the way Baptism and temptation of Jesus The calling of the first disciples Jesus Drives out an evil spirit Jesus heals many Jesus prays in a solitary place A man with leprosy 2) Jesus heals a paralytic The calling of Lent Jesus questioned about fasting 3) Lord of sabbath Crowds follow Jesus The appointing of the 12 apostles Jesus and Beelzebub Jesus' mother and brothers 4) The parable of the sower A lamp on a stand	1) Birth of John the Baptist foretold Birth of Jesus foretold Mary visits Elizabeth Mary's song The birth of John the Baptist Zechariah's song 2) Birth of Jesus The shepherds and the angels Jesus presented in the temple The boy Jesus at the temple 3) John the Baptist prepares the way Baptism and genealogy of Jesus (Joseph) 4) The temptation of Jesus Jesus rejected at Nazareth	1) The Word became flesh John the Baptist denies being the Christ Jesus the lamb of God Jesus' first disciples Jesus calls Philip and Nathaniel 2) Jesus changes water into wine Jesus clears the temple 3) Jesus teaches Nicodemus John the Baptist's testimony about Jesus 4) Jesus talks with a Samaritan woman The disciples rejoin Jesus Many Samaritans believe Jesus heals the official's son

Oaths An eye for an eye Love your enemies 6) Giving to the needy Prayer Fasting Treasures in heaven Do not worry 7) Judging others Ask seek knock The narrow and wide gates The wise and fool- ish builder 8) The man with leprosy The faith of the centurion Jesus heals many The cost of follow- ing Jesus Jesus calms the storm The healing of two demon pos- sessed men 9) Jesus heals a paralytic The calling of Matthew Jesus questioned about fasting A dead girl and a sick woman Jesus heals the blind and mute The workers are few 10) Jesus sends out the 12 Jesus and John the Baptist 11) Woe on unre- pentant cities Rest for the weary	The parable of the growing seed The parable of the mustard seed Jesus calms the storm 5) Healing of a demon pos- sessed man A dead girl and A sick woman 6) A prophet with- out honor Jesus sends out the 12 John the Baptist beheaded Jesus feeds the 5000 Jesus walks on the water 7) Clean and unclean Faith of a Syrophoenician Woman Healing of a deaf and mute man 8) Jesus feeds the 4000 Yeast of the Pharisees and Herod Healing of a blind man at Bethsaida Peter's confession of Christ Jesus predicts his death 9) The Transfiguration Healing of a boy with an evil spirit Who is the greatest Whoever is not against us is for us Cursing to sin	Jesus drives out an evil spirit Jesus heals many 5) The calling of first disciples The man with leprosy Jesus heals a paralytic The calling of Levi Jesus questioned about fasting 6) Lord of the Sabbath The 12 apostles Blessings and woes Love for enemies Judging others The tree and its fruit The wise and fool- ish builders 7) The Faith at the Centurion Jesus raises a wid- ow's son Jesus and John the Baptist Jesus anointed by a sinful woman 8) The parable of the sower A lamp on a stand Jesus' mother and brothers Jesus calms the storm The healing of a demon pos- sessed man A dead girl and a sick woman 9) Jesus sends out the Twelve Jesus feeds 5000 The Transfiguration	5) The healing at the pool Life through the Son Testimonials about Jesus 6) Jesus feeds the 5000 Jesus walks on water Jesus is the bread of life Many disciples desert Jesus 7) Jesus goes to feast of Tabernacle Jesus teaches at the feast Jesus is the Christ Unbelief of the Jewish leaders 8) The validity of Jesus' testimony The children of Abraham The children of the devil The claims of Jesus about himself 9) Jesus heals a man born blind The Pharisees to investigate the healing Spiritual blindness 10) The shepherd and his flock The unbelief of Jesus 11) The death of Lazarus Jesus comforts the sisters Jesus raises Lazarus from the dead The plot to kill Jesus 12) Jesus anointed at Bethany

12) Lord of the Sabbath God's chosen servant Jesus and Beelzebub The sign of Jonah Jesus' mother and brothers 13) The parable of the Sower The parable of the weeds The parable of the mustard seed and yeast The parable of the weeds explained The parable of the hidden treasure and the Pearl The parable of the net The prophet without honor 14) John the Baptist beheaded Jesus feeds the 5000 Jesus walks on the water 15) Clean and unclean Faith of Canaanite Women Jesus feeds 4000 16) The demand for a sign The yeast of Pharisees and Sadducees Jesus predicts his death 17) The Transfiguration healing of a boy with a demon The temple tax	10) Divorce The little children and Jesus The rich young man Jesus again predicts his death The request of James and John Blind Bartimaeus receives his sight 11) The triumphal entry Jesus clears the temple The withered fig tree The authority of Jesus questioned 12) The parable of the tenants Paying taxes to Caesar Marriage at the resurrection The greatest commandment Whose son is Christ The widow's offering 13) Signs of the end of the age The day and hour unknown 14) Jesus anointed at Bethany The Lord's supper Gethsemane Jesus arrested before the Sanhedrin Peter disowns Jesus 15) Jesus before Pilate The soldiers mock Jesus The crucifixion	Healing of a boy with evil spirits Who will be the greatest 10) Jesus sends out the 72 Parable of the good Samaritan At the home of Martha and Mary 11) Jesus teaching on prayer Jesus and Beelzebub The son of Jonah The lamp of the body Six woes Samaritan opposition The cost of following Jesus 12) Warnings and encouragements The parable of the rich fool Do not worry Watchfulness Not peace but division Interpreting the times 13) Repent or perish A crippled woman healed on the Sabbath Parables of the mustard seed and yeast The narrow door Jesus' surprise for Jerusalem 14) Jesus is at a Pharisees house The parable of the great banquet The cost of being a disciple	The triumphal entry Jesus predicts his death The Jews continue in their unbelief 13) Jesus washes his disciples' feet Jesus predicts his betrayal Jesus predicts Peter's denial 14) Jesus comforts his disciples Jesus' way to the father Jesus promises the Holy Spirit 15) The Vine and the branches The world hates the disciples 16) The work of the Holy Spirit The disciples' grief will turn to joy 17) Jesus prays for himself Jesus prays for his disciples Jesus prays for all believers 18) Jesus arrested Peter's first denial The high priest questions Jesus Peter's second and third denials Jesus before Pilate 19) Jesus sentenced to be crucified The crucifixion The death of Jesus The burial of Jesus 20) The empty tomb Jesus appears to Mary Magdalene

18) The greatest of the kingdom of heaven The parable of the lost sheep A brother who sins against you The parable of the unmerciful servant 19) Divorce The little children and Jesus The rich young man 20) The parable of the workers Jesus Again predicts his death A mother's request Two blind men receive sight 21) The triumphal entry Jesus at the temple The fig tree withers The authority of Jesus questioned The parable of the two sons The parable of the tenants 22) The parable of the wedding banquet Paying taxes to Caesar Marriage at the resurrection The greatest commandment 23) Seven woes 24) Signs of the end of the age The pay and the hour unknown 25) The parable of the 10 virgins	The death of Jesus The burial of Jesus 16) The resurrection	15) The parable of the lost sheep The parable of the lost coin The parable of the lost son 16) The parable of the shrewd Manager Additional teachings The rich man and Lazarus 17) Sin faith duty Ten healed of leprosy The coming of the kingdom of God 18) The parable of the persistent widow The parable of the Pharisee and tax collector The little children and Jesus The rich ruler Jesus again predicts his death A blind beggar receives his sight 19) Zacchaeus the tax collector The parable of the ten minas The triumphal entry Jesus at the temple 20) The Authority of Jesus questioned The parable of the tenants Paying taxes to Caesar The resurrection and marriage Whose son is the Christ	Jesus appears to his disciples 21) Jesus and his miraculous catch of fish Jesus reinstates Peter

The parable of the talents The sheep and the gates 26) The plot against Jesus Jesus anointed at Bethany Judas agrees to betray Jesus The Lord's supper Jesus predicts peter's denial Gethsemane Jesus arrested Before the Sanhedrin Peter disowns Jesus 27) Judas hangs himself Jesus before Pilate The soldiers mock Jesus The crucifixion The death of Jesus The burial of Jesus The guard at the tomb 28) The resurrection The guards report The great commission		21) The widow's offering Signs of the end of the age 22) Judas agrees to betray Jesus The last supper Jesus prays on the Mount of Olives Jesus arrested Peter disowns Jesus The Guards mock Jesus Jesus before Pilate and Herod 23) The crucifixion Jesus' death Jesus' burial 24) The resurrection On the road to Emmaus Jesus appears to the disciples The Ascension	

GOOD AFTERNOON

This will be the second half of my "rewriting the New Testament" project. My first half was focused on reading, studying, discerning, and rewriting the four Gospels. That exercise provided me with a much deeper understanding of the story of Jesus' life through the eyes of Matthew, Mark, Luke, and John.

At this point I feel like I am halfway up the mountain, and I need to keep going. My goal is to do the same with the rest of the New Testament. I find the stories in Paul's letters (as well as other writers) to be so inspiring because they share the inspired Word of God through the eyes of someone who is being persecuted as a believer. These letters were written by followers of Jesus who were building the early Church and their commitment and resiliency is a model to emulate. I believe that putting "pen to paper" to rewrite and interpret the lessons from these stories and letters will give me an even greater appreciation of what Jesus did for me and for all those who believe.

ACTS

The story of Acts is a close-up view of everything Jesus' followers did to grow the early Church after his death. In the 30 years after Jesus' death, the Church grew from what was considered an insignificant sect within the Jewish faith to a major force in the Roman empire. Most people believe that Luke was the Author of Acts, and he wrote it as an "add-on" to his original gospel. He wanted the world to know that Christianity was <u>not</u> a threat to the Roman empire. He wanted all to know that it was the work of God's Spirit building his kingdom for all who will follow Jesus. Most of Luke's writing focuses on Paul, who is viewed as "the apostle to the Gentiles". (Peter was the "apostle to the Jews".) Acts is the background information for all the Churches that Paul founded on his journeys.

ACTS 1

Acts picks up the story of Jesus where the Gospel of Luke ends. It reminds us of the commands that Jesus gave to the 11 apostles between his resurrection and when he was taken up to heaven. Over those 40 days, he appeared to them multiple times and spoke about the Kingdom of God. He told the 11 that they were not to leave Jerusalem until they received the Holy Spirit through baptism. They asked Jesus if he was going to restore the kingdom to Israel. He told them not to worry about "when" God would do his work. They will know when they will receive the Holy Spirit and when they do, they will be his witnesses to the ends of the earth. Then Jesus was taken into heaven right in front of their eyes. The 11 apostles chose Mattias to replace Judas as the 12th apostle. The group that was at this initial meeting was about 120. This is such a powerful picture of the beginnings of the growth of the Jesus movement and the **impact of being a true witness.**

ACTS 2

The Holy Spirit visits all the apostles as they were gathered together. It sounded like the blowing of a violent wind came from heaven and filled the whole house. They saw tongues of fire rest on each of them and they were filled with the Holy Spirit. This is just as Jesus promised! The crowds from the area heard the noise and came to the house where it occurred and despite the fact that many "races" came, they each heard the message in their own language. They thought that Jesus' followers were drunk!

Peter stood up in front of everyone and preached the story of Jesus. It was beautiful!

"Fellow Israelites, listen to this: Jesus of Nazareth was a man accredited by God <u>to you</u> by miracles, wonders, and signs, which God did among you through him, as you yourselves know. This man was handed over to you by God's deliberate plan and foreknowledge; and you, with the help of wicked men, put him to death by nailing him to the cross. But God raised him from the dead, freeing him from the agony of death because it was impossible for death to keep its hold on him". Peter also quoted David and said,

"The Lord said to my Lord:
'Sit at my right-hand
until I make your enemies
a footstool at your feet.'"

That is so reassuring as to the power of Jesus. David not only says 'don't worry about people who persecute you. He also says that Jesus will make them recognize you by bringing them down'. He told them that God made Jesus Lord and Messiah. They asked Peter what they should do.

Peter said, "Repent and be baptized, every one of you, in the name of Jesus Christ for the forgiveness of your sins. And you will receive the gift of the Holy Spirit. The promise is for you and your children and for all who are far off—for all whom the Lord our God will call...save yourself from this corrupt generation."

On that day 3000 people were baptized. This verse explains how these early followers of Jesus lived in community with each other, dined together "with glad and sincere hearts". The number of people being baptized grew every day. We need to remember the simple statement "and you will receive the Holy Spirit".

ACTS 3

Peter and John were going to the temple, and they came across a man who was a beggar, and he sat in front of the temple every day. He asked Peter and John for money. Peter said to him, "Silver or gold I do not have, but what I do have I give you. in the name of Jesus Christ of Nazareth, walk!" The man jumped for joy and the people were amazed.

Personally, I used to struggle with these stories of the apostles performing miracles. I have always attributed Jesus' ability to perform miracles to his divinity. So, when others perform those miracles, I don't want it to detract from Jesus' divinity as the only Son of God. I need to realize that all of these miracles were done in Jesus' name, and he said they would be able to do this. Peter goes on to preach to the people that all of this was done in the name of Jesus. He says, "Repent and turn to God, so that your sins may be wiped out, that Times of refreshing may come from the Lord."

He reminds them, as Jews, all of this was foretold through the prophets. "When God raised up his servant, he sent him first to you to bless you by turning each of you from your wicked ways".

ACTS 4

Peter and John were speaking to the people. The temple guard and the Sadducees were greatly disturbed because they were proclaiming the resurrection of the dead in Jesus. They seized Peter and John in jail for a day, but there were a lot of people there, so the number of Jesus' followers grew to 5000.

The high priest and his family asked Peter and John, "By what power or what name did you do this?"

Peter was filled with the Holy Spirit. He told them they did this in the name of Jesus Christ of Nazareth. (He reminded them they "crucified him".) Then Peter quoted Jesus, "The stone you builders rejected has become the cornerstone." That's like saying, "he's baaack"!

Peter continues, "Salvation is found in no one else, for there is no other name under heaven given to mankind by which we must be saved." **The apostles completely stuck to the script that salvation is found in no one else but Jesus. It was so brilliant that they did so because 2000 years later that is still the fundamental message of the power of faith in Jesus.**

This was such a spirit inspired speech by Peter! The people that were questioning Peter and John realized their courage and that they were just "ordinary men". But since they saw them heal the beggar, they could not deny it. But the leaders did not want the message to spread any further, so they instructed Peter and John to not teach anyone else. They replied, "which is right in God's eyes: to listen to you, or to him?" I love this! **They are telling the leaders upfront; 'we are listening to God!'**

All the people saw what happened and they raised their voices in prayer.

I love this verse. "They did what your power and will had decided beforehand should happen. Now Lord, consider their threats and enable your servants to speak your word with great boldness".

This is a powerful theme in acts. Against the opposition of the world, The Holy Spirit will provide us with our <u>boldness</u> and our conviction!

This chapter concludes by telling us how the followers of Jesus shared all their possessions with the group, including money from the sale of their land and houses. **They truly were one big team**, **that was committed to spreading the gospel of Jesus Christ.**

ACTS 5

Acts 5 is filled with several bizarre stories, many of which I struggle to reconcile with what Jesus would actually want us to do. It begins with the story of a man and his wife who sold their land and gave a majority of the proceeds to the apostles. But when they were questioned about "where the rest of the money was", they said that they gave it all to the apostles. at that moment, Both the husband and wife fell down and died. I am not sure if they died because they kept some of the money or because they lied, but in either case I don't think they warranted death. I believe Jesus realizes that keeping money for our families is the right thing to do. **As long as our hearts and our giving represent our total submission to him.**

The apostles go on doing many great works and healing people. They were brought in front of the full Sanhedrin to be questioned. The leaders reminded the apostles that they were given strict orders to not teach these lessons. Peter and the apostles replied, "We must obey God not human beings." The leaders wanted to put the apostles to death, but a Pharisee named Gamaliel made a brilliant plea to the leaders. He said, "If what they do is of human origin, it will fail. But if it is from God, you will not be able to stop these men, you will only find yourself fighting against God." So, they were not put to death, only flogged. They rejoiced as they left Sanhedrin. **Day after day, from house to house, they never stop teaching in proclaiming the good news that Jesus was the Messiah.**

ACTS 6

The Number of disciples was growing rapidly. There was a disagreement that occurred between the Grecian Jews and the Hebraic Jews about the distribution of food. The group decided to pick seven men who are known to be "Full of the spirit" to handle the responsibility. One of the most highly respected men of the group was Stephen—he had performed "wonders and miraculous works". Opposition arose and members of the synagogue began to argue with Stephen, but they "could not stand up against the wisdom or spirit by whom he spoke". So, they secretly stirred up some men to make up lies about him and say that Stephen had spoken words of blasphemy against Moses and against God. They brought him to the Sanhedrin and presented false witnesses against Stephen. "For we heard him say that this Jesus of Nazareth will destroy this place and change the customs Moses handed down to us".

"All who were sitting in the Sanhedrin looked intently at Stephen, and they saw that his face was like the face of an angel".

ACTS 7

Stephen's speech to the Sanhedrin is one of the most incredible speeches in the Bible. Recall from Chapter 6 that Peter was challenged by the Jews and they basically accused him (and Jesus) of destroying the laws of Moses. Stephen very eloquently and passionately connects the laws of Moses to the new covenant of Jesus. I would love to rewrite the two-page speech, but I will just summarize it here. Please read the whole speech!

- God appeared to Abraham and told him to "leave your country and your people. I will show you a land where you should go".

- Abraham settled in Harran. God promised him that he would someday possess the land, along with his descendants. At the time, Abraham had no children.

- God told him that for 400 years, his descendants will be slaves. But he will punish the nation, and afterward they will come out of that country and worship him in his place.

- Abraham became the father of Isaac and Jacob was Isaac's son, and Jacob became the father of the 12 patriarchs.

- The patriarchs were jealous of the youngest among them, so they sold him as a slave. God gave Joseph wisdom and he found favor with the Pharaoh, and so the Pharaoh made him ruler over all of Egypt.

- A famine struck Egypt. Jacob sent members of his family to Egypt, and Joseph told his brothers who he was.

- The new king came to power in Egypt. The population was increasing. The king forced "our ancestors to throw out their newborn babies so they would die".

- Moses was born and he was no ordinary child. Pharaoh's daughter took him and raised him in all "the wisdom of the Egyptians".

- When Moses turned 40, he decided to visit his fellow Israelites. He saw one being mistreated by an Egyptian, so Moses killed the Egyptian. He encouraged them not to fight amongst each other.

- 40 years later an angel appeared in a burning bush. He heard the Lord's voice: "I am the God of Abraham, Isaac and Jacob". Then the Lord said to him, "take off your sandals—this is holy ground." He then tells Moses what he has seen the oppression of his people in Egypt. So, he sent Moses back to Egypt to set them free. Moses became their ruler and deliverer and did many miraculous signs.

- Stephen reminds them that Moses told the Israelites that God would send a profit like me from your own people, and on Mount Sinai God gave Moses living words to pass on to us.

- Stephen tells the crowd that their forefathers refused to obey him. They turn back to Egypt and worshipped false Gods.

- One of those "Gods" was a tabernacle. (movie—Raiders of the Lost Ark) it was meant to be a dwelling place for the God of Jacob. Solomon also built a house for him. Stephen then says, "the most high does not live in houses built by men. Heaven is my throne. And the earth is my footstool. You stiff necked people…you resist the Holy Spirit. Was there ever a prophet your fathers did not persecute? They even killed those who predicted the coming of the righteous one. And now you have murdered him—You who have received the law that was put into effect through angels but have not obeyed it."

This is so powerful. Stephen basically tells them, "You waited for the messengers, God gave them to you. You persecuted them and killed them". They told you that Jesus was coming, and he did.

The people were furious with Stephen. But Stephen looked to heaven and said, "I see Heaven open and the Son of Man standing at the right hand of God."

The people dragged him out of the city and stoned him. Stephen said, "Lord Jesus, receive my spirit. Lord, do not hold this sin against them." Just like Jesus said. Stephen was the first martyr for Jesus; "proto martyr".

ACTS 8

After Stephen's death, there was great persecution of the church. The followers were scattered all over Judea and Samaria. Saul, himself began to destroy the church. He dragged off women and children and put them in prison.

Philip went to Samaria and performed great signs and preached to the people. There was great joy in the city.

When the apostles heard that Samaria had accepted the word of God, they sent Peter and John to tell them. They arrived and prayed that people might receive the Holy Spirit, in addition to being baptized in the name of Jesus. They laid their hands on people and they received the Holy Spirit.

Simon, who was a well-known "sorcerer" (magician) asked Peter to grant him the Holy Spirit. Peter said, "may your money perish with you, because you thought you could buy the gift of God with money. You have no part in this ministry because your heart is not right before God."

Simon asked Peter to pray for him.

Peter and John went on to preach in many Samaritan villages on their way back to Jerusalem.

Philip was on his way to Gaza (40 miles west of Jerusalem, The Gaza Strip) and he came upon an Ethiopian man who was reading the book of the prophet Isaiah. Philip asked him if he knew what he was reading. The man said he needed someone to explain it to him. He was reading:

> "He was led like a sheep to
> the slaughter,
> and a lamb before the
> shearer is silent,
> so he did not open his mouth.
> in his humiliation he was
> deprived of justice.
> who can speak of his
> descendants?
> for his life was taken
> from Earth".

Phillip used this passage to explain to him the good news of Jesus and the man asked Philip to baptize him, right then. And he did!

ACTS 9

This is one of the most exciting and most famous stories in the Bible.
The first chapter of Acts reminds us of the fact that Saul was perhaps the most significant and harshest persecutor of the Church and the followers of Jesus. At this point, Saul asked the high priest for permission to imprison anyone

he found that was a follower of Jesus while he was on his way to Damascus. While on his journey, a light from heaven flashed around him and he fell to his knees. He heard a voice: "Saul, Saul, why do you persecute me"? Paul said, "Who are you, Lord?" "I am Jesus who you are persecuting, now get up and go into the city and you will be told what to do".

When Saul got up, he was blind so the men that were with him led him by hand into Damascus. At the same time, the Lord appeared to a man named Ananias. He told them to "go to the house of judas on straight street". He told him that Saul would be there praying, and he should lay his hands on him to restore his sight. Ananias tells the Lord that he has heard about Saul, and all the distractions he has brought to the church. The Lord said to Ananias, "Go. This man is my chosen instrument to carry my name before the Gentiles and their kings and before the people of Israel. I will show him how much he must suffer in my name."

Ananias went to the house and told Saul what Jesus said, "The Lord sent me here so you could see again and so you may be filled with the Holy Spirit". Immediately scales fell from his eyes, and he could see it again.

Saul begins to immediately preach in the synagogues that Jesus is the Son of God. The people were confused because they knew that he was the one that had persecuted the church so harshly. But Saul became even more powerful in convincing the Jews that Jesus was the Christ. The Jews began to plot to kill Saul. Saul tried to join the apostles, but they were afraid of him. Barnabas told them about what happened to Saul, so they accepted him.

They continue to preach the good news and the Churches in Judea, Galilee and Samaria enjoyed a time of peace.

This story is so powerful. It is a reminder that God can use <u>anyone</u> to be a vehicle for spreading the good news. It is never too late. In Saul's situation, God didn't use someone who didn't really care about faith in Jesus—he used his biggest enemy. That is why it is called "Saul's conversion". God can turn anyone's heart in an instant!

Chapter 9 finishes with Peter performing great works in his travels through the countryside. All his works were done in the name of Jesus—so many people became believers.

ACTS 10

A man named Cornelius had a vision of God. The vision was God telling him to go to Joppa to get Peter. So, Cornelius sent two servants to find him. They did find him, and they brought him back to Cornelius' house. Cornelius had invited several guests. Peter said, "You are well aware that it is against our law for any Jew to associate with a Gentile. But God told me that I should not call any man unclean. May I ask why you sent for me?" Cornelius told Peter about his vision. Peter responds with beautiful words:

"I now realize how true it is that God does not show favoritism but accepts men from every nation who fears him and does what is right. You know the message God sent to the people of Israel, telling the good news of peace through Jesus Christ, who is the Lord of all. You know what has happened throughout Judea Beginning in Galilee after baptism that John preached—How God anointed Jesus of Nazareth with the Holy Spirit and power, and how he went about doing good things and healing all who were under the power of the devil, because God was with him. We are witnesses of everything he did in the country of the Jews and in Jerusalem. They killed him by hanging him on a cross, but cross raised him from the dead on the third day and caused him to be seen. He was not seen by all the people but by witnesses whom God had already chosen…he commanded us to preach to the people and to testify that he is the one whom God appointed as judge of the living and dead. All the prophets testify about him that everyone who believes in him receives forgiveness of sins through his name".

This is such a beautiful and succinct sermon by Peter of the impact of Jesus. I love how he leads with "God does not show favoritism". He welcomes all!

While he was speaking, "The Holy Spirit came upon all who heard the message". The people became believers and were baptized in Jesus' name.

ACTS 11

Chapter 10 and 11 can be slightly confusing. Remember that Jesus was a Jew, and his entire "movement" was in Israel. They talked a lot about "clean" and "unclean" people. In the mind of Jew, a Jew is clean because they are circumcised according to the law of Moses. A "non-Jew" is a Gentile. Jews did not associate with Gentiles because they were unclean and uncircumcised. Peter had just ministered and baptized a large group of Gentiles. When he returned to Jerusalem from Joppa, people heard about what he did, and they criticized him. Peter told them about the vision that he had that said, "do not call anything impure that God has made clean". In that vision, the Spirit told him to have no hesitation about sharing the message who some might think to be unclean. Peter said, "So if God gave them the same gift as they gave us, who believed in the Lord Jesus Christ, who was I to oppose God." When they heard this, they had no further objections and praised God saying, "so then, God has granted even the Gentiles repentance into life."

This message is about two things. 1) it's evidence from God that prejudice of any kind is wrong. God tells us, "If I made it, it is good." 2) Jesus is for everyone. His message is universal. His saving grace is for all people, and we need to make sure that everyone knows it.

The rest of chapter 11 is all about the Church expanding to more "non-Jewish" regions. **It's almost as if the veil has been lifted for the apostles and now, they were committed to spread the good news everywhere.** The people that had been scattered by the persecution of Stephen were in Phoenicia, Cyprus, and Antioch. Now they preached to Greeks as well as Jews.

ACTS 12

This is the story about Peter's miraculous escape from prison. King Herod was persecuting those who belonged to the Church. He had James, the brother of John, put to death by the sword. When he saw this pleased the Jews, he had Peter arrested. He was guarded by four squads of four soldiers each, around the clock. He was also chained.

While he was sleeping, an Angel appeared and told him to get up, grab his things and to "follow me". Peter did so and he escaped from prison.

Peter went to the house of Mary where many of us friends were praying. They could not believe Peter was free. The guards had no idea where Peter was. Herod had the guards cross examined, and when they could not explain how Peter escaped, he executed them.

The next part of this chapter is strange. Herod went to Caesarea from Judea. He was quarreling with the people of Tyre and Sidon. They wanted an audience with the King because they depended on the King's country for food. Herod delivered a speech from a throne and "because he did not give praise to God, an angel of the Lord struck him down and he was eaten by worms and died". (I don't know the point of this story.)

But the word of God continued to spread.

ACTS 13

While the group was in Antioch, the Holy Spirit told them to separate Barnabas and Saul from the group because he had more work for them to do.

The two traveled around the entire Island of Cyprus. They came upon a false prophet named Elymas and told him that he was full of the devil, and because of that he would go blind. Immediately, mist and darkness came over him and people that saw what happened—they believed.

This theme of false prophets will be presented many times in Paul's letters.

Paul and his companions traveled to Antioch, and they were praying in the synagogue. The synagogue rulers sent word to them saying, "Brothers, if you have a message of encouragement for the people, please speak."

Paul stood up and delivered a powerful message to them. Just like Stephen did to the Sanhedrin. Paul connected Abraham to Jesus. He continues by saying, "From this man's descendants, God has brought to Israel the Savior Jesus, as he has promised…it is to us that salvation has been sent." **Paul gives an inspired message of the life, death, and resurrection, and how this was all foretold by the prophets**. "Therefore, my brothers, I want you to know that through Jesus, the forgiveness of sins is proclaimed to you. Through him, everyone who believes is justified from everything you could not be justified from by the law of Moses". The whole crowd became inspired and the next Sabbath, the whole city gathered to hear them speak. The Jews scoffed at them and rejected the message. Paul and Barnabas told them they intended to speak to the Jews first, but since you reject it and don't consider yourself worthy of eternal life, we must now turn to the Gentiles.

Paul then quotes Isaiah 49:6 which says, "I have made you a light for the Gentiles that you may bring salvation to the ends of the earth". The Gentiles were glad and honored to have received the good news, but the Jews continue to persecute Paul and expelled them from the region. Paul and Barnabas shake the dust from their feet and moved on just like Jesus instructed in Matthew 10:14.

ACTS 14

Paul and Barnabas were together again in Iconium. "They spoke so effectively that a great number of Jews and Greeks believed". Some of the Jews refused to believe. Eventually there was a plot among some of the Gentiles and Jews to stone them, so they fled to some neighboring Lycaonian cities.

One of the cities was Lystra, where they came upon a lame man. Paul saw he had the faith to be healed so he told him to "stand up on your feet", and he did.

When the people saw this, they said, "The gods have come down on us in human form." They offered sacrifices to them like they were gods.

Paul and Barnabas assure the crowd they are only human and "we are bringing you good news". They continue by telling the crowd that God is telling them all to turn from worthless things, and that God shows kindness by "filling your hearts with joy". Once again, some Jews won the crowd over and they stoned Paul and dragged him outside because they thought he was dead. The disciples gathered around him, and they left for Derbe.

They preached in that city and won many disciples. They encouraged them to remain true to the faith. "We must go through many hardships to enter the kingdom of God".

They returned to Antioch and reported all that God had done and had "Opened the door of faith for the Gentiles". (Recall that Gentiles are non-Jews.)

ACTS 15

This is another chapter about historical Jewish teaching versus the good news of Jesus—Grace by Faith. People challenged Paul and Barnabas that the law of circumcision from Moses is required to be saved. Paul and Barnabas disagreed with them, so they were appointed to go to Jerusalem to see the elders and apostles about this question. On their way through Phoenicia and Samaria, they told everyone how the Gentiles had been converted. When they arrived in Jerusalem, they spoke about what God had done through them.

In Jerusalem, the Pharisees professed that, "Gentiles must be circumcised." Peter stood up and gives an inspirational speech about the fact that

"God knows the heart...does not discriminate...and it is through the grace of our Lord Jesus Christ that we are saved, just as they are".

This is such a powerful testimony that Jesus is for all! He tears down walls and builds bridges.

James spoke up and confirmed that the prophets confirm everything that Paul said. He says, "We should not make it difficult for Gentiles who are turning to God." The apostles and elders of the Church went to deliver a letter to the church in Antioch. It was to clarify their direction. It says the Holy Spirit does not want to burden them with anything except:

1) Abstain from food sacrificed to idols

2) Abstain from meat of strangled animals

3) Abstain from sexual immorality

Essentially, this was about removing the "law of circumcision" from the "law". The people were very encouraged by this letter.

After all this, Paul and Barnabas were going to return to some of the towns where they preached. Barnabas wanted to take John, but Paul didn't want to because John deserted them earlier and didn't want to continue the work. They had a strong disagreement, so Barnabas took John (also called Mark) and Paul Took Silas and they went separate ways.

ACTS 16

At this time, Timothy makes his first appearance and joins Paul and Silas on their journey. The Church continued to grow as they went from town to town. They preached everywhere except the province of Asia where "The Holy Spirit kept them from preaching". Paul had a vision of a man saying, "Come over to Macedonia and help us." So, they went! While they were in Philippi, they came across a young woman who became baptized, along with her entire family.

Next, they came across a woman who was following them and shouting, "These men are servants of the Most High God who are telling you the way to be saved." Paul became very annoyed with her and said, to the spirit, "in the name of Jesus Christ I command you to come out of her." I am not sure why Paul was annoyed with her message.

When her owners realized that she could not make any more money, they seized Paul and Silas (not sure what happened to Timothy) and they made them face the authorities. They had him beaten and thrown into prison.

At midnight Paul and Silas were singing hymns and praying and their fellow prisoners joined in. Suddenly a violent earthquake shook the foundations of the prison. All the doors flew open, and their chains came loose.

The Guard thought the prisoners escaped. He was going to kill himself, But Paul reassured him that they were still there. The guard then asked, "what must I do to be saved?" They replied, "Believe in the Lord Jesus Christ and you and your household be saved." The guard took them to his house where he and his family were baptized. He fed them a meal.

The magistrates sent officers to the house to release Paul and Silas. Paul said that they were beaten publicly without a trial, which is not right since they were Roman citizens. So, the magistrates themselves came to release them. Paul and Silas returned to Lydia's House to reunite with the group.

ACTS 17

Paul and his companions traveled to Thessalonica. They preached again in the synagogues. Some of the Jews believed the message about Jesus as did a large number of prominent Greeks. Some of the other Jews were jealous and so they wanted to drag Paul and Silas out into the crowd, but they couldn't find them. We are introduced to a man named Jason who became a believer. Jason has welcomed Paul and Silas into his home. They claimed that the believers were defying Caesar's decrees, saying there is another king—Jesus.

This supposed "rebellion against Caesar/Rome" is at the heart of the persecution of the early church. **They were not rebelling against anything!**

Paul and Silas traveled to Berea which is a city in northern Greece. The people there were very thoughtful in terms of their consideration for what Paul was saying to them. They examined scriptures to make sure that what he was saying was accurate. Because it was accurate, many of them were believers. When the Jews from Thessalonica heard that Paul was preaching, they went there to stir up trouble. The believers in Berea sent Paul to the coast (for safety I assume). They left instructions for Silas and Timothy to join him as soon as possible. When Paul got to Athens on the coast, he was upset because the city was full of idols. Paul began preaching the good news of Jesus. A group of philosophers thought he was a babbling idiot (literally) who was preaching about foreign Gods.

Paul told him that while he was walking, one of the things he saw was an altar that said, "to an unknown God". He said, "so you are ignorant of the very thing you worship."—brilliant.

So, Paul wanted to educate them on the truth—so he delivered this powerful testimony to God and Jesus:

"The God who made the world and everything in it is the Lord of heaven and earth and does not live in temples built by human hands. And he is not served by human hands, as if he needed anything. Rather, he gives everyone life and breath and everything else. From one man he made all nations, that they should inhabit the whole earth; and he marked out their appointed times in history and the boundaries of their lands. God did this so they would seek him and perhaps reach out for him and find him, though he is not far from any of us. For in him we live and move and have our being… We are his offspring. Therefore, since we are God's offspring, we should not think that the divine being is like gold or silver or stone—an image made by human design and skill. In the past God overlooked such ignorance, but now he commands all people everywhere to repent. for he has set a day when he will judge the world with justice by the man he has appointed (Jesus). He has given proof of this to everyone by raising him from the dead".

This speech by Paul has validated something that I did not understand until very recently. I used to think that we live life, and we have ups and downs, and we rely on God to get us through those ups and downs. I know now, that is not accurate. God put us here for one purpose—to seek him. Because he loves us. We don't seek him for some worldly gain. We seek him because he is God. Said another way, the purpose of our life is not to seek God <u>so we get something that we want</u>.

The purpose of our life is to seek God. Period. Because when we realize that he offers joy, hope, love, forgiveness, and grace, we realize that is all we need.

ACTS 18

Paul left Athens and went to Corinth. One of the nice things about truly understanding Acts is to watch Paul travel to the cities that are reflected in the letters he wrote later. While in Corinth, Paul continues to persuade the Jews and Greeks to believe his testimony about Jesus.

Silas and Timothy came from Macedonia. They opposed Paul and "became abusive". This is an interesting development in the relationship of the disciples. So, Paul "shook out his clothes" and focused on the Gentiles. Many of these Corinthians believed Paul and were baptized. At the same time, the Jews opposed him and brought him "to the place of judgment" for preaching ways contrary to historical Jewish law.

Paul stayed in Corinth for 18 months teaching them the word of God. One night he had a vision and the Lord spoke to him. "Do not be afraid; keep on speaking. Do not be silent. For I am with you, and no one is going to attack you or harm you, because I have many people in this city".

Then Paul left first Syria. He preached on the way in Ephesus. They asked him to stay but he declined. He did promise them that he would return. Paul continued to Antioch, Galatia, and Phrygia. Meanwhile a Jew named apollos came to Ephesus. He was a very intelligent man and had thorough knowledge of the Scriptures. He preached <u>fervently</u> about Jesus and vigorously refuted his Jewish opponents in public debate. He <u>proved from Scriptures</u> that Jesus was the Messiah!

Jesus' birth, life and death are easy to trace in the Old Testament. Everything was foretold, which is why the divinity of Jesus is so easily validated.

ACTS 19

Paul went to Ephesus and preached for three months. Many of the people there refused to believe, so Paul left with his disciples and went to the lecture hall of Tyrannus. He preached there for three years. During this time, God did extraordinary miracles through Paul. Some Jews began to drive out evil spirits in the name of Jesus. Word of this got out and the name of Jesus was held in high honor. People repented and the Word of the Lord "spread widely and grew in power".

Because there were so many false Gods at this time, one of the trades that was lucrative was being a silversmith. Because Paul was preaching a God who is not physical in nature, the silversmiths who made idols of these Gods became nervous that Paul would wipe out their industry. When Demetrius, the leader of the craftsmen, shared this with the rest of the craftsmen there was an uproar in the city that eventually became a riot. Paul wanted to speak to the crowd, but they would not let him. Eventually, because there were no real charges against Paul, the city clerk refused to proceed with the "uprising" until someone followed the rules of pressing charges, so the crowd was dismissed.

ACTS 20

Paul said goodbye to the disciples and set out for Macedonia and eventually settled in Greece for three months. Paul and his companions went to a town called Troas. Paul was speaking late one night, until midnight, and a young man named Eutychus was falling asleep. He fell to the ground from the third story and was picked up dead. Paul said, "Don't be alarmed, he is alive." he was alive, and the people were greatly comforted. The group of disciples traveled/sailed to many cities. Paul was in a hurry to get back to Jerusalem. He said to them, "I only know that in every city the Holy Spirit warns me that prison and hardships are facing me. However, I consider my life worth nothing to me; if only I may finish the race and complete the task the Lord Jesus has given me—the task of testifying to the gospel of God's grace."

The last sentence summarizes the entire second half of the New Testament, Paul preaching of God's grace through Jesus. God's grace is never ending. He begs us to accept it so we can spend eternity with him in heaven.

Paul tells them that they may not see him again. He tells him to keep watch over themselves and the flock that the Holy Spirit has entrusted them with. He says they should be shepherds of the church, and he warns them of the wolves that will try to destroy the flock, even from the "inside".

Paul finishes with, "I showed you that by this kind of hard work we must help the weak, Remembering the words of our Lord, 'It is better to give than to receive.'"

They all prayed together, realizing they might never see Paul again. Then he got on the ship.

ACTS 21

The opening paragraph in chapter 21 Is a great example of what type of commitment the followers of Jesus had:

"After we tore ourselves away from them, we put out to sea and sailed straight to Kos. The next day we went to Rhodes and from there to Patra. We found a ship crossing over to Phoenicia, went on board and set sail. After sighting Cyprus and passing to the south of it, we sailed on to Syria. We landed at Tyre, where our ship was to unload our cargo. Finding the disciples there, we stayed with them for seven days".

This was just a snapshot of what it was like to be part of the early believers. They went anywhere and everywhere to preach the good news, without consideration for the risk involved.

They reached Caesarea and a prophet named Agabus took Paul's belt and tied his own hands and feet with it and said, "The Holy Spirit says, 'in this way the Jews of Jerusalem will bind the owner of this belt and will hand him over to the Gentiles.'" because of this, the group pleaded with Paul not to go to Jerusalem. Paul answered, "Why are you weeping and breaking my heart? I am ready not only to be bound, but also to die in Jerusalem for the name of the Lord Jesus." Paul would not be dissuaded so they gave up and said, "the Lord's will be done."

Paul and the rest of the group arrived in Jerusalem and were welcomed warmly by the "Brothers"—which I assume is referring to the believers there.

After seven days, some Jews saw Paul in the temple. They stirred up the whole crowd and told them that Paul was teaching "against the law". The whole city was in uproar and people rushed to the temple area. They were going to kill him, but news reached the commander of the Roman troops. He and his men went to where they were beating Paul and because of their presence, the beatings stopped. The commander inquired who Paul was, and then he bound him with two chains and arrested him.

As the soldiers were taking Paul to the barracks, Paul asked the commander, "May I say something to you?" The commander asked Paul if he was the "Egyptian who led a revolt of 4000 terrorists"? Paul informed him that he was, "a Jew, a citizen of no ordinary city. Please let me speak to the people."

ACTS 22

Paul began speaking to the crowd. He recounts to them his testimony —exactly what happened to him in acts 9, "the conversion of Saul". He tells them how he was a zealot for God just like they are. He tells them how he was the biggest persecutor of Jesus in the region, and how he fell to the ground on the way to Damascus and was blinded by a bright light and heard the voice of Jesus. "The God of our ancestors has chosen you to know his will and to see the righteous one and to hear the words from his mouth. You will be his witness to all people of what you have seen and heard.

And now what are you waiting for? Get up, be baptized, and wash your sins away, calling on his name".

I believe this is what Jesus is asking for all of us to do. Be baptized, wash our sins away and profess to the world why we did it.

The crowd listened to Paul, and they shouted, "Rid the earth of him!" The commander ordered Paul to be taken into the barracks. He directed that he be flogged and interrogated because he wanted to know why people reacted so strongly to Paul's teaching. Paul reminds him that he is a Roman citizen and asks if it is legal for them to flog him. When they realized Paul was a Roman citizen, they released him, But the commander wanted to know why Paul was being accused by the Jews. So, he ordered the chief priests and all the members of the Sanhedrin to assemble. Then he brought Paul and had him stand before them.

ACTS 23

Paul stands before the Sanhedrin and tells them that he has fulfilled God's commands with a clean conscience. The high priest Ananias orders those standing near Paul to strike him on the mouth. He challenges them by saying, "God will strike you; you whitewashed wall. You sit there to judge me according to the law yet you yourself violate the law by commanding I be struck." **This is such a great hypocritical challenge against the Sanhedrin by Paul!**

Paul knew that there were both Sadducees and Pharisees in the crowd. Paul tells them that he is on trial because of the "Hope of the resurrection of the dead". (Jesus' good news) the Sadducees don't believe in angels or spirits, but the Pharisees do. Because of this difference of opinion, there was a great uproar. The pharisees said, "I find nothing wrong with the man." (Paul reminded them all that he was born a pharisee.) The commander was afraid Paul would be torn to shreds so he ordered that he be taken to the barracks. Paul had a vision the next night where the Lord said, "Take courage! as you have testified about me in Jerusalem, so you must also testify in Rome."

The next morning, 40 jews formed an oath to not eat or drink until they had killed Paul. Paul got word of this plot and asked one of the centurions to send a young man to the commodore to make him aware of this plot. The commander told the young man to not tell anyone about this conversation. Then he called two of his centurions and said, "get a detachment of 200 soldiers, 70 horsemen and 200 spearmen to go to Caesarea at 9 tonight. Provide horses for Paul so he can be taken safely to Governor Felix."

So, the group took Paul to Caesarea and presented a letter from the commander that explained everything. Felix read the letter and said, "I will hear your case when your accusers get here." then he sent Paul to be kept under guard in Herod's palace.

ACTS 24

A group of people went to the governor Felix to present the case against Paul. Their words were as follows: "We have found this man to be a troublemaker, stirring up riots among the Jews all over the world. He is a ringleader of the Nazarene sect and even tried to desecrate the temple; so, we seized him. By examining him yourself you will be able to learn the truth about all these charges we are bringing against him." I find the description of Paul as a "troublemaker" intriguing. He never makes trouble. Their explanation that he is a ringleader of a sect and "stirring up riots among the Jews" paints a great picture of what it's like for him to profess his faith. It's almost like as he talks, they fight with each other, not him. Paul articulates his faith to Felix, like this, "My accusers did not find me arguing with anyone at the temple or stirring up a crowd in the synagogues or anywhere else in the city. And they cannot prove to you the charges they are now making against me. However, I admit that I worship the God of our ancestors as a follower of the Way, which they call a sect. I believe everything that is in accordance with the Law and that is written in the Prophets, and I have the same hope in God as these men themselves have, that there will be a resurrection of both the righteous and the wicked. 16 So I strive always to keep my conscience clear before God and man." He aligns himself with the same God that they worship, our God, because he doesn't want them to see his faith in Jesus as a threat to anyone.

ACTS 25

Festus went from Caesarea to Jerusalem to hear the charges against Paul. The people that were charging Paul were plotting to kill him on the way to Jerusalem. Paul made his defense to Festus, saying, "I have done nothing wrong against the Jewish law or against the temple or against Caesar. Festus asks Paul if he was willing to go to Jerusalem to be charged. Paul reiterates that he has done nothing wrong, but he says, "if you find me guilty…worthy of death, I am willing to die. But if they are not true, no one has the right to hand me over. I appealed to Caesar!" Festus grants Paul's request to be seen by Caesar.

A few days later King Agrippa and Bernice arrive to pay their respects to Festus, who was procurator of all Judea. Festus tells them that he does not feel like those charging Paul really have a case against Paul. He says, "they had some points of dispute with him about their own religion about a dead man named Jesus who Paul claimed was alive." King Agrippa said he wanted to "see this man himself".

The next day, amid a lot to pomp and ceremony, Agrippa and Bernice enter the room with high-ranking military and prominent men of the city.

Festus begins the hearing by saying that he has found Paul guilty of nothing, but he is appealing to Agrippa before he decides to send Paul to Rome to see Caesar.

ACTS 26

King Agrippa gave Paul permission to speak for himself in defense against the charges brought before him. Paul began by assuring the King that has adhered to all the strictest laws of the Jewish faith for his whole life. He also assures Agrippa that all the people that are charging him know these facts about Paul. "They know how I have lived my life ever since I was a child". 'Jesus like'. **Being a follower Jesus is not about being against things, it's about being "for" love.**

Paul says, "Why should any of you question why God can raise the dead?" Paul reminds them all that he once was the biggest persecutor of Christ. He cast votes against Jesus' followers in public trial and he went so far as to hunt them down in foreign cities. And then he recounts his conversation to Agrippa.

This is obviously a story that repeats itself throughout Acts.

1) **Paul gets accused**

2) **Paul defends himself**

3) **Paul shares his testimony**

He then says to Agrippa that, "I have said nothing other than what the prophets and even Moses have told us what would happen."

Festus interrupted Paul and said, "Paul you are insane." Paul said, "I am not insane." And Agrippa asked Paul, "do you think that you can convince me to be a Christian in just one day?" **Paul said that he wants the same for all** people—that they may "become what I am, besides these chains." That's a powerful and slightly irreverently funny line by Paul.

Agrippa told Festus that Paul could have been set free had he not appealed to Caesar.

ACTS 27

This chapter is all about Paul and their group sailing to Rome—and their encounters with wild seas and intense storms. They sailed to many ports and islands. At one point, Paul warned the group that it would be disastrous to keep sailing—he said the ship would be damaged, they would lose cargo and risk their own lives. Instead of listening to Paul, the centurion convinced the group to "sail on".

While they were near Crete, a hurricane force storm overtook the boat, so much so that men began to throw cargo and tackle overboard. After the men had gone a long time without food, Paul gathered them together to encourage them. He tells them that an angel of God assured him that not one of their lives would be lost. He told them to maintain their courage.

There were 276 men on the ship. Paul encouraged them all to eat because they had all gone 14 days without food. The next morning, they ran the boat aground shipwrecked. The soldiers on board wanted to kill the prisoners (including Paul) but the centurion wanted to spare Paul's life. He ordered them all to jump overboard and swim to land. Everyone reached the shore safely.

ACTS 28

The island they shipwrecked on was called Malta. The people were very welcoming. They built a fire for the men and while Paul was placing some wood on the fire, a snake (viper) wrapped itself on Paul's hand. Paul just shook it off. The people thought the snake could have harmed or killed Paul. When nothing happened to him, they were convinced he was a god. The chief official of the island was Publius, who invited them to his home where his father was very sick. Paul healed him, and when the rest of the Islanders saw this, the sick came to be healed. After being on Malta for three months, the group set sail for Rome.

When they arrived in Rome, Paul is allowed to live by himself, under the watch of a guard.

Paul preaches while he is being guarded. He tells him the story of how he was charged with a crime, but was going to be released, until the Jews objected. Because the Jews objected to his release, He appealed to Caesar—and that is why he is here. The people basically tell Paul that they have no idea what he is talking about. "We have received no letter from Judea about you".

The Romans agree to meet Paul on a certain day to hear what he has to say. From morning to night, he spoke of the kingdom of God and Jesus. Some were convinced and others did not believe. They began to leave after Paul said this: "the Holy Spirit spoke the truth to your forefathers when he said through Isaiah the prophet:

> "Go to this people and say,
> "You will be ever hearing
> but never understanding.
> You will be ever seeing
> but never perceiving".
> For this people's heart has
> become calloused.
> They hardly hear with
> their ears,
> and they have closed
> their eyes,
> Otherwise, they might see
> with their eyes,
> hear with their ears,
> understand with their

hearts
and turn, and I will heal them".

"Therefore, I want you to know that God's salvation has been sent to the Gentiles and they will listen"! This is an "in your face" challenge to the Jews.

"For two whole years Paul stayed there in his rented house. He welcomed all who came to see him, boldly and without hindrance, he preached the kingdom of God and taught about the Lord Jesus Christ".

I love that last line to conclude Acts. What would happen if we all preached about Jesus like Paul did? Paul did it through constant hardship and persecution, imprisonment, torture, and threats. That was the most impressive thing about Paul. He didn't preach about Jesus because of the worldly gain it would bring him. He preached about Jesus because God asked him to.

ROMANS

Romans is an absolute life-changing book. The primary message is that anyone can be right with God on the final day of judgment, because right standing only comes through faith in Jesus Christ who died for our sins. Paul is clear in that none of us have an "edge" because none of us have kept the law. Our salvation lies in the lavish grace of God.

Romans is a bit of a different kind of letter in that Paul is introducing himself to the Church of Rome. Most of his letters are to Churches that he has already visited, and he has not visited Rome. There was a tension between the Jewish and Gentile believers and Paul wanted to clear up those intentions with his letter.

The most important lesson in Romans is "Romans road". This is a sequence of verses in the book that very clearly explain how salvation can <u>only</u> come through faith in Jesus. There is no other way. Understanding these verses can change your life.

> Romans 3:23   for <u>all</u> have sinned and fall short of the glory of God.

> Romans 6:23   for the wages of sin is <u>death</u> but the gift of God is <u>eternal life</u> through Jesus Christ our Lord.

Romans 5:8	but God demonstrates his own love toward us in that <u>while we were still sinners</u> Christ died for us.
Romans 10:9	if you confess with your mouth Jesus is Lord and believe in your <u>heart</u> that God raised him from the dead, you will be <u>saved</u>.
Romans 10:13	for <u>everyone</u> who calls on the name of the Lord will be saved.
Romans 5:1	therefore since we have been <u>justified through faith</u>, we have <u>peace</u> through our Lord Jesus Christ.
Romans 8:1	therefore there is now no condemnation for those who are in Christ Jesus.
Romans 8:38:39	for I am convinced that neither death nor life, neither angels nor demons, neither the present nor the future, nor any powers, neither height nor depth nor anything else in all creation will be able to separate us from the love of God that is in Christ Jesus our Lord.

So simple and understanding the message will change your life!! It simplifies the promise of Jesus in 8 verses!

ROMANS 1

Paul begins many of his letters with a greeting to the people that he is writing to—it's important to know that all Paul's writings are letters, and it helps to read them that way. He always tells his audience that he is grateful for them, he loves them, and he thinks of them often. "Grace and peace to you from God our Father and from our Lord Jesus Christ".

"Through him (Jesus) and for his namesake, we received grace and apostleship to call people from all the Gentiles to the obedience that comes from faith. and you also are among those called to Jesus Christ".

We <u>belong</u> to Jesus Christ.

Paul thanks the Romans because their "Faith is being reported all over the world". He tells them that he wants to impart a spiritual gift to them to "make you strong". Paul's words drip with wisdom and insight and are so very powerful.

"I am not ashamed of the gospel, because it is the power of God for the salvation of everyone who believes: First for the Jew, then for the Gentile. For in the gospel, a righteousness from God is revealed—a righteousness by faith from first to last, just as it is written: 'the righteous will live by faith'". **I believe Paul uses the word "live" as an action verb, not just as existence.**

Paul reminds them that God's presence has been made known to them since the beginning of time. So "men are without excuse". We can't say we don't know God. He is everywhere. Then he explains that while they knew God, they didn't glorify him or thank him. They became fools and exchanged the glory of the "immortal God for images made to look like mortal men and birds and animals and reptiles".

It's so true, people pray to images, statues, and pictures all the time. Just walk through some of the largest and most famous churches in the world, and see what people are praying to.

Paul says, "men served created things rather than the creator." he says, "since they did not think it worthwhile to retain the knowledge of God, he gave them over to a depraved mind." Paul says that essentially, "God let men do what they wanted to do, and men became filled with wickedness, evil, greed and depravity, envy, murder, strife, deceit and malice." **The important part is that this is what happens without God in our life. Left to ourselves, without God, we sin!**

ROMANS 2

The beginning of chapter 2 is powerful! "You therefore have no excuse, you who pass judgment on someone else, for at whatever point you judge the other, you are condemning yourself, because you who pass judgment are doing the same things". **Paul says that when God judges us, it is based on truth. He challenges us to realize that it is God's kindness that leads us to repentance.** "But because of your stubbornness and your unrepentant heart, you are storing up wrath against yourself for the day of God's wrath, when his righteous judgment will be revealed". This is an important point. **Paul tells us that not only is it wrong to pass judgment on others, the simple act of doing so condemns *ourselves*.**

Judging other people is such a recipe for being sad, lonely, and separated from God. It's not our job to judge. It is God's job to judge. One of the things he will judge is "did we judge others".

Since Paul is writing this letter to the Romans, most of them were Jews. He says if they are relying on "the law", and telling people about the law, and bragging about their relationship with the law, but not <u>following</u> the law, then there is no value in the law and they are dishonoring God. "a man is a Jew if he is one inwardly, and circumcision is circumcision of the heart, by the spirit, not by written code. Such a man's praise is not from men but from God".

It's important to understand that Jesus' coming was all about rewriting centuries of the Jewish law from "salvation through laws to salvation by grace".

That's why so is written "about" Jews and their customs. The Bible is largely about the conversion of the Jewish nation.

ROMANS 3

Romans 3 begins by talking about God's faithfulness and Paul talks about what the relationship is between our "unrighteousness and God's faithfulness", and then he begins his path down Roman's road, which as I said, is life changing because it succinctly explains why we believe in Jesus.

Roman's road #1, 3:11

"There is no one righteous.
Not even one.
There is no one who understands.
There is no one who seeks God.
all have turned away,
They have together become worthless.
There is no one who does good,
not even one.
Their throats are open graves.
Their tongues practice deceit.
The poison of vipers is on their lips.
Their mouths are full of cursing and bitterness".

This just tells me that we are all equal in God's eyes. We are not righteous by nature. We are held accountable to God. We only achieve righteousness through Jesus righteousness. "No one will be declared righteous in his sight by observing the law, rather through the law we become conscious of sin".

Romans Road #2, 3:22

"This righteousness comes through
faith in Jesus Christ to all who
believe. There is no difference, For

> all have sinned and fall short of
> the glory of God".

"And are justified freely by his grace through the redemption that came in Jesus Christ".

"God presented him as a sacrifice of atonement, through faith in his blood. He did this to demonstrate his justice, because in his forbearance He had left the sins committed beforehand unpunished—He did it to demonstrate his justice at the present time, so as not to be just and the one who justifies those who have faith in Jesus"

Paul concludes chapter 3 by discussing the role of "the law". He poses the question, "if we are justified by faith, why worry about the law?"

This is the beauty of following Jesus. We don't follow "the law" to get to Jesus. We follow the law <u>because</u> we follow Jesus! We do good things not to get a prize, we do good things because we already won the prize. And we want to show others how great the prize is and how to get it. The prize is Jesus.

ROMANS 4

This is a confusing chapter. It talks about the law (Jewish law), works according to that law, circumcision (which is essentially a Jewish custom that binds someone to that law), justification and faith. Paul first acknowledges that Abraham was our "forefather". He quotes the Old Testament (Gen 15:6) where it says, "Abraham believed God, so it was credited to him as righteousness." Paul goes ties all of these concepts together. Abraham believed that "God had power to do what he promised. Therefore, it was credited to him as righteousness. The words "it was credited to him" were not for him alone, but also for us, to whom God will credit righteousness—for us who believe in him who raised Jesus our Lord from the dead. He was delivered over to death for our sins and was raised to life for our justification."

While this is a slightly confusing and complex chapter, its message is simple, and it is a set up for the rest of Romans and a good foundation for the rest of Paul's letters. **He uses the historical laws of the Old Testament and bridges them to the new covenant established through the death and resurrection of Jesus. His message is simple. We are justified through our faith in Jesus.**

ROMANS 5

"Therefore, since we have been justified through faith, we have peace with God through our Lord Jesus Christ, through whom we have gained access by faith into his grace in which we now stand". This is an incredible passage. **Justification through faith in Jesus gives us peace! What is peace? Peace means that "everything will be okay"! It does not say life will be easy. Although we will face challenges in our lives, we know we have already won the game, because our faith in Jesus assures us our salvation.**

We have already won!

Romans Road #3

But God demonstrates his own love
for us in this: while we were still
sinners, Christ died for us.

That's how much God loves. Mankind were sinners, and God gave us his Son. We did not deserve it! I have often thought of how much someone must have to love someone to send his Son to die for someone else. I can't imagine it.

"For if, when we were God's enemies, we were reconciled to him through the death of his Son, how much more, having been reconciled, shall we be saved through his life"!

That's why following Jesus is so incredible. We get to live like he lived his life and enjoy the fruits that provides. And we defeat the enemy

by being reconciled to him through his death. We did not earn it and we don't deserve it.

Paul tells us that sin entered the world through one man, Adam, but goes on to say, "If by the trespasses of one man, how much more will those who receive God's abundant provision of grace and of the gift of righteousness reign in life through the one man, Jesus Christ?"

Jesus is bigger than sin. When we embrace that concept, we not only are forgiven for our prior sins, but also experience the joy of having Jesus in our lives that encourages us to stop sinning.

"Consequently, just as the result of one trespass was condemnation for all men, so also the result of one act of righteousness was justification that brings life for all men".

No matter the sin, God's grace is never ending.

ROMANS 6

Paul poses a great question to open Romans 6. Shall we go on sinning so that grace may increase? In Chapter 5 he said that God's grace grows and there is no end to it. So why not keep sinning so we can "get more grace". His answer to his own question. "We died to sin, so how can we live in it any longer? Or don't you know that all of us who were baptized into Christ Jesus were baptized into his death? We were therefore buried with him through baptism into death in order that, as Christ was raised from the dead through the glory of the Father, we too may live in a new life. for If we have been united with him in his death, we will certainly also be united with him in his resurrection". **We too may have a new life.**

Paul writes so eloquently—

We are united with Christ in his death (where he took away all my sins).

We are united with Christ in his resurrection (where he proved he was God) so that…I could have peace and joy of a new life in him!!

Paul challenges us to be dead to our old ways, be dead to sin (like Christ was), "For sin shall not be your master, because you are not under law, but under grace".

Because we are under grace, we no longer love sin. We hate sin. We are alive in Christ, and we want to live like him.

Romans Road #4

But now that you have been set free
from sin and have become slaves to God,
the benefit you reap leads to holiness,
and the result is eternal life.
For the wages of sin is death,
but the gift of God is eternal
Life in Jesus Christ our Lord.

So powerful! What is a wage? it's what you get paid for doing something. Live in sin, without Jesus—leads to damnation. Follow Jesus to heaven.

ROMANS 7

Paul uses marriage to illustrate the new covenant established by Jesus' death and resurrection. He says that a woman is bound to a man whom she is married to until he dies. Then she is not held to the laws of that marriage, and she can go and marry another man. "So, my brothers, you also died to the law through the body of Christ". He goes on to say, "We have been released from the law so that we serve in the <u>new way of the spirit, and not in the old way of the written code.</u>"

Paul talks about struggling with sin in a very powerful way. He says that we are slaves to sin. We just are! And the very presence of the commandment attracts us to that sin. It makes no sense, until we think about it. We are attracted to sin itself. We don't want to be, but we are.

"I do not understand what I do. For what I want to do I do not do, but what I hate I do. and if I do what I do not want to do, I agree that the law is good. As it is, it is no longer I who do it, but it is sin living in me. I know that nothing good lives in me that is in my sinful nature. For I have the desire to do what is good, but I <u>cannot carry it out</u>. For what I do is not the good I want to do, but the Evil I do not want to do—this I keep on doing. Now if do what I do not want to do. it is no longer I who do it but is sin living in me that does it".

"Who will rescue me from this body of death? Thanks be to God, through Jesus Christ our Lord".

I wish someone would have shared this passage with me when I was 10 years old. It is the key to combating sin in our lives. We are sinners. We were born that way. And though we follow Christ, we cannot figure out why we continue to sin. Paul's encouragement here is profound. Stop focusing on the sin! The more you think about it, the more you will be attracted to it. Think about Jesus, think about your love for him, and your desire to spend eternity with him. That thinking will replace your desire for sin!

ROMANS 8

"For what the law was powerless to do in that it was weakened by the sinful nature, God did by sending his own son in the likeness of sinful man to be a sin offering. And so, he condemned sin in sinful man in order that the righteous requirements of the law might be fully met in us, who do not live according to the sinful nature but according to the spirit".

The law was powerless because it is rooted in man's sinful nature. God fixed all that by making it based on the Spirit!

"Those who live according to the sinful nature have their minds set on what nature desires; But those who live in accordance with the spirit have their minds set on what the spirit desires. The mind of a sinful man is death, but the mind controlled by the Spirit is life and peace".

That is so appealing to me: To live a life of love and peace.

Paul tells us that because of God's promise of a life of love and peace we have an obligation to live according to that promise. "The Spirit himself testifies with our spirit that we are God's children. Now if we are children, then we are heirs—heirs of God and co-heirs with Christ, if we indeed share in his sufferings in order that we may also share in his glory."

"I consider that our present sufferings are not worth comparing with the glory that will be revealed to us".

How beautiful is that? That is why following Jesus is so awesome. No matter how tough life can get, we know that we have already won.

"If God is for us, who can be against us"? He who did not spare his own Son, but gave him up for us all—how will he not also, along with him, graciously give us all things"?

How powerful and poignant!!

"In the same way, the Spirit helps us in our weakness. We do not know what we ought to pray for, but the Spirit himself intercedes for us with groans that words cannot express".

When we don't know what we want to pray for—be quiet. The spirit will take over. Given that the primary purpose of prayer is to align to God's will (listening!) being quiet in prayer is so important.

"Who shall separate us from the love of Christ"?

Think about that question. Jesus came from God. God gave his Son to be killed. The ultimate sign of sacrifice and love. Do you think there is anything in this world that is bigger than that that can overpower God's love for us. No way!

"For I am convinced that neither death nor life, neither angels nor demons, neither the present nor the future, nor any powers, neither height nor depth, nor anything else in all creation, will be able to separate us from the love of God that is in Jesus Christ our Lord".

ROMANS 9

This chapter is a little confusing to read. It is essentially about God's mercy and compassion based on his wishes, based on our faith. Paul uses the history of Abraham, Isaac, and Jacob to explain how God chooses to demonstrate his mercy to us. When Jacob and Esau were born to Isaac and Rebekah, it is written in the Old Testament, "Jacob I loved, but Esau I hated". (God) Paul says, "Therefore God has mercy on whom he wants to have mercy and he hardens whom he wants to harden."

Then Paul poses a different question. "One of you will say, 'Then why does God still blame us for who is able to resist his will'"? he says, "does not the potter not have the right to make out of the same lump of clay some pottery for special purpose and some for common use?" Paul closes with an explanation and a strong statement about faith.

"What shall we say? That the Gentiles, who did not pursue righteousness, have obtained it, a righteousness that is by faith; But the people of Israel who pursued the law as the way of righteousness, have not attained their goal. Why not? because they pursued it not by faith but as if it were by works. They stumbled over the stumbling stone".

I love that. The "stumbling stone" is the belief that you can achieve salvation by works, race, ethnicity, or anything else. Don't fall for it. It is only achieved by faith in Jesus!

ROMANS 10

Paul Continues his narrative of his desire to pray for the Israelites. He knows they are zealous for God, but he explains that their zeal is about "zeal for the law" instead of knowledge and faith. He calls out that the Jew's sonship is directly traced from their heirs to Jesus, but they don't realize it.

Roman's Road #5

"If you declare with your mouth

'Jesus is Lord' and believe in your heart
that God raised him from the dead,
you will be saved"

"Everyone who calls on the name of the lord
will be saved"

That is what I love about the message of Jesus. Everyone is welcome. It does not exclude anyone ever. The only criteria to get into the club is that you must want to be in the club.

If Christ as the Messiah is the "good news" why did all the Israelites not accept it? Paul says that both Moses and Isaiah acknowledged that the good news would be available to all who seek it, but concerning Israel, Isaiah says:

"All day long I have held out
my hands to a disobedient
and obstinate people".

To this day the Jewish faith strongly denies that Jesus is the Messiah, and they continue to wait…

ROMANS 11

Paul continues his explanation of God's relationship with the Jews. It is in one sense complicated because the Israelites are God's chosen people, and they try to reach God by following the law, but they can never get there by doing it that way. Paul says, "At the present time there is a remnant chosen by grace. and if by grace, it <u>cannot be based on works; for if it were, grace would no longer exist</u>."

Think about that, if we could earn God's favor by doing good things, then why would we ever need his grace? It is another example about the whole story about Jesus is about who God IS, not about what we DO.

He also talks about the fact that the Gentiles have received the message more willingly than the Jews and the hope is that will be an inspiration to the Jews.

Once again Paul talks about the inclusiveness of the message of the good news of Jesus. "For God has bound everyone over to disobedience so that he may have mercy on them all".

ROMANS 12

This chapter is amazing. A must read. It is Paul telling the Romans (and us) how we should act as followers of Jesus. "Do not conform any longer to the pattern of this world but be transformed by the renewing of your mind. Then you will be able to test and approve what God's will is— his good, pleasing, and perfect will". Be transformed so you can attest to God's perfect will. not so you can achieve what is in your own will, but so we can point to God. Brilliant!

Paul tells us not to think of ourselves higher than we ought. We need to be honest with ourselves "in accordance with the faith God has given" us.

Paul also makes his often-quoted speech about the importance of using our spiritual gifts, because together they are all important in the body of Christ. "If it is serving, let him serve". He says the same thing about teaching, encouraging, generosity, leadership, governing and showing mercy. If we were given these gifts, we need to use them for God's purpose and glory.

Then he talks about love. We must be devoted to one another in brotherly love. We should be joyful, and patient and we should practice hospitality. Why? Because all these things point to God and our faith in Jesus!

We should bless everyone, even those who persecute you. We shouldn't curse. We shouldn't be conceited and always be willing to spend time with people in "low position". We need to live in peace with everyone. Because Jesus would.

"Do not be overcome by evil but overcome evil with good".

Why do we do all these things? Is it to earn points with God? No. Remember, we are already saved. We do these things out of true love, as a reflection of God's grace, mercy, and love for us. He gives it to us, and we pass it on, and in so doing, we point to God and attract others to him.

ROMANS 13

I struggled with this chapter. Not for what it says, but for how things have changed in the world since these words were written.

"Everyone must submit himself to the governing of authorities, for there is no governing authority except that which God has established. The authorities that exist have been established by God. Consequently, he who rebels against the authority is rebelling against what God has instituted, and those who do so will bring judgment on themselves".

"This is why you pay taxes, for the authorities are God's servants who give their full time to governing".

These verses deserve some "unpacking". Clearly, as of 2021, not all rulers are from God. Hitler, Mao, and Stalin are just a few examples of rulers that killed their own people. So that cannot be "of God", and to submit to them would not be the right thing to do. In these instances, we need to stand up for what is from God. While we don't have any rulers in the United States who are like that, we definitely have leaders who are more closely aligned with God's will than others. Our leaders are elected by people, and not all people are of God. **Today, false leaders are like false prophets, there are many and we need to be educated and aware. Most importantly, we need to pray and ask God which leaders are "of him" and which are not.**

The issue of taxes is similar. Tax collectors in the time of Jesus were viewed as very corrupt. The standard tax was 1% of a person's income. 1%! The tax collectors were free to charge people extra. (that's how they made their living.) All that said, I wonder what Jesus would say about taxation if he knew that we pay 60% of our income to our government, and other nations pay more. I do not think he would be in favor of that. That's just one man's opinion.

Paul finishes this chapter with a flurry. "Let no debt remain outstanding, except the continuing debt to love one another. The Commandments... are summed up in this one rule: "Love one another as yourself. Love does no harm to its neighbor. therefore, love is the fulfillment of the law". '**The continuing debt to love one another' is a beautiful depiction of how we are to treat others. We owe it to them to love them.**

He tells us that our salvation is nearer than we think, and we need to "wake up" and "clothe yourselves with the Lord Jesus Christ, and do not think about how to gratify the desires of sinful nature".

This is such a simple but critical message. If we clothe ourselves in Jesus, we focus on him and not the sin, and the allure of sin evaporates from our life!

ROMANS 14

This chapter is about the importance of not passing judgment on one another. People will do different things, eat different foods, choose different paths and live different lives. **It doesn't matter because the only thing that does matter is what we do for the Lord**. "For this very reason, Christ died and returned to life so that he might be the Lord of both the dead and the living. For why do you judge your brother or why do you look down on your brother? For we will all stand before God's judgment seat. It is written:

"As surely as I live, says the Lord,
every knee will bow before Me;
every tongue will confess to God".
"So then, each of us will give an account to God".

Everyone is equal; therefore, to look down or judge someone else is a waste of time.

Further, Paul encourages us to not put stumbling blocks in front of others. "For the kingdom of God is not a matter of eating and drinking, but of righteousness, peace, and joy in the Holy Spirit. because anyone who serves Christ in this way is pleasing to God and approved by men".

Paul talks in this chapter a lot about food. The reason is because he is writing to Roman Jews, and they have strict eating customs. Paul is telling them that it doesn't matter! It's all about serving God and following Jesus.

"Let us therefore make every effort to do what leads people to peace and mutual edification".

That is what Jesus would have done!

ROMANS 15

Paul tells us to build up our neighbors, especially the weak. He says to do that because that is what Jesus did. He says, "For everything that was written in the past was written to teach us, so that through endurance and encouragement of the scriptures we might have hope. May the God who gives endurance and encouragement give you a spirit of unity among yourselves as you follow Christ Jesus so that with one heart and mouth you may glorify the God and father of our Lord Jesus Christ."

This is important:

"Accept one another, then, just as Christ accepted
you, in order to bring praise to God".

Why do we do things that we are instructed to do? To bring praise and glory to God. That's it. That's the reason. That is why we are here. And if Jesus accepts us in our brokenness, who are we to reject others who are broken since we are called to be like him?

"May the God of hope fill you with all joy and peace as you trust in him, so that you may overflow with hope by the power of the Holy Spirit".

The God of hope. So incredibly beautiful. We need to remember that—God always brings us hope because all roads lead to him.

Paul tells the Romans that he will revisit them when he goes to Spain, and he asks them for their prayers of protection from the unbelievers in Judea.

ROMANS 16

Paul commends "our sister Phoebe" to the Roman people and he tells them that she has been a great help to many people, and he names several of them by name.

He tells them to watch out for people who put obstacles in their way that are contrary to what he has taught them. "Stay away from them for such people are not serving our Lord Jesus Christ, But their own appetites. by smooth talk and flattery, they deceive the minds of naïve people".

Do not be naïve. Seek truth. Seek knowledge. Seek wisdom.

"The God of peace will crush Satan under your feet"! **If we seek God consistently, he will crush Satan under our feet. It is so reassuring. We need to run for protection behind God's shield….Jesus.**

Paul closes the letter to the Romans with a beautiful "sendoff":

"Now to him who is able to establish you by my gospel and the proclamation of Jesus Christ, according to the revelation of the mystery hidden for long ages past, but now revealed and made known through the prophetic writings by the command of the eternal God, so that all nations might believe and obey him—to the only wise God be glory forever through Jesus Christ! Amen!

1 CORINTHIANS

The town of Corinth was a very busy city in the first century. It was large and wealthy. There was a Christian Church established there, but it was not thriving because there were disagreements, bitterness, focus on the pagan culture and hyper-spirituality. Paul's letter is an encouragement to the people of Corinth to turn from their sins of immorality, and he explains to them what a true Christian life looks like.

1 CORINTHIANS 1

Paul opens his letter (as he always does) very graciously with a reminder of their faith in Christ. "Our testimony about Christ has been confirmed in you". I think Paul is setting them up a bit. He is saying 'you know how to act, now it's time to do so'.

The first thing Paul does is encourage them to stop disagreeing. The Corinthians had idols to Apollo, Aphrodite and Cephas. Some Corinthians followed Christ, but some actually followed Paul. Paul emphatically defers to Jesus. He says, "Did Paul die for you? Were you baptized in the name of Paul?" **He reminds them that it is all about Jesus.**

He also "admits" that the message of Jesus conflicts with <u>conventional wisdom</u>.

"Where is the wise man? Where Is the scholar? Where is the philosopher of this age? Has not God made foolish the wisdom of the world? For since in the wisdom of God the world through its wisdom did not know him,

God was pleased through the foolishness of what was preached to save those who believe…for the foolishness of God is wiser than a man's wisdom, and the weakness of God is stronger than any man's strength '.

This is Paul's way of saying that God is always beyond our comprehension. We can't "outthink" God even when we are at our best! That's why I get a kick out of academic scholars trying to defend atheism. God said that would happen.

Paul tells them that not many of them were "wise" when they were called. "But God chose the foolish of the world to shame the wise. God chose the weak things of the world to shame the strong. He chose the lowly things of this world…and the things that are not to nullify the things that are, <u>so that no one may boast before him</u>". He reminds us that we are in Christ Jesus and that when we boast, we should "boast in the Lord".

We need to always point to the Lord. God is the ultimate contrarian. The things of this world are not the things of God and that is why Paul is writing to the Corinthians. We need to fix our eyes above.

1 CORINTHIANS 2

Paul addresses the Corinthians from a humble posture. "I did not come with eloquence or superior wisdom". He continues "My message and my preaching were not with wise and persuasive words, but with a demonstration of the spirit's power, so that your faith might not rest on men's wisdom, but on God's power".

Profound! Don't base your faith on your ability to reason—base it on God and only God. Paul is asking the Corinthians to believe him because of his faith through actions not just his words.

But then Paul speaks what is a truth about "God's secret wisdom" As it is written in Isaiah:

"No eye has seen, no ear has heard,

no mind has conceived—
what God has prepared for those who love him"!

That gives us confidence and a reason to believe! There will be a reward and that reward is God himself. (I think sometimes people use God as a conduit to other rewards.) If we do not live in the spirit, it is difficult for us to understand all these concepts. We sometimes fall into the trap of following Jesus because we want God to give us things like happiness, health, money, and other "worldly" things. Sometimes things like that do come into our lives, and sometimes they don't. But when we follow Jesus, he ALWAYS comes into our lives. And that gives us peace, joy, and hope.

"The man without the spirit does not accept the things that come from the Spirit of God, for they are foolish to him, and he cannot understand them because they are spiritually discerned. The spiritual man makes judgments about all things but he himself is not subject to any man's judgments".

Once we follow Jesus, and start submitting to God's will, we can stop worrying about what other people think of us!

1 CORINTHIANS 3

Paul challenges the Corinthians to not be "worldly". He tells them because there is still quarreling in the Church, they are not mature in their faith. He also tells them that they are following the wrong leaders at times. They follow him (Paul) or Apollos. He tells them, "I planted the seed, Apollos watered it, but God made it grow." Paul always defers to Jesus and his Father. He goes on to say, "we are God's fellow workers; you are God's field, God's building."

He says that by the grace of God he has laid a foundation for us. But we all need to be careful how we build "for no one can lay any foundation other than the one already laid, which is Jesus Christ". He tells us that, "If we build that foundation on anything else, gold, silver, costly stones; it will be brought to light and 'revealed with fire.'" **This is a very clear description of what happens when we try to build our life on anything but faith in Jesus. Our lives will crumble.**

"Don't you know that you yourselves are God's temple and God's Spirit lives in you? If anyone destroys God's temple, God will destroy him; for God's temple is sacred, and you are that temple".

Build our foundation on Christ, devote our lives to serving God, and as God's temple he will protect us.

He closes Chapter 3 with a warning to not deceive ourselves. Be careful about seeking worldly wisdom. "If any of you thinks he is wise by the standards of this age, he should become a fool so that he can become wise. For the wisdom of this world is foolishness in God's eyes. As it is written in Job, "he catches the wise in their craftiness".

The point is to start with God. Build your wisdom there. Learn the story of Jesus, and don't try to outthink your faith. Stay anchored to Jesus.

1 CORINTHIANS 4

"So then, men ought to regard us as servants of Christ and those entrusted with the secret things of God. Now it is required that those who have given a trust must prove faithful".

This is important. First, we <u>serve</u> God. We serve him by <u>sharing</u> his truth with others. This is our job. But we must also "walk the talk". If we can remember that other people's opinion of us doesn't matter, we will free ourselves to serve God.

Paul tells us that the only judgment that matters is the judgment by the Lord at the appointed time. Man's judgment of us is irrelevant.

"Already you have all you want. Already you are rich. You have become kings".

This simple statement by Paul is a reminder of one of the ultimate truths of following Jesus! We have already won. We are the victors. We do not need to spend our lives seeking worldly riches. "God has put us apostles on display at the end of the procession".

Paul also speaks of some of the arrogance of the leaders in Corinth, and he urges them to 'imitate me' because he "comes in love with a great spirit".

1 CORINTHIANS 5

For me, this is a controversial chapter. The primary focus of this chapter is about sexual immorality. I agree with Paul in that sexual immorality is "not right" and it is not at all in accordance with the teachings of Jesus. However, Paul encourages the Corinthians to "expel the wicked man from among you". He also says, "hand this man over to Satan so that the sinful nature may be destroyed, and his spirit saved on the day of the Lord."

That is just not logical to me. How could Satan "destroy sinful nature"? Satan creates sinful nature. Further, Jesus not only did not expel sinners, but he also welcomed them and forgave them. Now he did encourage them to sin no more and talked about forgiving "7 times 70 times".

Sexual immorality is a sin, not unlike other sins. It destroys our relationships—with those close to us and with Jesus. But God forgives and Jesus instructs us to stop sinning. (Woman at the well). As Paul says in Romans, Jesus transcends sin, and he forgives us when we repent. That is the cornerstone of his new covenant.

1 CORINTHIANS 6

It is important to realize that Paul's letter to the Corinthians was intended to both chastise and encourage them. Corinth had turned into a city of sin, and he was trying to redirect them to Jesus. Many of them are fighting amongst each other via disputes and lawsuits. He tells them to settle them among themselves as believers. "The very fact that you have lawsuits among you means you have been completely defeated already. Why not rather be wronged? Why not rather be cheated? Instead, you yourselves cheat and do wrong, and you do this to your brothers". Paul makes a confusing statement about all these sinners and says, "they will not inherit the kingdom of God." He then rescues it by saying, "But you were washed, you were sanctified, you were justified in the name of the Lord Jesus Christ and by the Spirit of God."

This is important. People sin. We all do. But the beauty of following Jesus is that he absorbed that sin for us, and because of that love we strive to love him back and it reduces the allure of sin in our lives.

Paul returns to the topic of sexual immorality. This time he says something that resonates, "All other sins a man commits are outside his body, but he who sins sexually, sins against his own body. Do you not know that your body is a temple of the Holy Spirit? You are not your own; You were <u>bought</u> at a price. Therefore, honor God with your body!"

I believe the statement "honor God with your body" is transcendent. It refers to sex, food, drink, health, exercise, tattoos, piercings, all of it. My intent is not to judge, my intent is to remind ourselves that our body is a gift from God and when I present it back to him, my hope is that he will say, "well done, my good and faithful servant".

1 CORINTHIANS 7

Paul provides instruction on marriage. Recall, 1 Corinthians is all about Paul trying to re-educate the people and what it means to be a Christian. Hence, this chapter is about who should marry, whom they should marry, how they should marry, what happens if there is a divorce, if there is a death, etc. Honestly, there are some circular messages within the teaching. One of his messages that he does communicate is that no matter what, our mission is to serve "what is above". Therefore, (at least from his vantage point) it is easier to serve God when you are unmarried because you can devote your whole life to serving "what is above". I understand his logic, but the Kingdom of God is God's people and serving his people is serving him, and it is what he would want us to do. **And marriage, along with a family, can serve as the greatest builder of the kingdom of all. So, I think a little discernment over Paul's words are important.**

"I am saying this for your own good, not to restrict you, but that you may live in a right way in undivided devotion to the Lord".

1 CORINTHIANS 8

Paul shares with us the importance of separating the one true God from the many Idols that exist in the world. He does this by discussing food. In the Jewish faith, there was food sacrificed to idols. It was sacrificial eating—the faith was very intertwined with food. Paul instructs them that:

1) **what you eat or drink is not any part of your faith. It is unrelated.**

2) **Idols mean nothing. Therefore, to sacrifice food for them is a waste of time.** "Yet for us there is but one God the Father, from whom all things came and for whom we live; and there is but one Lord, Jesus Christ, through whom all things came and through whom we live". **We continue to see food being woven into various faiths, and we certainly see idol worship on a regular basis. Both things take our eyes off Jesus.**

1 CORINTHIANS 9

I will begin this summary with the final verses of the chapter.

"Do you know that in a race all run, but only one gets the prize? Run in such a way as to get the prize. Everyone who competes in the games goes into strict training. They do they do it to get a crown that will not last, but we do it to get a crown that will last forever. Therefore, I do not run like someone running aimlessly; I do not fight like a boxer beating the air. No, I strike a blow to my body and make it my slave so that after I have preached to others, I, myself, will not be disqualified for the prize". **This is a powerful athletic metaphor that resonates for me. Running to Jesus is certainly not running aimlessly.**

The title of this chapter is "Paul's rights as an apostle" and it is a bit of a confusing read. It is essentially Paul explaining to the people that he has the right to "benefits" from preaching the gospel. I believe this is in response to the criticism he is receiving from the Corinthians regarding food or money from those he is preaching to. "Don't you know that those who serve in the temple get their food from the temple, and those who serve at the altar share in what is offered on the altar"?

This is an important point. If a minister doesn't earn money from the people, where else could he earn it? The problem emerges when ministers twist the gospel so they can get rich at the expense of others. That is why we carefully choose the earthly "leaders" that we choose to listen to. An honorable pastor deserves to be "fed" from the Church. A pastor who twists Jesus' words (prosperity gospel) to gain earthly riches needs to be avoided like the plague.

1 CORINTHIANS 10

Paul warns the Corinthians that what they are facing is not new. Temptations, idolatry, food sacrificed to those idols; all of it was experienced by their ancestors. He talks about how they died in the desert due to their failure to recognize what they were doing. "These things happened to them as examples and were written down as warnings for us, on whom the culmination of ages is to come. So, if you think you are standing firm, be careful that you don't fall. No temptation has overtaken you except what is common to mankind. And God is faithful; you will not be tempted beyond what you can bear. But when you are tempted, he will also provide you a way out so you can endure it".

I love the warning Paul provides: "If you think you are standing firm, be careful that you don't fall". We just need to stay "on guard."

This is so important. It's almost as if we need to stay a little uncomfortable in our faith. We need to seek a "life learner" mentality, never being too confident in where we are because Satan is lurking and is ready to pounce on our arrogance.

"So, whatever you do, do it all <u>for the glory of God</u>. Do not cause anyone to stumble, whether Jews, Greeks, or the Church of God". **So, to a certain degree, we are not only responsible for ourselves, but we are also responsible for others because we know the truth. Imagine you are traveling with friends, and you are lost in the woods. There is only one path out of the woods, and you know what that path is because you have been there before. What friend would keep that a secret. Of course, we would lead our friends out of the woods and out of danger. When we know the truth of Jesus, which is the path to Heaven, why don't we share it with them?**

1 CORINTHIANS 11

This is a frustrating chapter for me. Most of it talks about what men and women should or should not wear on their heads when they go to church. I am trying to remember that Paul is instructing Jews from 2000 years ago. Hats, veils, hair, all those things were a major part of Jewish culture, and in some Jewish synagogues, they still are. They were also a part of Christian culture just 75 years ago. Paul says that a man should not cover his head because he is the image of God, and a woman should cover her head because she is made in the image of man. **I find it interesting that in the previous chapter Paul says, "what you eat, doesn't matter." And here he says, "what you wear on your head does matter." Seems a bit inconsistent. I will simply chalk it up to differences in times. God cares about our hearts.**

1 CORINTHIANS 12

This chapter is about spiritual gifts which is an important topic for all Christians to understand. If we truly believe we were put here by God, for God's glory, then we need to also believe that God was going to equip us with the gifts and talents necessary to carry out that mission. "There are different kinds of gifts, but the same spirit distributes them. There are different kinds of service, but the same Lord. There are different kinds of working, but in all of them and in everyone it is the same God at work".

Paul says that some receive a message of wisdom, to another a message of knowledge, to another faith, gifts of healing, miraculous powers, prophecy, distinguishing between spirits and interpretations of tongues".

Paul tells us we all have a part to play in the "body of Christ". He likens it to the body itself. "Now if the foot should say because I am not a hand, I do not belong to the body...if the whole body were an eye what would the sense of hearing be"? **The point is that we need to <u>identify</u> and <u>use</u> our spiritual gift. In other words, if we are not able to <u>sing</u> that does not mean that we can't serve in Church. We can still speak, read, usher, console, teach. We all have gifts and responsibilities.**

He also encourages us all to work together. "God has put the body together...so that there can be no division in the body, but that its parts should have equal concern for each other. If one part suffers, every part suffers with it; If one part is honored every part rejoices with it. **United, we are a powerful force against the evils of this world.**

1 CORINTHIANS 13

This chapter is eloquent, impactful, important, and beautiful. I love it so much that it was a reading at our wedding, and we have it hanging in our bedroom. For that reason, I am going to rewrite the chapter.

"And now I will show you the most excellent way. If I speak in tongues of men and angels, but have not love, I am only a resounding gong or a clanging cymbal. If I have the gift of prophecy and can fathom all mysteries and all knowledge, and if I have a faith that can move mountains, but have not love, I am nothing. If I give all I possess to the poor and surrender my body to the flames, but have not love, I am nothing.

Love is patient, love is kind. It does not envy, it does not
boast, it is not proud. It is not rude, it is not self-seeking, it
is not easily angered, it keeps no record of its wrongs.
Love does not delight in evil but rejoices with the truth.
It always protects, always trusts always hopes, always perseveres.

Love never fails. But where there are prophecies, they will cease; where there are tongues, they will be stilled; where there is knowledge, it will pass away. For we know in part, and we prophesy in part, but when perfection comes, the imperfect disappears. When I was a child, I talked like a child. I thought like a child, I reasoned like a child. When I became a man, I put childish ways behind me. Now we see but a poor reflection as in a mirror; Then we shall see face to face. Now I know in part; then I shall know fully, even as I am fully known.

And now these three remain:
Faith hope and love.
But the greatest of these is love.

Jesus asked us to what do one thing: Love. Nothing matters without it. When we default to the kind of love that Jesus demonstrated, and asked us to emulate, we experience the true peace and joy that God promises. And the beauty is that we experience it here on earth and are promised eternal peace and joy in heaven with God. It's the ultimate Win-Win proposition! And the best evangelism and discipleship we can ever do to attract people to the Kingdom of God is to walk around this earth loving people. They will see that love, and want to seek it with us.

1 CORINTHIANS 14

Once again Paul transitions from an impactful chapter to a slightly unusual one. But it may not have been all that unusual at the time. He writes about speaking in tongues and prophesies. He tells them (us) that speaking in tongues is a sign to be used for unbelievers, not believers. He says, "What good is it if you use words that no one understands." Regarding prophecies, "unless you speak intelligible words, how will anyone know what you are saying"? I agree with this completely and never really understood the role of speaking in tongues as it relates to sharing the good news of Jesus. Paul says, "I would rather speak five intelligible words to instruct others than 10,000 words in a tongue." He also returns to the topic of spiritual gifts and says, "try to excel at gifts that build up the church."

It is important that I call out a controversial section of this chapter. Paul says very specifically that women are not to speak in church. He says it is, "disgraceful for a woman to speak in church," and, "a woman should ask her own husband at home."

While I disagree with this statement, I don't hold Paul in contempt for writing it. As it is more about the fact that it was a sign of the times and part of the Jewish culture, so it was in line with all of that. In my opinion, it's not appropriate nor accurate for today.

1 CORINTHIANS 15

We're approaching the end of Paul's letter and he is trying to "bring it home". He reminds them of the gospel he preached, "By this gospel you are saved, if you hold on firmly to the Word I have preached you. Otherwise, you have believed in vain." He reminds them that Christ died for their (our) sins and rose from the dead. He also testifies that Jesus appeared before 500 people after he rose. He admits to them that he does not deserve to be an apostle because he persecuted the Church. "But By the grace of God, I am what I am".

This is important. God's grace can repair all of us, no matter what we have done. It can happen at any time, up to our final days on this earth.

Paul challenges the Corinthians who claim that there is no resurrection of the dead. He states that if there is no resurrection of the dead (us going to heaven), then Christ did not rise from the dead. And if Christ did not rise from the dead "our faith is useless". **This is so important. It is a very logical explanation of why we believe what we believe. These sections of scripture that explain God's sacrifice of his Son Jesus to our daily faith is so compelling for me. He then makes another profound statement. "If only for this life we have hope in Christ, we are pitied more than all men".**

His point is that following Jesus is not about what happens here. It's a pathway to heaven, and it's not easy. So, if we anchor ourselves in the fact that following Jesus Is about what happens here, we are missing the point.

Paul says death came from Adam (original sin) but life came from Jesus. He says that the "last enemy to be destroyed is death". **How great is that? The beauty of following Jesus is that we never truly die!! We remain alive in Jesus.**

After so much discussion about the resurrection of the dead, the people start to wonder what happens to our bodies after we are raised from the dead. Paul tells them that there are earthly bodies and there are heavenly bodies "so will it be with the resurrection of the dead. The body that is sown is perishable, it is raised imperishable; It is sown in dishonor, it is raised in glory; It is sown in weakness, it is raised in power; It is sown in a natural body, it is raised in a spiritual body...for the Trumpet will sound, the dead will be raised imperishable, and we will be changed.

"The sting of death is sin, and the power of sin is the law. But thanks be to God. He gives us the victory through our Lord Jesus Christ. Therefore, my dear brothers, stand firm. Let nothing move you. Always give yourselves fully to the work of the Lord because you know that your labor in the Lord is not in vain".

The last sentence is so important. Nobody wants to "work" for no reason. When we work for the Lord, it always pays off. <u>The value is intrinsic</u>! When we work for Jesus, we get Jesus. And when we get Jesus, we get heaven!

1 CORINTHIANS 16

The beginning of this chapter is about Paul providing instructions while he is away. He is unafraid to talk about money and the importance of it. This is an important lesson for all of us. We cannot be afraid, or uncomfortable, of talking about money in the Church. Sharing the gospel requires resources. The people who spend their lives doing the Lord's work need to eat too. If we truly believe that it is God's money from the start, then we need to be willing to share it willingly with all people.

He goes on to provide instructions to them about how to be hospitable to Timothy, whom Paul trusts implicitly, as well as several other believers.

And then he shares with them this often shared, timeless and powerful advice. "Be on your guard; stand firm in the faith; be men of courage; be strong. do everything in love".

Sometimes we believe that strength and love are mutually exclusive. They are not! With Jesus, they are mutually dependent.

2 CORINTHIANS

Paul's first letter to Corinth is known as "the warning letter" to the people who were living sinful lives. His second letter was written in about 55 a.d. And refers to an upheaval among Christians there. They were very critical of his ministry and his message. That said, Paul receives word the people have repented and is full of joy. There is so much debate about how many letters Paul actually wrote to Corinth, and some believe 2 Corinthians is actually two letters because 1-9 is quite different than 10-13. Some say he wrote four letters to Corinth. In 2 Corinthians Paul spends considerable time defending himself and his ministry. It is a deeply personal letter.

2 CORINTHIANS 1

"Praise be to the God and Father of our Lord Jesus Christ, the Father of compassion and the God of all comfort, who comforts us in all our troubles, so that we can comfort those in any trouble with the comfort we ourselves receive from God. For just as we share abundantly in the sufferings of Christ, so also our comfort abounds through Christ".

Wow!! "The Father of compassion". What a beautiful nickname for God and the beauty of Paul's comments are that it depicts "the circle of following Jesus" in a beautiful way. We follow Jesus, he comforts us, so we can comfort others.

The love of Jesus is boundless.

Paul tells us of the "troubles" they experienced when they were in Asia. I assume he is referring to persecution. He says they "were under great pressure, far beyond our ability to endure, so that we despaired of life itself." He then tells us something important, "But this happened that we might not rely on ourselves but on God, who raises the dead". Sometimes God takes us to a place that the only thing we can do is rely on him. The magic is to always experience his love and not to wait until you are in the depths to realize that he is right there with you.

Paul says, "Now this is our boast: our conscience testifies that we have conducted ourselves in the world, and especially in our relations with you, with integrity and Godly sincerity. We have done so, relying not on worldly wisdom but on God's grace."

"For no matter how many promises God has made, they are 'yes' in Christ. Now it is God who makes both us and you stand firm in Christ. He anointed us, set his seal of ownership on us, and put his Spirit in our hearts as a deposit, guaranteeing what is to come".

2 CORINTHIANS 2

Paul tells the Corinthians that he is writing to them out of "distress and anguish of the heart". In short, I believe he is trying to tell them that, "I was down, and because I love you so much, I wanted to write a letter to you to tell you that, and that made me happy." Paul is no different than us. We reach out to friends when we are down. He also speaks about forgiveness. "Anyone you forgive, I also forgive. and what I have forgiven—if there was anything to forgive—I have forgiven in the sight of Christ for your sake, in order that Satan might not outwit us. For we are not unaware of his schemes".

Paul had traveled to a city called Troas because "God opened a door for me". (**We should all be so aware as to see God's open doors!**) But he did not find Titus (his traveling companion), so he left there. He follows with this:

"But thanks be to God, who always leads us as captives in Christ's triumphal procession and uses us to spread the aroma of the knowledge of him everywhere. For we are to God the pleasing aroma of Christ among those who are being saved and those who are perishing. To the one we are an aroma that brings death; to the other an aroma that brings life".

That is so beautiful. When we live in the Spirit, we are the pleasing aroma of Christ to God!

If you hear God's word and reject it—death. If you hear God's word and embrace it—Life!

2 CORINTHIANS 3

Paul compares the old covenant of Moses to the new covenant of Jesus. "You show that you are a letter from Christ…written not with ink but with the Spirit of the living God, not on tablets of stone, but on tablets of human hearts".

This is such a great depiction of the difference between "following the law written on stone and changing someone's heart", which is what happens when you follow Jesus.

Paul also says that our confidence comes through Jesus Christ and our competence comes from God himself. We cannot take credit for that.

He continues to depict the difference between the old and new covenant by saying "If the ministry that condemns men (not following the written law) is glorious, how much more glorious is the ministry that brings righteousness? Because we have the confidence that exists in following Jesus, we have hope, and we are bold." He very clearly talks about in the old Jewish customs, people put veils over their faces "to keep the Israelites from gazing at it while the radiance fades away". He says, "For their minds were made dull for to this day the same veil remains when the old covenant is read." Recall, Moses lived 800 years before this. **Paul is saying, 'Open your eyes and see the true glory that can only be found in Jesus.'** "But when anyone turns to the Lord. The veil is taken away. <u>Now</u> the Lord is the spirit, and where there is a spirit of the Lord, there is freedom".

We need to remove the veil of this world and see the glory that is only found in Jesus!

2 CORINTHIANS 4

"Therefore, since through God's mercy we have this ministry, we do not lose heart. Rather, we have renounced secret and shameful ways; we do not use deception nor, do we distort the word of God. On the contrary, by setting forth the truth plainly we commend ourselves to every man's conscience in the sight of God. And even if our gospel is veiled, it is veiled to those who are perishing. The God of this age (Satan) has blinded the minds of unbelievers, so they cannot see the light of the gospel of the Glory of Christ, who is the image of God. For we do not preach ourselves, but Jesus Christ as Lord, and ourselves as your servants for Jesus' sake. For God, who said, 'let light shine out of darkness' made his light shine in our hearts to give us a light of knowledge of the Glory of God in the face of Christ".

This chapter is so rich! Bottom line is that Jesus is the light. The light shows in us. Satan blinds people to that light. That is why it is so hard to convince nonbelievers that Jesus is real. They have been blinded by the lies of this world (money will make you happy!).

"But we have this treasure in jars of clay to show this all-surpassing power is from God and not from us. We are hard pressed on every side, but not crushed; perplexed but not in despair; persecuted, but not abandoned; struck down but not destroyed. We always carry around in our bodies the death of Jesus, so that the life of Jesus may also be revealed in our mortal body. So then, death is at work in us, but life is at work in you."

It is written: "I believed; therefore, I have spoken. With the same spirit of faith, we also believe and therefore speak, because we know that the one who raised the Lord Jesus from the dead will also raise us with Jesus and present us with you in his presence. All this is for your benefit, so that the grace that is reaching more and more people may cause thanksgiving to overflow to the glory of God".

"Therefore, we do not lose heart. though outwardly we are wasting away, yet inwardly we are being renewed day by day. For our light and momentary troubles are achieving for us an eternal glory that far outweighs them all. So, we fix our eyes not on what is seen, but on what is unseen, for what is seen is temporary, what is unseen is eternal".

This chapter is both brilliant and beautiful!

2 CORINTHIANS 5

"Now we know that if the earthly tent we live in is destroyed, we have a building from God, an eternal house in heaven, not built by human hands".

This is a great way to look at our bodies and existence on earth. It is a "tent", a perfect example of a temporary structure, as opposed to the beautiful palace that God has prepared for us. "Now it is God who has made us for this very purpose, and has given us the spirit as a deposit, guaranteeing what is to come".

"Therefore, we are always confident and know that as long as we are at home in the body we are away from the Lord".

We need to remember this is not our true home. Our true home is what is to come. "For we all must appear before the judgment seat of Christ, that each one may receive what is due him for the things done in the body, whether good or bad".

"For Christ's love compels us, because we are convinced that one died for all, and therefore all died. And he died for all, that those who live should no longer live for themselves but for him who died for them and was raised again".

And then Paul hits us with one of his strongest statements:

"Therefore, if anyone is in Christ, he is a new creation; the old is gone, the new life has come"!! We are new beings who see the world through the eyes of Jesus.

"All of this is from God, who reconciled himself through Christ and gave us the ministry of reconciliation: That God was reconciling the world to himself in Christ, not counting men's sins against them".

This is tricky. Earlier in the chapter, he says we will stand before the judgment seat of Jesus and pay for what we've done. How can we have to "pay" and "not have our sins count against us"? It is all about reconciliation.

"We are therefore Christ's ambassadors, as though God were making his appeal through us. We implore you on Christ's behalf: be reconciled to God. God made him who had no sin to be sin for us, so that in him we might become the righteousness of God". **Our faith in Jesus, and our journey through this life is all about a process of our sinful nature pushing us away from God and the gift of reconciliation which pulls us to the Father.**

2 CORINTHIANS 6

"As God's fellow workers we urge you not to receive God's grace in vain. for he says,

"In the time of my favor
I heard you, and in the day
of salvation I helped you".

"I tell you, now is the time of Gods favor, now is the day of salvation".

"We put no stumbling block in anyone's path, so that our ministry will not be discredited. Rather as servants of God we commend ourselves in every way: In great endurance; in troubles, hardships and distresses; in beatings, imprisonments and riots; in hard work, sleepless nights and hunger; in purity, understanding, patience and kindness; in the holy spirit and in sincere love;

in truthful speech and in the power of God; with weapons of righteousness in the right hand and in the left; through glory and dishonor, bad report and good report; genuine, yet regarded as impostors; known, yet regarded as unknown; dying, and yet we live on; beaten, and yet not killed; sorrowful, yet always rejoicing; Poor, yet making many rich; Having nothing, and yet possessing everything".

This is a beautiful testament of what it means to follow Jesus. No matter how hard things get, no matter what troubles we face, we are cloaked in the glory of Jesus, and we always end up the victors!

2 CORINTHIANS 7

This is an important chapter about repentance and reconciliation. Paul refers to his first letter to the Corinthians and acknowledges to them that while he may have initially regretted writing the letter to them, because it may have appeared too harsh in its chastisement of them, and their behavior, he no longer regrets it because it had a significant impact on them. He tells them that while Paul and his team were in Macedonia, they were "harassed at every turn" and yet, Titus informed Paul about their "longing for me, your deep sorrow, your ardent concern for me, so that my joy was greater than ever". "Even if I caused you sorrow by my letter, I do not regret it. Though I did regret it—I see that my letter hurt you, but only for a little while--yet now I am happy, not because you were made sorry but because your sorrow led you to repentance". **It's very much like how a parent feels after disciplining a child. Sometimes a parent says, "it hurts me more than it hurts you". But it is worth in the end because the child learns and changes. As do we when we truly approach God's throne of grace and repent for our sins.**

This is an important concept, if you tell someone they did something wrong and they just feel bad, and don't repent, it doesn't fix anything. When they repent, it fixes it for both parties.

"For you became sorrowful as God intended and so were not harmed in anyway by us. <u>Godly sorrow</u> brings repentance that leads to salvation and leaves no regret, but worldly sorrow brings death. See what this Godly sorrow has produced in you: what earnestness, what eagerness to clear yourselves, what indignation, what alarm, what longing, what concern, what readiness to see justice done".

This is so beautiful! I did not experience true <u>Godly sorrow</u> until the second half of my life. It's the feeling you get when you literally get on your knees and beg God to forgive you for a sin, and he always forgives. And the best part is, you feel it. You truly feel it. You feel the weight lifted off your shoulders and the grace of God is palpable!

2 CORINTHIANS 8

This chapter is about money. Paul testifies to the generosity of the churches in Macedonia. "In the midst of a very severe trial, their overflowing joy and their extreme poverty welled up in rich generosity". Paul is doing this to encourage the Corinthians to do the same. He tells them, "But since you excel in everything—in faith, in speech, in knowledge, in complete earnestness and in the love we kindled in you—see that you also excel in this grace of giving". He also says, "for you know the grace of our Lord Jesus Christ, that though he was rich, yet for your sake he became poor, so that you through his poverty might become rich!"

Such is the paradox of following Jesus. It is sometimes when we are lowest and poorest when we see his richness.

Paul encourages them to not just give, but also to "have the desire to do so". We need to give because we want to, not just out of obligation. That's where the true love flows. "Now finish the work so that your eager willingness to do it may be matched by your completion of the task, according to your means. for if the willingness is there, the gift is acceptable according to what one has, not according to what one does not have".

He continues, "At the present time your plenty will supply what they need, so that in turn their plenty will supply what you need. The goal is equality." As it is written: "The one who gathered much did not have too much, and the one who gathered little did not have too little".

Money is such a tricky subject. It is said that if you want to see someone's priorities, look at their checkbook and their calendar. Where do we spend our money and our time? If Jesus saw those two things, what would he say? He does see, and he is talking to us. We need to listen.

I have found that the more I give of my time and money, the more I am willing to surrender my heart, and that is when the magic happens!

2 CORINTHIANS 9

This chapter is extremely important, but one needs to avoid the land mines that it contains.

"Remember this: whoever sows sparingly will reap sparingly, and whoever sows generously will also reap generously. Each man should give what he has decided in his heart to give, not reluctantly or under compulsion, for God loves a cheerful giver. And God is able to make all grace abound in you, so that in all things at all times, having all what you need, you will abound in every good work.

> "He has scattered abroad his gifts
> to the poor, his righteousness
> endures forever".

This is a message to the Corinthians to encourage them to give generously to his ministry for Christ:

"Now he who supplies seed to the sower and bread for food will also supply and increase your store of seed and will enlarge the harvest of your righteousness. You will be made rich in every way so that you can be generous on every occasion, and through us your generosity will result in Thanksgiving to God".

This is a very tricky reading. It reads like the genesis of the prosperity gospel which has done more harm to Christianity than almost any other movement. The prosperity gospel teaches, "give money to <u>my</u> church and God will multiply your money and send it back to you."

That is <u>not</u> true. He who supplies seed to the sower above is talking about giving money to Paul (Church), but Paul's sowing is sowing of the seeds of belief in new followers of Christ. He says, "increase your harvest of righteousness." It's not like your own "favor with God". Once we give our heart to God, we get closer to him. Giving our money to God is a first step in giving our heart to him.

Paul goes on, "Because of the service by which you have proved yourselves, men will praise God for the obedience that accompanies your confession of the gospel of Christ…and in their prayers for you their hearts will go out to you, because of the surpassing grace God has given to you."

The formula is:

1) **we want to get closer to God.**
2) **we give our money back to God because we realize it's his in the first place.**
3) **that helps us to progressively turn our lives over and give our hearts to God.**
4) **we get closer to Him, and we see his glory, greatness and grace in our lives.**
5) **others see how he has blessed us and the joy in our hearts.**
6) **people want that grace, and they follow us to follow Jesus.**

2 CORINTHIANS 10

Paul defends his ministry. He tells them (us) that he is "timid when face-to-face but bold when away." **That's kind of a cool description of a "man on a mission". He does not want to be bold in a traditional way and acknowledges that he doesn't want to be thought of as bold according to the standards of this world.**

"For though we live in the world, we do not wage war as the world does. The weapons we fight with are not the weapons of the world. On the contrary, they have divine power to demolish strongholds. We demolish arguments and every pretension that sets itself up against the knowledge of God". **Powerful! The evidence of God is irrefutable! The evidence demolishes arguments. The case for Jesus is that strong!**

What follows is an introspection into Paul. He says that he will not apologize for his letters. He says he will not be ashamed of lifting up others in Christ. "Some say his letters are weighty and forceful, but in person he is unimpressive and his speaking amounts to nothing". Paul has a good sense of self-awareness! He knows his strengths and he uses them to spread the word!

He talks about his group continuing their ministry and he talks about not boasting about their work. "But let him who boasts, boast in the Lord. For it is not the one who commends himself who is approved but the one whom the Lord commends".

We work for God!

2 CORINTHIANS 11

There is a lot covered in this chapter, and some of it is complex and confusing. The important part for me is where Paul shares his summary of things he has endured on his mission. When comparing himself to other false apostles, he says, "are they servants of Christ? I am more. I have worked much harder, been in prison more frequently, been flogged more severely, and been exposed to death again and again. Five times I received from the

Jews the forty lashes minus one, three times I was beaten with rods, once I was stoned, three times I was shipwrecked, I spent a night and a day in the open sea, I have been constantly on the move. I have been in danger from the rivers, in danger from the bandits, in danger from my own countrymen, in danger from the Gentiles, in danger in the city, in danger in the country, in danger at sea, and in danger from false brothers. I have labored and toiled and gone without sleep. I have known hunger and thirst and have gone without food. I have been cold and naked."

For me, this is important for us to understand what Paul went through on his mission. This is him saying, 'what else do I have to do to prove to you that I am 'All in' for Jesus?'. How do I measure up to that? It can be difficult for us to be attracted to a faith like the one Paul is describing. It doesn't sound like much fun. Paul's point to us is that 'it's worth it'. We just can't comprehend the joy and peace that Christ provides until we experience it. And when we do, we just can't let go.

2 CORINTHIANS 12

Paul shares some revelations that he has had but he apologizes because he believes it sounds like he is boasting—being the one who received these revelations from God. In one of the revelations, he was given a thorn in his flesh, and three times he pleaded with the Lord to remove the thorn. The Lord said to Paul, "My grace is sufficient for you, for my power is made perfect in weakness."

This is so important. we need to remember that God's grace is all we need. We don't need his grace for any other reason, (so that we can get x). His grace is enough, and it is especially important for us to realize that we will see that grace and greatness when we are at our lowest. "That is why, for Christ's sake, I delight in weakness, in insults, in hardships, in persecutions, in difficulties. for when I am weak, I am strong". How can you be strong when you are weak? Because when you are weak is when you are lifted up by God's strength. And that is stronger than yourself.

Paul tells the Corinthians that he is going to visit them for a third time. "What I want is not your possessions, but you".

Paul goes on to tell them how much he loves them. He says that everything they do is for "your strengthening. for I am afraid that when I come", I may not find you as I want you to be, and you may not find me as you want me to be. I fear that there may be quarreling, jealousy, outbursts of anger, factions, slander, gossip, arrogance, and disorder." Basically, Paul is worried that when he returns, he will find a Corinth still full of unrepentant sinners.

2 CORINTHIANS 13

A powerful chapter!! it Is entitled "Final warnings" and it is Paul encouraging (threatening) the Corinthians to listen to his word and to stop sinning.

"On my return I will not spare those who sinned earlier or any of the others, since you are demanding proof that Christ is speaking through me. He is not weak in dealing with you but is powerful among you. for to be sure, he is crucified in weakness, yet he lives by God's power. Likewise, we are weak in him, yet by God's power we will live with him to serve you. Examine yourselves to see whether you are in the faith; test yourselves. Do you not realize that Christ Jesus is in you—unless, of course, you failed the test? And I trust that you will discover that we have not failed the test. Now we pray to God that you will not do anything wrong—Not so that people will see that we have stood the test but so that you will do what is right even though we may have seemed to have failed. For we cannot do anything against the truth, but only for the truth. We are glad whenever we are weak, but you are strong; and our prayer is for your perfection".

"Finally, brothers, goodbye. Aim for perfection. Listen to my appeal, be of one mind, live in peace. and the God of love and peace will be with you"!

While Corinthians 1 and 2 can be challenging to read, it oozes with Paul's commitment to Jesus and demonstrates his heartfelt caring for the people—he longs for them to find the truth and to follow Jesus!

GALATIANS

This letter was written by Paul between a.d. 48-5. This is most likely the earliest surviving letter of Paul. The theme of Galatians is very similar to Romans in that our justification is by faith alone, and salvation is a free gift, and it cannot be earned. While Romans reflects Paul being calm and logical, Galatians is an emotionally charged letter with Paul vehemently making the point that the old Jewish customs are not the key to earning favor with God. We must follow Jesus.

GALATIANS 1

"I am astonished that you were so quickly deserting the one who called you by the grace of Christ and are turning to a different gospel—which is really no gospel at all. Evidently some people are throwing you into confusion and are trying to pervert the gospel of Christ. But even if we or an angel from heaven should preach a gospel other than the one we preached to you, let him be eternally condemned".

There is Paul's emotion coming out and him wearing his heart on his sleeve. He is drawing a line in the sand!

"I want you to know brothers, that the gospel I preached is not something that man made up. I did not receive it from any man, nor was I taught it; rather, I received it by my revelation from Jesus Christ".

Paul shares his history to the Galatians—how he was one of the great persecutors of the church until he was "called by grace" by God to reveal his

Son "in me" and preach to the Gentiles. Many of Paul's travels were to gentile nations. He says that wherever he went, the only thing that people knew about him was "the man who formerly persecuted us is now preaching the faith he once tried to destroy."

Paul is making a statement that the message of Jesus is so strong, that it convinced one of his biggest enemies to switch teams!

GALATIANS 2

Paul essentially "explains" his ministry to the Galatians. He tells them that he was accepted by the apostles. He also uses a term that I love. While they were preaching and traveling, he says, "Some false brothers had infiltrated our ranks to spy on the freedom we have in Christ Jesus." **To spy on the freedom! Wow. Freedom is exactly what faith in Jesus provides for us; Freedom from the false opinions of people, freedom from the troubles of this world and freedom from worry. We just need to remember that freedom and know that it is available to us 24/7.**

He reminds us that his ministry has been primarily to the Gentiles, while Peter has ministered to the Jews.

This is important because the next section is where he details his partial opposition to Peter.

When Peter came to Antioch, Paul "opposed him to his face". He did so because he felt like Peter withdrew from the Gentiles because he didn't want to "separate himself from the circumcision group". Paul is basically calling Peter out. He is telling Peter that he is a hypocrite. It is similar to someone saying "you are more than willing to share the good news of Christ with a "non-believer", but you are afraid to speak to someone who is in "X" religion"

Paul says, "When I saw that they were not acting in line with the truth of the gospel, I said to Peter in front of them all, 'you are a Jew, yet you live like a Gentile and not like a Jew. How is it, then, that you force gentiles to follow

Jewish customs.'" "We who are Jews by birth and not sinful Gentiles know that a man is not justified by observing the law but by faith in Jesus Christ".

The next paragraph Is critically important because it explains why a life of following Christ is so radically different than the life of following laws.

"If while we seek to be justified in Christ, it becomes evident that we ourselves are sinners, does that mean that Christ promotes sin? Absolutely not! If I rebuild what I destroyed, I prove that I am a lawbreaker. For through the law, I died to the law so that I might live for God. I have been crucified with Christ and I no longer live, but Christ lives in me. The life I live in the body, I live by faith in the Son of God, who loved me and gave himself for me. I do not set aside the grace of God, for if righteousness could be gained through the law, Christ died for nothing".

The last sentence is the key to our faith. If you can gain righteousness, salvation, etc., by doing something, <u>anything</u>, then Jesus' death means nothing! This closes the "logic loop" in our faith. Logic shouldn't be necessary when we are talking about God, but it's nice when the story makes sense!

GALATIANS 3

"You foolish Galatians…before your very eyes Jesus Christ was clearly portrayed as crucified. I would like to learn just one thing from you: Did you receive the Spirit by observing the law or by believing what you heard? After beginning with the spirit, are you now trying to attain your goal by human effort".

Paul explains that if they are still following Jewish law they are cursed because it <u>says in the law</u>, "cursed is everyone who does not continue to do everything written in the book of the law." He then says, "He (God) Redeemed us in order that the blessing given to Abraham might come to the Gentiles through Christ Jesus, so that by faith we might receive the promise of the spirit."

Paul tries to explain that the laws in the old Jewish covenant were not necessarily bad "but the scripture declares that the whole world is a prisoner of sin, so that what was promised, being given through faith in Jesus Christ, might be given to those who believe." **What an awesome gift!**

"Before this faith came, we were held prisoners by the law, locked up until faith should be revealed. So, the law was put in charge to lead us to Christ, that we may be justified by faith. Now that faith has come, we are no longer under the supervision of the law".

As we read this, it is important to understand that this battle, this debate, is what Paul (and Peter I'm sure, although we have no record) faced every day on his mission. He had to explain how Jesus changed everything! We were "locked up until faith should in Jesus would be revealed".

GALATIANS 4

Paul is working so hard to convince the Galatians that their old ways were slavery to the law, and the new way is total freedom in Christ. All they need to do is accept it. "You are sons of God through faith in Christ Jesus for all of you who were baptized into Christ have clothed yourself with Christ. There is nothing Jew, nor Greek slave, nor free, male nor female, for you are all one in Christ Jesus. If you belong to Christ Jesus, then you are Abraham's seed, and heirs according to the promise. The Galatians are committed to being sons and daughters of Abraham and Paul is trying to say, "That's okay. You are heirs to the freedom found in Jesus just like everyone else".

He says, "When we were children, we were in slavery under the basic principles of this world. But when the time had fully come, God sent his son, born of a woman, born under law, to redeem those under law, that we might receive Full rights of sons."

He's saying 'Don't you see what happened? Why can't you connect the dots. There is a new way.'

He challenges them to not go back to their old ways. "For many, when you did not know God, you were slaves to those who by nature are not God's but now that you know God, or rather are known by God, how is it you are turning back to those weak and miserable principles? Do you wish to be enslaved by them all over again"?

Paul is really going after them <u>hard</u> with the truth. He warns them about the people that are trying to win them over with the "old way". "Those people are zealous to win you over, but for no good. What they want is to alienate you from us, so that you may be zealous for them". Paul uses a historical story about Abraham's children to demonstrate.

Abraham had two sons—one was born from Hagar, a slave woman. One was born from Sarah, His wife. He says the child born from Hagar was born in "an ordinary way", but the child from Sarah (Isaac) was born out of a promise (marriage). **He uses history to demonstrate that we are children of a promise. God made a promise, and we are heirs to that throne. "Therefore, we are not children of the slave woman, but of the free woman". A brilliant analogy.**

GALATIANS 5

"It is for freedom that Christ has set us free. Stand firm then, and do not let yourselves be burdened again by a yoke of slavery". "You who are trying to be justified by the law have been alienated from Christ; you have fallen away from Grace".

This is an important concept—critically important. This does not say that doing good things is bad, or following laws is bad. It says that if you believe your justification comes from doing that, you are alienated from Christ, because you do not believe that your justification and salvation comes from following Christ. This is a terrific articulation of the reason you cannot earn your way to heaven without faith in Jesus.

Paul continues by challenging the Galatians for being persuaded by the wrong people. "You were running a good race. Who cut in on you and kept you from obeying the truth? That kind of persuasion does not come from the one who calls you".

"You my brothers were called to be free. But do not use your freedom to indulge the sinful nature, rather serve one another in love".

There it is. The universal message of the New Testament. Love.

"So, I say, live by the spirit, and you will not gratify the desires of the sinful nature. For the sinful nature desires what is contrary to the spirit, and the spirit what is contrary to sinful nature". The spirit does what is contrary to sin! So profound!

Paul finishes chapter 5 with a reminder that if we live in the spirit, we will not "gratify the desires of the sinful nature". That's the reason to live and love because it is more powerful than sin.

"But the fruit of the Spirit is love, joy, peace, patience, kindness, goodness, faithfulness, gentleness, and self-control. Those who belong to Christ Jesus have crucified the sinful nature with its passions and desires".

GALATIANS 6

This is a powerful chapter. So much so that I named my company after verse 9!

"Brothers, if someone is caught in a sin, you who are spiritual should restore him gently. But watch yourselves, or you also will be tempted". This is wise guidance. Sin is powerful and tempting. When you dive into someone's sinful life it can attract to our human sinful nature. So, I agree with Paul. We all need to be 'on guard'".

"Do not be deceived: God cannot be mocked. A man reaps what he sows. The one who sows to please his sinful nature, from that nature will

JESUS: HIS LIFE, HIS LOVE, HIS PROMISE

repeat destruction. The one who sows to please the Spirit, from the Spirit will reap eternal life".

> "Let us not become weary
> in doing good, for at the
> proper time we will reap
> a harvest if we do not give up".

That's what I believe, and that's why I named my company "Team G6 consulting". Do the right thing. Don't be tired. There will be a payout. Sometimes it's an earthly payout, sometimes it's not. It may be a lesson learned but if you operate in the spirit, you will always see God's hand. And the harvest that Paul is talking about here is Jesus.

EPHESIANS

Paul wrote this letter from prison in approximately 60 A.D. Interestingly, about half of the verses in Ephesians also appear in Colossians, which was also written at the same time while in prison. It's almost as if Paul identified common themes for local problems, that he wanted to be a part of a universal message.

My application bible summarized the theme of Ephesians perfectly.

"In this letter, Paul takes us to the mountain tops of Christian truth and invites us to look at the breathtaking view. Paul reaches into his eternity, past and future, to demonstrate, out of his love and glory, calls people to be reconciled to himself and to one another through the cross of Christ".

Part one of this letter (1-3) deals with doctrine—new life in Christ. Part two (4-6) deals with ethics, the new relationships expected of believers.

EPHESIANS 1

Paul comes out of the gates fast!

"Praise be to the God and Father of our Lord Jesus Christ, who has blessed us in the heavenly realms with every spiritual blessing in Christ. For he chose us in him before the creation of the world to be holy and blameless in his sight. In love he predestined us to be adopted as his sons through Jesus Christ, in accordance with his pleasure and will—to the praise of his glorious grace, which he has freely given us in the one he loves. In him we have redemption through his blood, the forgiveness of sins, in accordance with the riches of God's grace that he lavished on us. With all wisdom and understanding, he made known to us the mystery of his Will according to his pleasure, which he purposed in Christ, to be put into effect when the times will reach their fulfillment—to bring all things in heaven and on earth together under one head, even Christ".

There it is! That's the story. God knew what he was doing from the beginning. God did all this because he wanted to reconcile us to himself because he loved us.

"Having believed, you were marked in him with a seal, the promised Holy Spirit, who is a deposit guaranteeing our inheritance until the redemption of those who are God's possession to the praise of his glory".

We have a guaranteed inheritance. Think about that. Our salvation is guaranteed! How comforting is that? There are so few guarantees in life, it's nice to have this one. The most important one!

Paul tells the Ephesians that he prays for them always." I keep asking that the God of our Lord Jesus Christ, the glorious Father, may give you the spirit of wisdom and revelation, so that you may know him better. I pray also that the eyes of your heart may be enlightened in order that you may know the hope to which he has called you, the riches of his glorious inheritance in the Saints, and his incomparably great power for us who believe".

"That power is like the working of his mighty strength which he exerted in Christ when he raised him from the dead and seated him at his right hand in the heavenly realms, far above all rule and authority, power and dominion, and every title can be given, not only in the present age but also in the one to come".

This is so powerful. This is what God has given us. The greatest gift ever known. It's free and it's awesome and we just have to take it! Envision this: It's Christmas morning, and your child is sitting by the Christmas tree, with a beautiful gift-wrapped present sitting next to him. It's the

only present your child asked you for, and you know she will love it. All she has to do it open it. And she sits there, staring at you, waiting to earn your praise, trying to earn your love before she opens it. As a parent, you are thinking, "Open it! It's from me! Because I love you!" That is the story of God's gift of salvation through his Son Jesus. He just wants us to open the gift.

EPHESIANS 2

The people in Ephesus were primarily gentiles. Paul acknowledges to them that they were looked down upon by Jews. He also tells him that they, like most people live a sinful life, craving the things of this world.

"But because of his great love for us, God, who is rich in mercy, made us alive with Christ even when we were dead in our transgressions—it is by grace you have been saved. And God raised us up with Christ and seated us with him in the heavenly realms in Christ Jesus, in order that in the coming ages He might show the incomparable riches of his grace, expressed in his kindness to us in Christ Jesus. For it is by grace you have been saved, through faith—and this is not from yourselves, it is a gift from God—not by works, so that no one can boast".

The last sentence is the great differentiator between true faith in Jesus and other religions who profess to know what that means. Imagine if "earning your way to heaven" was real. When you approach the throne, you tell God all the good things you did. How badly does that compare to what Jesus did on the cross for us? God does not want us to boast before him or before others. He wants us to acknowledge and worship him and follow his Son!

"For he himself is our peace, who has made the two, one, and has destroyed the barrier, the dividing wall of hostility…he came and preached peace to you who were far away and peace to those who were near. For through him we both have access to the Father by one spirit".

Paul then encourages the Ephesians by explaining that they are part of God's kingdom.

"Consequently, you are no longer foreigners and aliens, but fellow citizens with God's people and members of God's household, built on the foundation of the apostles and prophets, with Christ Jesus himself as the cornerstone".

We need to remember that we have an open invitation to join the most elite club that the world has ever known. That elite club is the kingdom of God. All we must do is accept the invitation! How many clubs do we get to join where someone else paid our initiation fee?

EPHESIANS 3

There are a handful of absolute golden nuggets in this chapter!

Paul talks about the revelation of Christ and says, "this mystery is that through the gospel the Gentiles are heirs together of one body and sharers together in the promise in Christ Jesus."

We are one family of believers! Paul is trying to unite everyone.

Paul tells them that he became a servant of the gospel through God's grace, and he is to "preach to the Gentiles the unsearchable riches of Christ." **The unsearchable riches! That is such a great explanation of what we receive when we seek God. It is so awesome that we don't even understand it because nothing we have ever experienced on this earth compares to it.**

"In him and through faith in him we may approach God with freedom and confidence". **Another awesome thought! When we believe in Jesus, we have the confidence of knowing that we have accepted God's grace and can freely stand before him! So often when we sin, we are embarrassed to stand before God. God's unending grace encourages us to never let that be the case. If we come with repentant hearts, God waits for us with open arms.**

"I pray that out of his glorious riches he may strengthen you with power through the Holy Spirit in your inner being".

Glorious riches! We inherited <u>glorious riches</u> by following Jesus. <u>Glorious riches</u>! We can't get that anywhere else!

"And I pray that you, being rooted and established in love, may have power, together with all the saints to grasp how wide and long and high and deep is the love of Christ, and to know this love surpasses knowledge—that you may be filled to the measure of all the fullness of God".

If we all realized that this last sentence was true, oh, what a wonderful world it would be!

EPHESIANS 4

This chapter is a plea to live lives worthy of the love of Christ. "I urge you to live a life worthy of the calling you have received. Be completely humble and gentle; be patient, bearing with one another in love. Make every effort to keep the unity of the Spirit through the bond of peace".

Peace is what Jesus offers us. Peace does not mean that bad things won't happen. It doesn't mean we won't experience pain, suffering and loss. It does mean that when those things happen, we will find peace of mind knowing that God has a bigger plan, and it allows us to see God's hand in our lives. It allows us to experience God's refuge when we run to him with reckless abandon.

"So, Christ himself gave the apostles, the prophets, the evangelists, the pastors and teachers, to equip his people for his works of service, so that the body of Christ may be built up until we all reach unity in faith and in the knowledge of the Son of God and become mature, attaining to the whole measure of the fullness of Christ".

This is an important topic because it explains the reasons we do acts of service. It's not to earn favor with God—it's to give him glory and to build up his kingdom.

Paul encourages us to live a new life in Christ. "Speak truthfully to your neighbor, for we are all members of one body. In your anger do not sin. Do not let the sun go down while you are still angry". Great advice! If you are angry with someone, try to settle it before you go to sleep. "Get rid of all bitterness, rage and anger, brawling and slander, along with every form of malice. Be kind and compassionate to one another, forgiving each other, just as in Christ, God forgave you"!

We can never forget that God forgives us always. Because human nature keeps us from forgiving others. If we remember that God forgives all, how can we hold others to a standard that is higher than God's? How can we not forgive, when God forgives?

EPHESIANS 5

"Be imitators of God, therefore, as dearly loved children and live a life of love, just as Christ loved us and gave himself up for us as a fragrant offering and sacrifice to God". That is beautiful! Be imitators of God and live a life of love!!

Paul then reminds us to live lives worthy of that love—no sexual immorality, impurity or greed, obscenity, foolish talk, or course joking. These kinds of behavior do not honor our God. He encourages us to not "be partners" with people who do these things.

"For you were once in darkness, but now you are the light in the Lord. Live as children of light, for the fruit of light consists in all goodness, righteousness, and truth". He also tells us to avoid "darkness" because "everything exposed by the light becomes visible". **Live in the light and show the world that we are followers of Jesus.**

We should live our lives "wisely" and by "making the most of every opportunity". "Sing and make music in your heart to the Lord, always giving thanks to God the Father for everything".

Put those three sentences together and they make so much sense! A wise life is one that thanks God every chance one gets!

Paul provides some marital advice, and he starts out by saying that wives should submit to their husbands because the husband is "the head of the wife just as Christ is the head of the church". This is a difficult topic to unpack in today's time. Personally, I don't like to think of a husband being "head of his wife". It is difficult to see a hierarchy in a functional marriage. I do think that a father can be the "leader of the family" in a loving way. I believe the family wants to view the father as the leader if for no other reason than physical protection. Men are called to be men to lead, but not in a domineering way. **We need to lead just like Jesus led**. With Love.

"Husbands, love your wives". Boom! Undisputed! People love to be loved. It is said that women want to be loved and men want to be respected. His words to describe this love are awesome:

"Husbands, love your wives, just as Christ loved the church and gave himself up for her to make her holy, cleansing her by the washing with water through the word, and to present her to himself as a radiant church, without stain or wrinkle or any other blemish, but holy and blameless. In this same way, husbands ought to love their wives as their own bodies. He who loves his wife loves himself".

That is a beautiful description of how committed we should be to loving our wives!!

He finishes with a very specific direction about what marriage means for those that are believers. "For this reason, a man will leave his father and mother and be united to his wife, and the two will become one flesh". **Crystal clear! We are one. That's why Jesus says a Godly marriage cannot be separated. Because you can't separate "1". Especially when "1" was created by God.**

EPHESIANS 6

One of the all-time great chapters in the Bible!! It is both instructional and inspirational. "Children, obey your parents, honor your father and mother…so that it may go well with you and that you may enjoy long life on earth". Pretty sound advice, followed by the benefit for doing so. Paul then provides guidance for "Masters" and "slaves". I think the message still applies today in terms of the employers and employees. Employees should serve wholeheartedly as if they are serving the Lord, and employers should treat their employees the same way with respect.

Then we get to one of the most often quoted and recited verses in the New Testament. It is a beautiful depiction of what it means to be a follower of Jesus.

The Armor of God

"Finally, be strong in the Lord and his mighty power. Put on the full armor of God, so that you can take your stand against the devil's schemes. For our struggle is not against flesh and blood, but against the rulers, against the authorities, against the powers of this dark world and against the spiritual forces of the evil in the heavenly realms. Therefore, put on the full armor of God, so that when the day of evil comes, you may be able to stand your ground, and after you have done everything, to stand. Stand firm then, with the belt of truth buckled around your waist, with the breastplate of righteousness in place, and with your feet fitted with the readiness that comes from the gospel of peace. In addition to all this, take up the shield of faith, with which you can extinguish all the flaming arrows of the evil one. Take the helmet of salvation and the sword of the spirit, which is the word of God".

The belt of truth—
>   **the story of Jesus is true!**

Breast plate of righteousness—it is our
>   **badge and our protection and our**
>   **righteousness only found in Jesus.**

Shield of faith—protection against
     The temptations of this world.

Helmet of salvation—it's our uniform
     And our ticket to eternity.

Sword of the spirit—God's word in
     The Bible is our weapon
     against lies!

PHILIPPIANS

The theme of this book is that we must have hope, humility, and love in our hearts as we serve Christ, because we may endure trials and suffering along the journey. That is the tone of Paul's writing. 'I am literally in chains for Christ—and I love it because the good news is being preached because of it.' This letter was written in approximately 62 a.d. while Paul was in prison in either Rome or Ephesus.

PHILIPPIANS 1

I love the opening of Paul's letters. They are such a joyful greeting! "I thank God every time I remember you. In all my prayers for all of you, I always pray with joy because of your partnership in the Gospel from the first day and until now, being confident in this, that he who began a good work in you will carry it on to completion until the day of Christ Jesus".

"And this is my prayer: That your love may abound more and more in knowledge and depth of insight, so that you may be able to discern what is best and you may be pure and blameless until the day of Christ, filled with the fruit of righteousness that comes through Jesus Christ—to the glory and praise of God".

This is such a beautiful prayer. Paul is praying that we will all have true understanding of the gospel because he knows that once you have that, you have all you need.

"Because of my chains, most of the brothers in the Lord have been encouraged to speak the work of God more courageously and fearlessly".

That is when the word of God is most powerful. When people give glory to God when times are tough, that is when the message is most important. And we need to be careful that we don't just pray that God will take our cross away. We need to pray that we <u>seek</u> God, no matter what. 'Let me see your hand in my current situation, Lord'!

Paul talks about his pending death in a unique way. He looks forward to it because he knows he will be in heaven. "I am torn between the two: I desire to depart and be with Christ, which is better by far; but it is more necessary for you that I remain in the body".

This is such a vivid depiction of what Christian death is all about, "departing to be with Jesus".

"Whatever happens, conduct yourselves in a manner worthy of the gospel of Christ". Simple, but Important. Not to earn points, but to accurately reflect our <u>faith</u>!

"For it has been granted to you on behalf of Christ not only to believe in him but also to suffer for him, since you go through the same struggle you saw I had, and now hear that I still have".

Struggle is a part of our faith and our life. And in those struggles, it is so important that we lean into Jesus because that is how we reflect God's glory. People will wonder how we can reflect peace in the most difficult times in our lives. It is also by leaning into Jesus that we will have the clarity of mind to make Christ like decisions as we carry those crosses.

PHILIPPIANS 2

"If you have any encouragement from being united with Christ, if any comfort from his love, if any fellowship with the spirit, if any tenderness and compassion, then make my joy complete by being like-minded, having the same love, being one in spirit and purpose. Do nothing out of selfish ambition or vein conceit. But, in humility consider others better than yourselves, each of you should not look only to your own interests but also to the interests of others".

I like this passage so much because it is how I try to view others. It does not say, "don't think about yourself."—it says, "don't _only_ think about yourself." If everyone spent a little more time caring for others, oh, what a wonderful world it would be! The compound effect of the 8 billion people on earth thinking about the other 8 billion would be incredible.

Paul explains to us _why_ he is giving us this instruction:

"Your attitude should be the same as Christ Jesus who, being in the very nature, God, did not consider equality with God something to be grasped, but made himself nothing by taking the very nature of a servant, being made in human likeness. And being found in appearance as a man, he humbled himself and became obedient to death—and even death on a cross. Therefore, God exalted him to the highest place and gave him the name above every other name, that at the name of Jesus every knee should bow, in heaven and on earth and under the earth, and every tongue confess that Jesus Christ is Lord, to the glory of God the Father".

So, we should be humble, don't be selfish, and make other's interests a priority because that is "what Jesus would do". Jesus was the ultimate servant and became the greatest servant leader who ever lived.

"Continue to work out your salvation with fear and trembling, for it is God who works in you to will and an act according to his good purpose".

God is going to do what God is going to do, and he always has a purpose for it—and that is to make his glory known to all mankind.

"Do everything without complaining or arguing, so that you become blameless and pure, 'children of God without fault in a crooked and depraved generation'. Then you will shine like stars in the universe as you hold to the word of life, in order that I may boast on the day that I did not run or labor for nothing". **We need to stop complaining about our struggles; it's part of the deal. Become blameless and pure so we can shine like stars in the universe—that is why we follow Jesus!**

PHILIPPIANS 3

"But whatever was to my profit I now consider loss for the sake of Christ. What is more, I consider <u>everything</u> a loss compared to those surpassing greatness of knowing Christ Jesus my Lord, for whose sake I have lost all things. I consider them rubbish, that I may gain Christ and be found in him, not having a righteousness of my own that comes from the law, but that is through faith in Christ—the righteousness that comes from God and is by faith. I want to know Christ and the power of his resurrection and the fellowship of sharing in his sufferings, becoming like him in his death, and so, somehow, to attain the resurrection of the dead".

The surpassing greatness of knowing Christ Jesus. It is only when realizing that what we gain in losing our attachment to earthly things will we be able to achieve oneness with him! The things of this world are rubbish in comparison to Jesus. As we chase worldly things, we need to remember we are chasing rubbish. Maybe then we will chase it less.

Pressing on toward the goal:

"Not that I have already obtained all this, or have already been made perfect, but I press on to take hold of that for which Christ Jesus took hold of me. Brothers, I do not consider myself yet to have taken hold of it. But one thing I do know: forgetting what is behind and straining toward what is ahead, I press on toward the goal to win the prize for which God has called me heavenward in Christ Jesus". **I love this. Paul is saying 'enjoy the journey'. While it may be difficult, the "striving" of following Jesus is worth it. Because the more we strive, the closer we get and the image and "realness" of Jesus becomes clearer.**

Paul warns us to stay away from enemies of the cross. "Their destiny is destruction, their God is their stomach, and their glory is in their shame. Their mind is on earthly things. But our citizenship is in heaven".

We are all a "work in progress" and that is okay! We must press on, stay focused on the ultimate prize. We may sin on our journey but staying on path is the key!

PHILIPPIANS 4

This chapter includes some incredible verses, as well as one of the misunderstood verses in the Bible.

"Therefore, my brothers, you whom I love and long for, my joy and my crown, that is how you should stand firm in the Lord, dear friends"

"Rejoice in the Lord always. I will say it again: rejoice. Let your gentleness be evident to all. The Lord is near. Do not be anxious about anything, but in everything by prayer and petition, with thanksgiving, present your requests to God. And the peace of God, which transcends all understanding, will guard your hearts and your minds in Christ Jesus".

Wow! Be joyful! That is how we demonstrate our love for Christ to the world. Be gentle because Jesus was gentle. Don't be anxious because we have nothing to be anxious about! And God's peace transcends all understanding. It's so great, no matter what we do, we can't understand it.

"Finally, Brothers, whatever is true, whatever is noble, whatever is right, whatever is pure, whatever is lovely, whatever is admirable—if anything is excellent or praiseworthy—Think about such things. Whatever you have learned or received or heard from me or seen in me—put it into practice. and the God of peace will be with you".

God is good. God is really good! Everything that comes from God is true, noble, right, pure, lovely and admirable! And it brings peace!

Then we get to the verse that is misunderstood and quoted out of context. Paul thanks the Philippians for their concern for him—as he is in a tough spot, being persecuted, imprisoned, etc. but he basically says, "don't worry about me, I got this."

"I have learned to be content whatever the circumstances. I know what it is to be in need, and I know what it is to have plenty. I have learned the secret of being content in any and every situation, whether well fed or hungry, whether living in Plenty or in want. I can do this through him who gives me strength". **This is Philippians 4:13. This verse is plastered all over billboards, tattoos, shirts and even faces. This verse is about contentment in Jesus. it is <u>not</u> about running marathons, winning games, building businesses or anything unrelated to Jesus. It sounds so awesome that people apply it to earthly endeavors. While it's not tragic that people are pointing to God, it is <u>not</u> about those earthly endeavors. It is about the fact that faith in Jesus will be all you need to achieve contentment during difficult times! Paul is saying his love for Jesus allows him to sustain his current imprisonment, because the reward is Jesus. Affirmation that our pursuit of Jesus is to get Jesus. Nothing else.**

COLOSSIANS

This letter from Paul to the Church in Colossae was written to affirm Jesus as the Lord of the Church, and to allow their lives to be transformed by following him.

COLOSSIANS 1

This letter begins with a beautiful prayer of thankfulness and hope. First Paul thanks the people for their faithfulness. Then he says, "For this reason, since the day we heard about you, we have not stopped praying for you, and asking God to fill you with the knowledge of his will through all spiritual wisdom and understanding, and we pray this in order that you may live a life worthy of the Lord and may please him in every way; bearing fruit in every good work, growing in the knowledge of God, being strengthened with all power according to his glorious might so that you may have great endurance and patience, and joyfully giving thanks to the Father, who has <u>qualified you to share in the inheritance</u> of the Saints in the kingdom of light. For he has rescued us from the dominion of darkness and brought us into the kingdom of the Son he loves, in whom we have redemption, the forgiveness of sins."

Incredible! Awesome summary of what we believe and why we do what we do. The characterization of our faith as a journey from darkness to light Is just so poignant. Following Christ allows us to live in the light of truth. 'Qualifies us to share in the inheritance' is such a reassuring statement that tells us that we have a special place in God's will.

The Supremacy of Christ

"He is the image of the invisible God, the firstborn over all creation. For by him all things were created: things in heaven and on earth, visible and invisible, whether thrones or powers or rulers or authorities; all things were created by him and for him…for God was pleased to have all his fullness dwell in him, and through him to reconcile to himself all things, whether things on earth or things in heaven, By making peace through his blood, shed on the cross".

"Once you were alienated from God and were enemies in your mind because of your evil behavior. But now he has reconciled to you by Christ's physical body through death to present you Holy in his sight, without blemish and free from accusation".

The concept of "enemies in your minds" is important and powerful. When we sin, and are not in concert with God. We find ourselves in a state of turmoil and discontent. It is painful. When we sin as followers of Jesus, we quickly remember we are reconciled to him, by him, and we return to living freely by grace. More importantly, we desire <u>not</u> to sin!

Paul explains that he has become Christ's servant to "present the word of God in its fullness—the mystery that has been kept hidden for ages and generations but now it is disclosed to the Saints…The **glorious riches** of this mystery, which is Christ in you, the hope of glory".

COLOSSIANS 2

"My purpose is that they may be encouraged in heart and united in love, so that they may have the full riches of complete understanding, in order that they may know the mystery of God, namely, Christ, in whom are hidden all the treasures of wisdom and knowledge. I tell you this so that no one will deceive you by fine-sounding arguments".

This is Paul encouraging us to know the <u>truth</u> so that we can <u>combat the lies</u>! The story of Jesus is a true one—and it makes no sense to listen to

any story that is a diversion from that. When we know the truth of what scripture says, we can see the perversions of it from this world. When we don't know the truth, we are influenced by the lies. If we just exist in our own truth, then everyone can exist in their own truth and the real truth of Jesus is lost. 'Let people believe what they want to believe' feels good, and it feels nice, but it is not we are called to do. We are called to share the real truth.

"See to it that no one takes you captive through hollow and deceptive philosophy, which depends on human tradition and the basic principles of this world, rather than on Christ!...God made you alive in Christ. He forgave all our sins, having <u>canceled the written code</u>, with its regulations, that was against us and then stood opposed to us, he took it away and nailed it to the cross".

That was a righteous passage. The laws have been canceled, the sins have been forgiven and the picture of God nailing that to the cross is a beautiful one! We have total freedom in Jesus!

"Do not let anyone who delights in false humility and the worship of angels disqualify you for the prize. Such a person that goes into great detail about what he has seen, and his unspiritual mind puffs him up with idle notions. He has lost connections with the head...".

Therefore, we don't worship the angels, saints, Mary, Paul, Peter or anyone except Jesus, his Father and the Holy Spirit. Anything else takes our focus away from the only thing that matters. And those individuals don't want to be worshipped because they want our eyes on Jesus. I'm confident those other folks don't even want us praying to them either. They are pointing to God. At times, people say "I feel more comfortable praying to X than I do praying directly to God". My question is 'why is that, and when God is begging us to talk to him on a daily basis and we don't feel comfortable doing that, whose fault is that?' As a parent, think about what it is like when you know your child is struggling with something.

Encouraging our kids to pray to anyone except God, Jesus, or the Holy Spirit is like telling our child to go ask the neighbors if they will come talk to you about your child's problem. If we believe that only God can answer prayers, and he is begging us to run to him, why would we pray to anyone else who can't answer those prayers? God hears our prayers and he talks to us. We need to hone our listening skills so we can hear the VOICE OF GOD. When we are listening to a voice that is not God, we lose our ability to hear HIS voice.

"Since you died with Christ to the basic principles of this world, why, as though you still belong to it, do you submit to its rules".

We need to ask ourselves that question! Are we in or are we out? Do we believe the world, or do we believe Jesus? Are we writing both rails or are we living to pick a track? The track that leads to Jesus.

COLOSSIANS 3

This is another one of those "all-time great chapters" in the Bible. Paul challenges us to change to a new life in Jesus.

"Since, then, you have been raised with Christ, set your heart on things above, where Christ is seated at the right hand of God. Set your mind on things above, not on earthly things. For you died, and your life is now hidden with Christ in God. When Christ, who is your life, appears, then you also will appear with him in glory".

"Put to death, therefore, whatever belongs to your earthly nature: sexual immorality, impurity, lust, evil desires and greed, which is idolatry. Because of these, the wrath of God is coming. You used to walk in these ways, in the life you once lived. But now you must rid yourself of all such things as these: anger, rage, malice, slander, filthy language from your lips. Do not lie to each other, since you have taken off your old self with its practices and have put on the new self, which is being renewed in knowledge in the image of its creator. Here there is no Greek or Jew, circumcised, barbarian, Scythian, slave or free, but Christ is all, and is in all".

"Therefore, as God's chosen people, holy and dearly loved, clothe yourself with compassion, kindness, humility, gentleness, and patience. Bear with each other and forgive as the Lord forgave you. And over all these virtues <u>put on love</u>, which binds them all together in perfect unity".

"Let the peace of Christ rule in your hearts, since as members of one body you were called to peace. And be thankful. Let the word of Christ dwell in you richly as you teach and admonish one another with all wisdom, and as you sing psalms, hymns, and spiritual songs, with gratitude in your hearts to God. And whatever you do, whether in word or deed, do it all in the name of the Lord Jesus, giving thanks to God the Father through him".

This is an incredible synopsis of the reason for our faith, the beauty and simplicity of our faith, and a way to demonstrate our faith. Love People Way Jesus did.

Paul provides instruction "for households". Again, he tells wives to submit to your husbands, and husbands to love their wives. He also says, "Fathers do not embitter your children, or they will become discouraged."

It is a fine line between discipline and encouragement. I think if both are rooted in love, we can navigate that fine line.

COLOSSIANS 4

Paul finishes with instructions to "devote yourselves in prayer, being watchful and thankful...let your conversations always be full of grace, seasoned with salt". **Seasoned with salt! Be nice but be true! Remember in Matthew 5:13 Jesus spoke of saltiness. It flavors everything around it. We need to be the saltiness for Jesus for the world.**

1 THESSALONIANS

This was either the first or second letter written by Paul (Galatians was first). The letter was written most likely from Corinth. The theme of this letter is thanksgiving to the Thessalonians for their "deep conviction" and for becoming "imitators of us (Paul and team)" in the Lord.

1 THESSALONIANS 1

"We continually remember before our God and Father your work produced by faith, your labor prompted by love, and your endurance inspired by hope in our Lord Jesus Christ…you became imitators of us and of the Lord, despite severe suffering you welcomed the message with joy given by the Holy Spirit. And so, you became a model to all the believers in Macedonia and Achaia". Paul is thanking them for their faith and for validating that the message they heard from Paul about Jesus is true. It's like he considers them partners in his ministry. I love this depiction of their actions; 'Labor prompted by love and your endurance sponsored by hope". **Jesus is not about duty and obligation. Rather he is about love and hope.**

1 THESSALONIANS 2

Paul acknowledges that his group had been "insulted in Philippi" and had "suffered" there. "But with the help of our God we dared to tell you his gospel in spite of strong opposition". He professes his love for them by saying we "cared for you like a mother caring for her little children. We loved you so much that we were delighted to share with you not only the gospel, but our lives as well, because you had become so dear to us". He also tells them that he is grateful that they received a message as it was from <u>God</u> not from men. And that word "is at work in you who believe". That is a powerful message. **The word of God is at work in us when we believe!**

Paul then tells them that they were "torn away" and Satan kept them from returning to see them.

1 THESSALONIANS 3

Paul explains to them that he decided to stay in Athens and to send to Timothy to visit them to strengthen and encourage them in their faith, so they could persevere through the persecution they were enduring. Timothy reports back that their faith is strong. "For now, we really live, since you are standing firm in the Lord". He asks God to create a path so he can visit them, and he encourages them by saying, "may the Lord make your love increase and overflow for each other and for everyone else, just as ours does for you. May he strengthen your hearts so that you will be blameless and holy in the presence of our God and Father when our Lord Jesus comes with all his holy ones."

1 THESSALONIANS 4

Paul provides some direction for them in terms of how to live a holy life. He acknowledges that they are doing so…but to do it even more. "It is God's will that you be sanctified: that you should avoid sexual immorality; that each of you should learn to control his own body in a way that is holy and honorable, not in passionate lust like the heathens, who do not know God; and in this matter no one should wrong his brother or take advantage of him". He encourages them to love each other and says, "Make it your ambition to lead a quiet life, to mind your own business and to work with your hands, just as we told you, so that your daily life may win the respect of outsiders and so that you will not be dependent on anybody." **In many ways, this is** 'life advice' that still applies today. 'Win the respect of outsiders' is only to attract more people to Jesus.

Paul wraps up Thessalonians with some serious warnings and instructions: "We do not want you to be ignorant about those who fall asleep, or to grieve like the rest of men who have no hope". He tells them that those who believe will be reunited with God, along with Jesus, before those who have fallen asleep (nonbelievers). "For the Lord himself will come down from heaven with a loud command, with the voice of the Archangel and with the trumpet call of God, and the dead in Christ will rise first. After that, we who are still alive and are left will be caught up together with them in the clouds to meet the Lord in the air. And so, we will be with the Lord forever. Therefore encourage each other with these words".

1 THESSALONIANS 5

"For you know very well that the day of the Lord will come like a thief in the night…but you, brothers, are not in darkness…you are sons of the light and sons of the day…so then, let us not be like others, who are asleep, but let us be alert and self-controlled…Putting on the faith and love as a breastplate, and the hope of salvation as a helmet. For God did not appoint us to suffer wrath but to receive salvation through our Lord Jesus Christ. He died for us so that, whether we are awake or asleep, we may live together with him. Therefore encourage one another and build each other up". **This is important. We all have tough days. Sometimes those turn into tough years. We need to remember (and remind each other) that salvation is ours; we have already won and that gives us peace and the stamina to continue.**

We need to remember that as Christ's family, we need to encourage each other to continue to "walk in the word"!

"Now we ask you, brothers, to respect those who work hard among you, who are over you in the Lord and who admonish you. Hold them in the highest regard in love because of their work. Live in peace with each other.

And we urge you, brothers, warn those who are idle, encourage the timid, help the weak, be patient with everyone. Make sure nobody pays back wrong for wrong, but always try to be kind to each other and to everyone else. Be joyful always, pray continually, give thanks in all circumstances; for this is God's will for you in Christ Jesus. Do not put out the spirit's fire. Do not treat prophecies with contempt, test everything, hold on to the good, avoid every kind of evil. May God himself, the God of peace, sanctify you through and through. May your whole spirit, soul and body be kept blameless at the coming of our Lord. The one who calls you is faithful, and he will do it!" This is a powerful blessing from Paul. I need to share this blessing with others.

2 THESSALONIANS

Paul continues his efforts of thanking the Thessalonians for their faithfulness and acknowledges that their faith is growing. He dedicates some time in his letter to discuss the second coming of Christ.

2 THESSALONIANS 1

"All this evidence that God's judgment is right, and as a result you will be counted worthy of the kingdom of God, for which you are suffering. God is just: he will pay back trouble to those who trouble you and give relief to you who are troubled, and to us as well. This will happen when the Lord Jesus is revealed from Heaven in blazing fire with his powerful angels. He will punish those who do not know God and do not obey the gospel of our Lord Jesus Christ. They will be punished with everlasting destruction and shut out from the presence of the Lord and from the majesty of his power on the day he comes to be glorified in his holy people and to be marveled at among all those who have believed".

Wow! That is a powerful warning as to what happens when we don't follow Jesus. Better yet—how great it will be when we do! It seems that sometimes people want to ignore the second half of the salvation message. They love John 3:16, but don't read John 3:17. Same here. The price for NOT following Jesus is everlasting destruction and the bible is very clear about that.

"With this in mind, we constantly pray for you, that our God may count you worthy in his calling, and that by his power he may fulfill every good purpose of yours and every act prompted by your faith. We pray this so that the name of our Lord Jesus may be glorified in you and you in him, according to the grace of our God and the Lord Jesus Christ".

2 THESSALONIANS 2

This is a bit of an apocalyptic chapter. Paul is telling the Thessalonians to not be deceived about the false teachings that may say that the second coming has already occurred. It has not! He reminds them that the second coming will not occur until the rebellion occurs, and that "the man of lawlessness" is revealed and he will exact himself and proclaim himself to be God. And he says Jesus will overthrow that man with the very breath of his mouth.

I do not know who the man of lawlessness is. It is not Satan, because Paul says, "His coming is in accordance with the work of Satan." So, this is someone sent by Satan to deceive people. He says people will perish because "They refuse to love the truth." He tells them to "stand firm and hold on to the teachings we passed on to you by word of mouth or by letter." Then he shares a beautiful prayer for them: "May our Lord Jesus Christ himself and God our Father, who loved us and by his grace gave us eternal encouragement and good hope, encourage your hearts and strengthen you in every good deed and word".

Encourage our hearts!!

2 THESSALONIANS 3

Then Paul asked for a return prayer: "Pray for us that the message of the Lord may spread rapidly and be honored, just as it is with you...may the Lord direct your hearts into God's love and Christ's perseverance".

I love how Paul spends so much effort talking about our <u>hearts</u>! That is where we will find our relationship with Jesus! The only thing Jesus asks us for is our loving hearts.

Paul tells them to keep away from every brother who is "idle". He reminds them that when they were together "we worked night and day, laboring and toiling so that we would not be a burden to any of you". He instructs them, "if a man shall not work…he shall not eat."

Very timely advice that stands true today!

He tells them to "never tire of doing what is right."—I love this. And he also says that they should not associate with those that do not follow this instruction "but don't regard him as an enemy but warn him as a brother". **That is our role as a follower of Jesus; to help people see the truth and find the right path. That doesn't mean we have to be friends with everyone, but it doesn't mean that our "non-friends" are our enemies either!**

1 TIMOTHY

Timothy and Titus were recommended to Paul, as faithful disciples of Christ, when Paul heard of some false teachings that were occurring in the church of Ephesus. So, Paul excommunicated those leaders and put Timothy in charge. This letter was designed to encourage Timothy and his leadership of the Church. The primary focus of his letter was to describe the kind of characteristics that church leaders need to have. There are also some doctrinal teachings that are shared, some of which are time bound and not totally appropriate for today, in my opinion—particularly as it relates to women's role in the church.

1 TIMOTHY 1

"As I urged you when I went into Macedonia, stay there in Ephesus so that you may command certain men not to teach false doctrines any longer or to devote themselves to myths and endless genealogies. These promote controversies rather than God's work—which is by faith. The goal of this command is <u>love</u> which comes from a pure heart and a good conscience and a sincere faith".

Paul thanks "Christ our Lord, who has given me strength, that he considered me faithful, appointing me to his service...the grace of our Lord was poured out on me abundantly, along with the faith and love that are in Christ Jesus".

Paul tells them that Jesus came to save sinners, and he is the worst of them. And in so doing, Jesus "might display his unlimited patience as an example for those who might believe in him and receive eternal life". **In other words, Paul is saying, "if Jesus saved me, He will save anybody"**! He tells Timothy that he will provide this instruction so that "following them you may fight the good fight".

1 TIMOTHY 2

Instructions on worship

Paul says to pray for everyone. "That we may live peaceful and quiet lives in all Godliness and holiness. This is good, and pleases God our Savior, who wants all men to be saved and to come to knowledge of the truth. For there is one mediator between God and men, the man Christ Jesus".

This is a critically important sentence. Our <u>only only only</u> pathway to God is Jesus. He is the only one who can direct our prayers and He is the only one who can provide salvation. Prayers to Saints, Mary, ancestors, or anyone else are a waste of breath. It might make people feel good, but God is the only one who can answer prayers and to think that our prayers are being answered by someone else is truly idolatry. Those individuals never asked for a divine crown. Humanity gave it to them.

Paul shares some direction on women's role in the faith, and in the church. That direction should be taken under discernment by everyone individually. I have seen this direction work effectively in churches, and I have seen it lead to the destruction of churches. Bottom line, we need to love and respect everyone, man, or woman.

1 TIMOTHY 3

This is the chapter where Paul gets very specific on what kind of men should lead the Church Regarding overseers (elders) and deacons. He essentially says they must be self-controlled, respectable, hospitable, gentle, not a lover of money. It also says he must not be a recent convert or he may become conceited. He also says deacons must not pursue dishonest gain and they must be "tested" before they can become trusted.

For me it is important to realize that Paul is writing this letter to Timothy 2000 years ago. Nowhere in the letter does say "It needs to be this way forever". I believe that churches that take this teaching literally are taking the verses out of context relative to women's role in the church. I do think the "not a recent convert" qualifier is an important one. I know what it's like to be 'young in my faith' and I know what it feels like to mature from that young faith. And I know what it's like to know that I have so much to learn about my relationship with Christ. When someone is very young in their faith, it is a tall task to help lead a church.

1 TIMOTHY 4

Paul warns Timothy that in later times "some will abandon the faith and follow deceiving spirits and things taught by demons". Paul encourages Timothy to point these lies out to current and future believers; tell them the truth about Christ Jesus.

He also tells him to not let anyone look down on him because he is young. Because he is young, he has the opportunity to "set an example for believers in speech, in life, in love, in faith and in purity...do not neglect your gift".

It's interesting that this section about "young" follows the section about a "recent convert". The delineation is about 'age' vs 'spiritual maturity' and those are different. It is so important that each of us recognize and use our spiritual gifts. They were given to us by God for a reason and that is so others could seek God's greatness in us.

1 TIMOTHY 5

Some of chapter 5 is full of wisdom, and some of it includes more instructions that seem to be further outdated. We need to remember that Paul is writing a letter to Timothy as an individual, and some of the instruction is to him as such (health related, as an example).

"Do not treat an elderly man harshly but exhort him as if he were your father. Treat younger men as brothers, older women as mothers, and younger women as sisters, with absolute purity".

Paul also gives lengthy guidance on how widows should behave, and how people should treat widows. Paul says to take care of widows, but only if they are over 60 (?) And only do so if they have done good deeds (?). He encourages younger widows to get remarried. This is another example of instruction that is based on the times. Example: I find it interesting that Paul doesn't talk about widowers (I don't think ever). I have to believe this is because back then a widower just went back to work and women did not work 'for money' in 64 a.d. Hence, much sympathy was heaped upon widows and rightly so. Not that Paul's advice is bad, I just think it needs to be looked at through the lens of 64 a.d.

I do like what Paul says about accusations against elders. He says don't believe it unless it is brought to you by two or three witnesses. This is sound advice, not just regarding elders, but anybody. People are accused by others all the time. Don't pay attention to it unless you hear it from multiple sources.

"The sins of men are obvious, reaching the place of judgment ahead of them; the sins of others trail behind them. In the same way, good deeds are obvious and even those that are not, cannot be hidden".

The greatest teller of truth is <u>time</u>. This applies to character, reputation, work, faith, parenting, sports, and life.

1 TIMOTHY 6

Love of money

"If anyone teaches false doctrines and does not agree to the sound instruction of our Lord Jesus Christ and to Godly teaching, he is conceited and understands nothing. He has an unhealthy interest in controversies and quarrels about words that result in envy, strife, malicious talk, evil suspicions, and constant friction between men of corrupt mind, who have robbed of the truth and who think that Godliness is a means to financial gain".

<u>Very wise words</u>. This is speaking directly to people who teach that giving to the church is the key to wealth. "God will return that money 10 times". That is not true!! We give to God as a sign of thanksgiving and worship because it is his money to begin with! And our gain is we move closer to God because we submit our hearts to his will.

Paul explains this clearly: "But Godliness and contentment is great gain. For we brought nothing into the world, and we can take nothing out of it. But if we have food and clothing, we can be content with that. People who want to get rich fall into temptation and a trap and into many foolish and harmful desires that plunge men into ruin and destruction. For the love of money is the root of all kinds of evil. Some people, eager for money, have wandered from the faith and pierced themselves with many griefs".

There is a big difference between having <u>money</u> and <u>loving</u> money. When you love money, you serve money. And it is clear that you cannot serve <u>both</u> money and God!

Paul challenges Timothy, "But you, man of God, flee from all of this and pursue righteousness, faith, love, endurance, and gentleness. Fight the good fight of the faith. Take hold of the eternal life to which you were called when you made your good confession in the presence of many witnesses. In the sight of God, who gives life to everything, and of Christ Jesus, who while testifying before Pontius Pilate made the good confession, I charge you to keep this command without spot or blame until the appearing of our Lord Jesus Christ, which God will bring about in his own time—God, the blessed and only ruler, the King of Kings and Lord of lords, who alone is immortal and who lives in unapproachable light, whom no one he has seen or can see. To him be honor and might forever. Command those who are rich in this present world not to be arrogant nor put their hope in wealth, which is so uncertain, but to put their hope in God, who richly provides us with everything for our enjoyment. Command them to do good, to be rich in good deeds, and to be generous and willing to share. In this way they will lay up treasure for themselves as a firm foundation for the coming age, so they take hold of the life that is truly life"! These are some of the most brilliant words in the bible that every follower of Jesus should read frequently.

2 TIMOTHY

This letter was written by Paul after he was thrown in prison while on his way to Ephesus (I assume to visit Timothy). This was during the time of Nero's persecution of the Christians. Paul did not expect to be released from prison, so he wrote this very personal letter to Timothy. It differs from 1 Timothy in that the first letter was very instructional in nature. This one is heartfelt.

2 TIMOTHY 1

Paul thanks Timothy for his faithfulness and tells him that he misses him. He says because of Timothy's sincere faith, "I remind you to fan into flame the gift of God…for God did not give us a spirit of timidity, but a spirit of power, of love and of self-discipline". **I love the word picture: When you fan a flame, it grows!** He tells Timothy we cannot control its power, then he says to Timothy, "Here is a trustworthy saying":

> If we died with Him,
> We will also live with Him;
> If we endure, we will also
> reign with Him. if we disown Him,
> He will disown us; if we
> are faithless, He will remain
> faithful, for He cannot disown himself."

Paul tells Timothy to not "quarrel about words". **In other words, don't waste our time with mindless debate about frivolous things. It's a waste of**

time. "Do your best to present yourself to God as one approved, a workman who does not need to be ashamed and who correctly handles the word of truth. Avoid Godless chatter because those who indulge in it become more and more unGodly".

We, as believers, must remove ourselves from gossip rings and conversations that tear others down. "Nevertheless, God's solid foundation stands firm, sealed with this inscription: "the Lord knows those who are his," and, "everyone who confesses the name of the Lord must turn away from wickedness".

"Flee the evil desires of youth and pursue righteousness, faith, love, and peace, along with those who call on the Lord out of pure heart. Don't have anything to do with foolish and stupid arguments because you know they produce quarrels. Instead, he must be kind to everyone, able to teach, not resentful. Those who oppose him must gently instruct in the hope that God will grant them repentance leading them to a knowledge of the truth, and that they will come to their senses and escape from the trap of the devil, who has taken them captive to do his will".

Oh my gosh! This is how to live life. This is how to be a disciple. This is how to teach others. This is how to witness. It is so easy to be offended when someone challenges our faith. Paul says, take a breath, be calm, pray for that person right then in your heart, be nice, don't get rattled. You have the power of truth on your side!

2 TIMOTHY 3

"But mark this: There will be terrible times in the last days. People will be lovers of themselves, lovers of money, boastful, proud, abusive, disobedient to their parents, ungrateful, unholy, without love, unforgiving, slanderous, without self-control, brutal, not lovers of the good, treacherous, rash, conceited, lovers of pleasure rather than lovers of God—having a form of Godliness but denying his power. Have nothing to do with them!"

This is Paul's view of what things will be like just before Jesus returns. The challenge is this is how things are now and it has been that way for quite a while. The key is to not worry about the wicked force on God. Paul says, "But they will not get very far because, as in the case of those men, their folly will be clear to everyone."

He also reminds Timothy that the Lord rescued him from all his trials and persecutions. He also says that "everyone who lives a Godly life in Christ Jesus will be persecuted." **We need to remember that! 1) Lead a Godly life. 2) We will be persecuted. 3) God will rescue us! 4) And we need to be ready to defend the faith with the truth!** "All Scripture is God-breathed and is useful for teaching, Rebuking, correcting and training in righteousness, so that the man of God may be thoroughly equipped for every good work".

2 TIMOTHY 4

"I give you this charge: preach the word; be prepared in season and out of season; correct review and encourage—with great patience and careful instruction. For the time will come when men will not put up with sound doctrine. Instead, to suit their own desires, they will gather around them a great number of teachers to say what their itching ears want to hear. **This is so critical. People long to hear anything that validates their own narratives or beliefs. This is an incredibly dangerous way to grow in our faith. It compounds. The more we believe what we want to believe, the more we believe it. It leads us down trails of falseness. Some are useless and some are harmful. The only way to avoid that is to learn the truth.** "They will turn their ears away from the truth and turn aside to myths. But you, keep your head in all situations, endure hardship, do the work of an evangelist...". Remember all Scripture is God-breathed. It's our job to share it! Paul tells Timothy that he will be dying soon. "I have fought the good fight, I have finished the race, I have kept the faith. Now there is in store for me the crown of righteousness, which the Lord, the righteous judge, will award me on that day!"

TITUS

TITUS 1

This is a letter from Paul to Titus. It provides Titus with specific directions on how to set up the Church on the island of Crete. Paul introduces himself in the letter in a profound way. (He always introduces himself at the beginning of his letters.) This one stuck out for me:

"Paul, a servant of God and apostle of Jesus Christ to further the faith of God's elect and their knowledge of the truth that leads to Godliness—in the hope of eternal life, which God, who does not lie, promised before the beginning of time, and which now at His appointed season he has brought to light through the preaching entrusted to me by the command of God our savior".

Paul tells Titus that he left him in Crete to "finish the job" and to appoint elders in every town. "An elder must be blameless, faithful to his wife, a man whose children believe and are not open to the charge of being wild and disobedient. Since an overseer manages God's household, he must be blameless—not overbearing, not quick-tempered, not give into drunkenness, not violent, not pursuing dishonest gain. Rather, he must be hospitable, one who loves what is good, who is self-controlled, upright, holy and disciplined. He must hold firmly to the trustworthy message as it has been taught, so that he can encourage others by sound doctrine and refute those that oppose it".

I think many (most) Christian churches still use this criterion in the selection of Church elders, which is fine so long as the church realizes the importance of casting a wider net and realizing that no person is perfect.

Paul tells Titus to silence rebellious people who are "Full of meaningless talk and rebellion because they are teaching the wrong things for dishonest gain". He says to, "rebuke them (with scripture) so that they will be sound in the faith."

TITUS 2

"You, however, must teach what is appropriate to sound doctrine. Teach the older men to be temperate, worthy of respect, self-controlled, and sound in love, faith, and endurance."

"Likewise, teach older women to be reverent and the way they live, not to be slanderers or addicted to much wine, but to teach what is good. Then they can urge the younger women to love their husbands and children, to be self-controlled and pure, to be busy at home, to be kind, and to be subject to their husbands, so that no one will malign the word of God".

Most of this text is a good template for how people should be, and their delineation between men and women is a bit unnecessary in my opinion. Moreover, while I believe strong male leadership is critical for any household to function effectively, suggesting that wives be "subject" to their husbands is a bit overboard for my tastes. I think it is not ill-intended, just a sign of the times.

"Similarly, encourage the young men to be self-controlled. In everything set them an example by doing what is good. In your teaching show integrity, seriousness, and soundness of speech that cannot be condemned, so that those who oppose you may be ashamed because they have nothing bad to say about us".

"For the grace of God has appeared that <u>offers salvation to all people</u>. It teaches us to say 'no' to ungodliness and worldly passions, and to live self-controlled, upright and Godly lives in this present age, while we wait for the blessed hope—the appearing of the glory of our great God and Savior, Jesus Christ, who gave himself for us to redeem us from wickedness and to purify for himself a people that are his very own, eager to do what is good".

We do these things <u>because</u> we believe, not to earn points with God!

TITUS 3

Paul tells Titus that he needs to remind everyone that they need to be "subject to the authorities, to be obedient, to be ready to do whatever is good, to slander no one, to be peaceable and considerate, and to show true humility toward all men"!

He says that at one time "we" were foolish and disobedient people that hated each other. "But when the kindness and love of God our savior appeared, he saved us, not because of righteous things we had done, but because of his mercy. He saved us through the washing of rebirth and renewal by the Holy Spirit, whom he poured out on us generously through Jesus Christ our Savior, so that, having been justified by his grace, we might become heirs having the hope to eternal life".

"But avoid foolish controversies and genealogies and arguments and quarrels about the law because these are unprofitable and useless. Warn a divisive person once, and then warn him a second time. After that, have nothing to do with him. You may be sure that such a man is warped and sinful; he is self-condemned.

Usually, Paul talks about the old law first then the new law. In this passage he describes the grace and mercy of life with Jesus, followed by the uselessness of the old law. We need to not waste our time talking about laws and customs because they have no place in our lives! We need to talk about Jesus' covenant that is based on love.

PHILEMON

This is the shortest book in the Bible. it Is a short letter from Paul to his friend Philemon. This letter is generally cited when people are discussing the topic of forgiveness. At this time, there were about 60 million slaves in the Roman empire. It was a little different than how we think about slavery today, in that it was not based on race, and slaves could purchase their way into mainstream society. Onesimus was Philemon's slave, and he ran away from him. He met Paul in Rome and became a Christian. When he told Paul that he had run away from Philemon, Paul encouraged Onesimus to return to Philemon. This letter is Paul asking Philemon to accept Onesimus back without retaliation, along with Paul's promise to pay Philemon back for any losses occurred during Onesimus' absence. **It's a beautiful example of the extent to which we should all be willing to go to forgive others.**

HEBREWS

This letter was written to the Christian Jews who were being persecuted at the time and were being coerced into turning away from Jesus back to the old Jewish law. While many believe that Paul wrote this letter, the author is not universally agreed upon. For purposes of this book, we will refer to Paul as the author. "A marvelous portrait of Jesus Christ seen through the lens of the Old Testament. The author's intent is to show the superiority of Jesus over the prophets, angels, Moses, priests, and the whole Old Testament system. Jesus is the new priest with the new sacrifice that establishes a new covenant between people and God". (NIV Summary)

HEBREWS 1

"In the past God spoke to our forefathers through the prophets at many times in various ways, but in the last days he has spoken to us by his Son, whom he also appointed heir of all things, and through whom He made the universe. The Son is the radiance of God's glory and the exact representation of his being, sustaining all things by his powerful word".

Paul comes right out of the gate declaring Jesus is King. There is no other, he is above all, and he sits with God eternally. Paul says that God never said such things to the Angels (the things that he said about Jesus). The minute he introduced us to his son Jesus, everything changed about God. He said in Psalms, "Your throne, o God, will last for ever and ever and righteousness will be the scepter of your kingdom. You have loved

righteousness and hated wickedness; therefore God, your God, has set you above your companions by anointing you with the oil of joy". Comparing to the Angels, Paul says, "to which of the angels did God say, 'sit at my right hand until I make your enemies a footstool at your feet'?" This is important—Paul is setting the stage for the rest of this letter which is a plea to Jewish Christians to hold on to Jesus as the "cornerstone of their faith".

HEBREWS 2

"We must pay careful attention, therefore, to what we have heard so that we do not drift away".

Paul explains to them that Jesus was made "a little lower than the angels" but that is only so he could come to earth, show us how to live, and be crucified for our sins. Then God "crowned him with glory".

"In bringing many sons to glory, it was fitting that God, for whom and through whom everything exists, should make the author of their salvation perfect through suffering...since the children have flesh and blood, he too shared in their humanity so that by his death he might destroy him who holds the power of death—that is, the devil—and free those who all their lives were held in slavery by their fear of death...because he himself suffered when he was tempted, he is able to help those who are being tempted".

In the first two chapters of Hebrews there are 14 verses that Paul quotes from the Old Testament to make the case for Christ. This is brilliant on Paul's part. He is using a language that these Jewish Christians understand to help them bridge from their old faith to their new faith.

HEBREWS 3

Paul speaks very directly to the Hebrews by comparing their past way to the new way. He continues to use Jewish history and customs as a foundation to lead them to Jesus.

"Therefore, holy brothers, who share in the heavenly calling, fix your thoughts on Jesus, the apostle and high priest whom we confess. He was faithful to the one who appointed him, just as Moses was faithful in all God's house. Jesus has been found worthy of a greater honor than Moses, just as the builder of a house has greater honor than the house itself. For every house is built by someone, but God is the builder of everything". **This had to be difficult for the Jews to hear, as Moses is the foundation of their faith.**

He warns them against "unbelief" by quoting Psalm 95:7-11:

"So, as the Holy Spirit says: today, if you hear his voice, harden not your hearts as you did in the rebellion, during that time of testing in the desert".

"See to it, brothers, that none of you has a sinful, unbelieving heart that turns away from the living God. But encourage one another daily, as long as it is called today so that none of you may be harmed by sin's deceitfulness. We have come to share in Christ if we hold firmly till the end the confidence we had at first".

Paul reminds them what happened to those who did not believe, who sinned while they wandered in the desert with Moses. "Whose bodies fell into the desert? And to whom did God swear that they would never enter his rest"? That's a heavy price to pay for not believing the truth!

HEBREWS 4

"Therefore, since the promise of entering his rest still stands, let us be careful that none of you be found to have fallen short of it". **That's an encouragement by Paul to the Hebrews to share the truth and hold each other accountable to it—in belief and actions. He says that many have heard the story "but the message was of no value to them, because they did not combine it with faith". In other words—hearing does not mean believing!**

Paul makes an interesting point about resting on the Sabbath. He says, "God's work has been finished since the creation of the world" then

God rested. He reminds us that those who do God's work deserve a day of rest as well.

I believe Paul is challenging them to realize that there is no excuse for non-belief. This is a profound verse:

"For the word of God is living and active, sharper than any double-edged sword. It penetrates even to dividing soul and spirit, joints, and marrow; it judges the thoughts and attitudes of the heart. Nothing in all of creation is hidden from God's sight. Everything is uncovered and laid bare before the eyes of him who we must give account".

We have been given the answers to the test. We know what to do, how to act, and how to treat people. We just need the courage and discipline to do it. We also need to remember that the "Word of God" is not just a phrase. The "completeness" of the Bible is amazing. It is the original life manual, and the paragraph above eloquently articulates how it can be used as the template to build faith and character.

HEBREWS 5

Hebrews really is a collection of brilliant lessons from Paul. In chapter 5 he writes that Jesus is the real high priest who is not like most high priests who are "unable to sympathize with our weaknesses". Jesus was tempted in every way, yet without sin.

"Let us approach the throne of grace with confidence so that we may receive mercy and find grace to help us in our time of need". **To view God sitting on the "throne of grace" is so comforting.**

Paul reminds us that high priests are appointed—no one takes that honor upon himself. In Jesus' case, he was appointed by God. He was appointed when God said, "You are my Son. Today I have become your Father." He also said, "You are a priest forever, in the order of Melchizedek."

"During Jesus' life on earth, he offered up prayers and petitions with loud cries and tears to the one who could save him from death, and he was heard because of his reverent submission".

How beautiful of a term is that? That is how we should approach God—reverent submission. But with confidence because we know he is merciful and provides us with everlasting grace.

"Although he was a Son, he learned obedience from what he suffered and, once made perfect, became the source of all who obey him and was designated by God to be high priest in the order of Melchizedek. (Melchizedek was the king of Salem and is first mentioned in Genesis.)

Paul finishes chapter 5 by saying that his audience is slow to learn so he has to feed them milk like a baby before he feeds them solid food. What a great analogy!

HEBREWS 6

Paul says he will now move on to mature teaching. "Therefore, let us leave the elementary teachings about Christ and go on to maturity, not laying again the foundation of repentance from acts that lead to death, and of faith in God, instruction about baptism, the laying on of hands, the resurrection of the dead, the eternal judgment. And God permitting, we will do so".

"It is impossible for those who have once been enlightened, who have tasted the heavenly gift, who have shared in the Holy Spirit, who have tasted the goodness of the word of God and the powers of the coming age, if they fall away, to be brought back to repentance. To their loss they are crucifying the Son of God all over again and subjecting him to public disgrace".

Oh my gosh. As believers of God's word, and followers of Jesus, every time we reject Jesus, and sin, we are crucifying him, and giving the world an opportunity to ridicule him. Incredible! This is important! When we exemplify Jesus, we attract followers. When we claim to be Christians, but don't walk the walk, we do more damage than if we had never followed.

"Land that drinks in the rain…receives the blessing of God. Land that produces thorns and thistles is worthless and is in danger of being cursed. In the end it will be burned".

"God is not unjust; he will not forget your work and the love you have shown him…we do not want you to become lazy, but to imitate those who through faith and patience inherit what has been promised".

"Men swear by something greater than themselves, and the oath confirms what is said and puts an end to all argument. Because God wanted to make the unchanging nature of his purpose clear to the heirs of what was promised, he confirmed it with an oath. (I think his oath was Jesus.) God did this so that, by two unchangeable things in which it is impossible for God to lie, we who have fled to take hold of the hope offered to us may be greatly encouraged. We have this hope as an anchor for the soul, firm and secure. It enters the inner sanctuary behind the curtain where Jesus, who went before us, has entered on our behalf".

Incredible. The hope of Jesus is an anchor for our soul!

HEBREWS 7

Melchizedek was the high priest that blessed Abraham when he was returning from the defeat of the Kings. For that, Abraham gave him 1/10 of everything.

Paul gets into some heavy genealogy as it relates to Melchizedek, Aaron, Levi and Jesus. In short, Melchizedek was different in that he was viewed as "having no father or mother, without genealogy, without beginning of days or end of life, like the Son of God, he remains a priest forever". The point Paul makes is that there are many high priests, and almost all of them inherit their role from their lineage, not from their greatness and righteousness like Melchizedek and Jesus. That is why God said, "you are a priest forever in the order of Melchizedek."

"If perfection could be attained through the Levitical priesthood—why was there another priest to come—not in the order of Aaron"? **His point was that the Jews are all waiting for this next high priest, but it was not going to come the traditional way.**

"The former regulation was set aside because it was weak and useless (for the law made nothing perfect), and a better hope is introduced, by which we draw near to God. And it was not without an oath. Others became priests without any oath, but he became a priest with an oath when God said to him:

> "The Lord has sworn
> And will not change his mind:
> 'You are a priest
> forever'".

"Because of this oath, Jesus has become the guarantor of a better covenant. Now there has been many of those priests, since death prevented them from continuing in office; but because Jesus lives forever, he has a permanent priesthood. Therefore, he is able to save completely those who come to God through him, because he always lives to intercede for them".

"Such a high priest meets our need—one who is holy, blameless, pure, set apart from sinners, exalted above the heavens. unlike other high priests, he does not need to offer sacrifices day after day, first for his own sins, and then for the sins of the people. He sacrificed for their sins <u>once</u> for all when he offered himself. For the law appoints as high priests men who are weak; but the oath, which came after the law, appointed the son, who has been made perfect forever".

This is incredible scripture. It is certainly one of Paul's more impassioned, emotional plea for these people about why Jesus is different, and the host of a new way of life. A new covenant.

HEBREWS 8

"The point of what we are saying is this: We do have such a high priest, who sat down at the right hand of the throne of the majesty in heaven, and who serves in the sanctuary, the true tabernacle set up by the Lord, not by man. Every high priest has done things according to the law as a shadow of what is in heaven…but the ministry Jesus has received is superior to the old one, and it is founded on <u>better promises</u>".

"For if there had been nothing wrong with the old covenant, no place would have been sought for another. But God found fault with the people and said:

"The time is coming, declares the Lord, when I will make a new covenant with the house of Israel and with the House of Judah. It will not be like the covenant I made with their forefathers when I took them by the hand and led them out of Egypt, because they did not remain faithful to my covenant, and I turned away from them, declares the Lord. This is the covenant I will make with the house of Israel after that time, declares the Lord. I will put my laws in their minds and write them on their hearts. I will be their God, and they will be my people. No longer will a man teach his neighbor, or a man his brother saying, 'know the Lord', because they <u>all know me</u>, from the least of them to the greatest. For I will forgive their sins no more". That is all from Jeremiah 31:31-34.

"By calling the covenant new, he has made the first one <u>obsolete</u>; and what is obsolete and aging will soon disappear".

God replaced laws with himself.

HEBREWS 9

This is a bit of a wild chapter. Paul tries to explain the difference between historical high priests and Jesus as the new high priest. He describes the history of the design of the sanctuary and the Tabernacle; everything about it and everything in it was designed for a reason. He says that part of the high priest's ceremony was to offer some of his own blood to offer forgiveness for the people's sins. The high priest had to do this every year, because the conscience needed to be cleared continuously.

"How much more will the blood of Christ, who through the eternal Spirit offered himself unblemished to God, cleanse our consciences from acts that lead to death (condemnation), so that we may serve the living God. For this reason, Christ is the mediator of a new covenant, that those who are called may receive the promised eternal inheritance—now that he has died as a ransom to set them free from the sins committed under the first covenant."

Paul draws on a powerful metaphor to make his point. "In the case of a will, it is necessary to prove death of the one who made it, because a will is in force only when somebody has died; it never takes effect when the one who made it is living".

He talks about how Moses used the blood of animals as a sign of the Commandments becoming law. The blood was the covenant. "Without the shedding of blood, there is no forgiveness". Regarding Jesus, however, "Christ did not enter A man-made sanctuary that was only a copy of the true one; he entered heaven itself, now to appear for us in God's presence". He also explains that he only did it once, otherwise he would have had to be killed again and again. "So, Christ was sacrificed once to take away the sins of many people; and he will appear a second time not to bear sin, but to bring salvation to those who are waiting for him". **While it is a 'wild' chapter, it is remarkably accurate. Our faith is rooted in the actual blood of Jesus.**

HEBREWS 10

This is an "all-time chapter". It is so very powerful, and it is a detailed description of how Jesus rewrote the rules of forgiveness and salvation. Paul basically says, 'we can't keep doing this year after year.' He makes a case of, if the blood offerings and ceremony worked, why didn't we just do it once? In other words, if something worked, why is there a need to

do it twice? Because "it is so impossible for the blood of goats and bulls to take away sins". That's why Jesus repeatedly said, "Here I am, I have come to do your will…and by that will we have been made holy to the sacrifice of the body of Jesus Christ once and for all".

In Jeremiah the Holy Spirit says, "This is the covenant I will make with them after that time, says the Lord. I will put my laws in their hearts, and I will write them on their minds". Then he adds, "their sins and lawless acts I will remember no more. And where are these have been forgiven, there is no longer any sacrifice for sin". This is a beautiful prelude to the covenant that Jesus created when he was born.

A Call to Persevere

"Therefore, brothers, since we have confidence to enter the most holy place by the blood of Jesus, by a new and living way opened for us through the curtain, that is, His body, and since we have a great priest over the house of God, let us draw near to God with a sincere heart in full assurance of faith, having our hearts sprinkled to cleanse us from a guilty conscience and having our bodies washed with pure water. Let us hold unswervingly to the hope we profess, for he who promised is faithful. And let us consider how we may spur one another on toward love and good deeds". **This is incredible. For me it's like a pregame speech by Paul. "We can do this!"**

What follows is a warning. A warning of the dangers of avoiding what we know to be true.

"If we deliberately keep on sinning after we have received the knowledge of the truth, no sacrifice for sins is left, but only a fearful expectation of judgment and of raging fire that will consume the enemies of God". **Wow! This really is Paul telling us that if we know the truth, and do nothing, the Jesus' sacrifice means nothing. We know the truth! <u>We</u> must find the courage and develop the discipline to follow it.** "How much more severely do you think a man deserves to be punished who has trampled the Son of

God underfoot, who has treated as an unholy thing the blood of the covenant that sanctified him, and who has insulted the spirit of grace"?

Do not spit in the face of Jesus! And whenever we act in a way that is not in accordance with our 'professed' belief in him, that's exactly what we do.

"So do not throw away your confidence; it will be richly rewarded".

"You need to persevere so that when you have done the will of God, you will receive what he has promised. For, "in just a little while, he who is coming will come and will not delay" and "but my righteous one will live by faith. And if he shrinks back, I will not be pleased with him". hab 2:3-4

"But we do not belong to those who shrink back and are destroyed, but to those who believe and are saved".

Hebrews 11

This chapter absolutely must be read in its entirety. There are approximately 20 paragraphs in this chapter and the majority of them begin with "by faith" and they go on to share great examples of faith in biblical history. I will summarize the ones that resonate most with me.

"Now faith is being sure of what we hope for and certain of what we do not see".

"By faith we understand that the universe was formed at God's command, so that what is seen was not made out what was visible".

— Abel offered a better sacrifice than Cain did—out of faith.

— Without faith it is impossible to please God because anyone who comes to him must believe that He exists and that He rewards those who earnestly seek him.

— Noah built the ark through faith. He rejected the world and sought God.

— Abraham, Isaac, and Jacob did everything through faith. Abraham "was looking forward to the city with foundations whose architect and builder is God".

— By faith Abraham and Sarah conceived a child and from that came countless generations.

— By faith Abraham offered his son Isaac as a sacrifice, and God saved him.

— By faith Moses' parents hid him for three months because they were not Afraid of the King's edict.

— By faith Moses refused to be known as the son of the rich pharaoh's daughter. "He regarded disgrace for the sake of Christ as of greater value then the treasures of Egypt".

— By faith the people pass through the Red Sea while the Egyptians drowned.

Paul lists many more champions of faith by name. He mentions all the trials and tribulations of all of them. "These were all commended for their faith, yet none of them received what had been promised. God had planned something better for us so that only together with us would they be made perfect". **For all the people who were waiting, and for us, God ultimately delivered on his promise in Jesus.**

HEBREWS 12

This chapter reads like it could have been written last week! This entire stretch of Hebrews is all about recognition of the power of faith, the importance of being disciplined in our efforts, and the role that perseverance plays in staying strong followers of Jesus. This chapter is about discipline.

"Therefore, since we are surrounded by such a great cloud of witnesses, let us throw off everything that hinders and the sin that so easily entangles.

And let us run with perseverance the race marked out for us. <u>Let us fix our</u> <u>eyes on Jesus,</u> the author and perfecter of our faith who for the joy set before him endured the cross, scorning its shame, and sat down at the right hand of the throne of God. Consider him who endured such opposition from sinful men, so that you will not grow weary and lose heart".

Paul is telling us to remember Jesus' struggles when we are struggling. Build on our own perseverance by recalling Jesus' inspiration.

"In your struggle against sin, you have not yet resisted to the point of shedding your blood. And you have forgotten that word of encouragement that addresses you as sons:

> "My son, do not make light of the
> Lord's discipline, and do not lose
> heart when he rebukes you, because
> the Lord disciples those that he
> loves, and he punishes everyone
> he accepts as a son".

I have come to realize that following Jesus is <u>simple but not easy</u>. He is the answer, and we can make that simple decision. But it's not easy to follow him your whole life because it requires discipline and perseverance.

Paul compares the discipline from God to the discipline imposed on us by our earthly fathers. They do it for a reason and it builds our character. "Later on, it produces a harvest of righteousness and peace for those who have been trained by it. Therefore, strengthen your feeble arms and weak knees. make level paths for your feet, so that the lame may not be disabled, but rather healed. make every effort to live in peace with all men and to be holy; without holiness no one will see the Lord".

Paul encourages us to be witnesses so people can see God through us. He tells us that, "we have to come to the city of the living God…and to Jesus the mediator of a new covenant."

"Therefore, since we are receiving a kingdom that cannot be shaken, let us be thankful, and so worship God acceptably with reverence and awe, for God is a consuming fire"! **God is a consuming fire! That word picture is so powerful. Like a fire, it consumes everything in its path, in a good way!**

HEBREWS 13

Paul encourages the Hebrews and gives them instructions in his final chapter:

— keep on loving each other as brothers

— entertain strangers and remember prisoners

— honor your marriage and do not commit adultery

"Through Jesus, therefore, let us continually offer to God a sacrifice of praise—the fruit of lips that confess his name".

"May the God of peace, who through the blood of the eternal covenant brought back from the dead our Lord Jesus, that great shepherd of the sheep, equip you with everything good for doing his will, and may he work in us what is pleasing to him, through Jesus Christ, to whom be glory forever and ever. Amen".

JAMES

The book of James is a unique one. It is assumed that James is the brother of Jesus and was a leader of the church of Jerusalem. It is not exactly clear who James is writing to. James uses a lot of questions in his writing style, and he also uses commands frequently. **The theme of this book is Christianity in action**. For those who favor works based on Christianity (as opposed to faith), they usually cite James' writings. Interestingly, it says very little about Jesus (does not mention his death or resurrection) and does not mention the Holy Spirit. While Jesus is not mentioned often, his teachings from the Sermon on the Mount are the cornerstone of this book.

JAMES 1

"Consider it pure joy, my brothers, whenever you face trials of many kinds, because you know that the testing of your faith develops perseverance. Perseverance must finish its work so that you may be mature and complete, not lacking anything. If any of you lacks wisdom, you should ask God, who gives generously to all without finding fault, and it will be given to him. But when he asks, he must believe and not doubt, because he who doubts is like a wave of the sea, blown and tossed by the wind".

"The brother in humble circumstances ought to take pride in his high position. But the one who is rich should take pride in his low position— because he will pass away like a wild flower".

"Blessed is the man who perseveres under trial because, when he has stood the test, he will receive the crown of life that God has promised to those who love him".

Stay faithful no matter what the circumstances.

"Everyone should be quick to listen and slow to speak and slow to become angry, for man's anger does not bring about the righteous life that God desires"! **Great life advice!**

"Do not merely listen to the word, and so deceive yourselves. Do what it says. Anyone who listens to the word but does not do what it says is like a man who looks at his face in a mirror and, after looking at himself, goes away and immediately forgets what he looks like". **Don't be hypocrite.**

This is a phenomenal analogy by James. We can't have our faith lie in the reading of Scripture alone. That puts our faith into a silo, in a very small portion of our life. It needs to be visible the entire day, every day. That is how we attract people to follow Jesus.

"Religion that God our father accepts as pure and faultless is this: to look after orphans and widows in their distress and to keep oneself from being polluted by the world".

JAMES 2

James tells us not to judge people. Don't give special favoritism to the rich and look down on the poor. Do not discriminate! "Listen, my dear brothers: has not God chosen those who are poor in the eyes of the world to be rich in faith and to inherit the kingdom he promised those who love him"? That is straight from the Sermon on the Mount.

James draws an analogy that if you break any part of the law (adultery, murder, etc.) you break all of it. He also says, "judgment without mercy will be shown to anyone who has not been merciful."

We then arrive at the most quoted passage from James, "What good is it my brothers, if a man claims to have faith but has no deeds? Can such faith save him...In the same way, faith by itself, if it is not accompanied by action, is dead".

Paul cites Abraham offering Isaac in sacrifice as a sign of faith backed up by works. So...what does this all mean? It is complex and simple at the same time. Some misinterpret James' writing by thinking this means that salvation is works based. In other words, we earn our way to heaven by doing good things. This is <u>not</u> what James is saying. He is suggesting that works comes from a position of love and obedience; you <u>act</u> like Jesus because he told you to, not to earn points with his Father. <u>Because you love, you do</u>! Just like Abraham did. He loved God, so he did what he told him to do.

JAMES 3

Taming the Tongue

This is an important chapter about the importance of speech and the role that it plays in good and evil. James says that teachers will be judged more strictly because of their influence on others. He also draws on some great analogies to demonstrate the power of the tongue. The bit in the mouth of a horse Controls the entire horse. A small rudder on the bottom of a ship controls the direction of the entire ship. And "with the tongue we praise our Lord and Father, and with it we curse men, who have been made in God's likeness. out of the same mouth come praise and cursing. My brothers, this should not be".

What a strong statement by James! Who are we going to be? <u>Choose</u> how we are going to use our words.

"Who is wise and understanding among you? Let him show by his good life, by deeds done in the humility that comes from wisdom".

He also tells us to not be full of envy and selfishness. "For where you have envy and selfish ambition, there you find disorder and every evil practice".

That statement cuts deeply because it is so true. Selfish ambition can lead to greed, pride, and conceit! "But the wisdom that comes from heaven is first of all pure; then peace-loving, considerate, submissive, full of mercy and good fruit, impartial and sincere. peacemakers who sow in peace reap a harvest of righteousness".

Heavenly wisdom is a beautiful thing to strive for!

JAMES 4

Submit Yourselves to God

This chapter is brief but very impactful because it reaches right into our daily lives.

"What causes fights and quarrels among you? Don't they come from your desires that battle within you? You want something but you don't get it. You kill and covet but you cannot have what you want. You quarrel and fight. <u>You do not have because you do not ask God</u>. When you ask, you do not receive, because you ask with the wrong motives, that you may spend what you get on your pleasures".

Wow! We definitely do this! We ask God for things that will make our earthly lives better. We need to ask God for the things that will draw us closer to him because this is all he wants!

"You adulterous people, don't you know that friendship with the world is hatred toward God? Anyone who chooses to be a friend of the world becomes an enemy of God… "God opposes the proud but gives grace to the humble." prov 3:34

"Submit yourself, then, to God. Resist the devil, and he will flee from you come near to God and he will come near to you". I never remember

reading the last statement before, but I believe it to my core. People ask, "why has God abandoned me?" God abandons no one. Ever. When we feel distant from God, we need to ask ourselves, "who moved?". The answer is, "we moved." Because God is unchanging. He doesn't move. We need to return to God, and he will change our hearts! And when we do, Satan will run from us because he knows he is powerless over God.

"Brothers do not slander one another. Anyone who speaks against his brother or judges him speaks against the law and judges it…who are you to Judge your neighbor"?

Don't boast about tomorrow. "Now listen, you who say, 'today or tomorrow we will go to this city or that city, spend a year there, carry on business and make money'. Why, you do not even know what will happen tomorrow. what is your life? You are a mist that appears for a little while and vanishes. Instead, you ought to say, 'if it is the Lord's will, we will live and do this or that'".

This is how we should pray! —Lord, help me submit to your will. Draw me closer to you! Once again, the "Our Father" is a beautiful prayer for a reason!

JAMES 5

This is a warning to the rich! "Now listen, you rich people, weep and wail because of the misery that is coming upon you. Your wealth has rotted, and moths have eaten your clothes. Your gold and silver have corroded. Their corrosion will testify against you and eat your flesh like fire. You have hoarded wealth in the last days"! James gives us a powerful vision of the transient joys and lingering dangers of wealth. The corrosion of our gold will eat our flesh like fire. Such a powerful word picture.

"Be patient, then, brothers, until the Lord's coming…don't grumble against each other, brothers, or you will be judged. The judge is standing at the door". God is watching!! James tells us to be patient in our perseverance of following Jesus and waiting for his return because, "the Lord is full of compassion and mercy".

"Above all, my brothers, do not swear—not by Heaven or by Earth or by anything else". **I wish people would experience the joy of removing swearing from their vocabulary. It makes such a strong statement about who you are as a person.**

"Is anyone of you in trouble? He should pray. Is anyone happy? Let him sing songs of praise. Is any one of you sick? He should call the elders of the Church to pray over him and anoint him with oil in the name of the Lord. And the prayer offered in faith will make the sick person well; the Lord will raise him up. If he has sinned, he will be forgiven. Therefore, confess your sins to each other and pray for each other so that you may be healed. The prayer of a righteous man is powerful and effective".

James has a great statement about Elijah who prayed for rain after a 3 1/2-year drought. "Again, he prayed, and the Heavens gave rain". He also tells us that we are accountable to teach each other: "whoever turns a sinner from the error of his way will save him from death and cover a multitude of sins". **We need to help each other remain faithful!**

1 PETER

This letter was written by the apostle Peter before he was arrested. It was written in the final years of Nero's reign, which caused great persecution among Christians. Peter encourages Jewish and Gentile believers to turn to Jesus and live a holy life, regardless of persecution.

1 PETER 1

"Praise be to God and Father of our Lord Jesus Christ. In his great mercy he has given us new birth into a living hope through the resurrection of Jesus Christ from the dead, and into an inheritance that can never perish, spoil or fade. This inheritance is kept in heaven for you, who through faith are shielded by God's power until the coming of the salvation that is ready to be revealed in the last time". Paul goes on to say that we will face all kinds of trials, but "these have come to show the genuineness of our faith—of greater worth then gold, which perishes even though refined by fire—may result in praise, glory, and honor when Jesus is revealed. Though you have not seen Him, you love Him; and even though you do not see Him now, you believe in Him and are filled with inexpressible and glorious joy, for you are receiving the end result of your faith, the salvation of your souls".

Shielded by God's power—genuineness of our <u>faith</u>—<u>greater worth</u> <u>than gold</u>—<u>refined by fire</u>—<u>glorious joy</u>—Beautiful imagery!

"Therefore, with minds that are alert and fully sober, set your hope on the grace to be brought to you when Jesus Christ is revealed at his coming".

He encourages us to be holy because as Jesus said, "Be holy because I am holy". He tells us to abandon the world we inherit from our ancestors because we "are redeemed from the precious blood of Christ, a lamb without blemish or defect." He was chosen before the creation of the world but was revealed in these last times for your sake".

"Now that you have purified yourselves by obeying the truth so that you have sincere love for each other, love one another deeply, from the heart. For you have been torn again, not of perishable seed, but of imperishable, through the living in and enduring Word of God. All people are like grass, and all their glory is like the flowers of the field; the grass withers and the flowers fall, but the word of the Lord endures forever".

1 PETER 2

"Therefore, rid yourselves of all malice and all deceit, hypocrisy, envy, and slander of every kind. Like newborn babies, crave pure spiritual milk, so that by it you may grow up in your salvation, now that you have tasted that the Lord is good".

Think about that one! Crave pure spiritual milk so that you may grow up in your salvation. The "pure spiritual milk" is the word of God—the Bible—Study it so you can grow!

Peter draws on "stones" to make a great point. He says, "The living stone (Jesus)—was rejected by humans but chosen by God—you also are being built into a spiritual house." Then he cites Isaiah and psalms:

"See, I lay a stone in Zion, a chosen and precious cornerstone, and the one who trusts in him will never be put to shame". But to those who do not believe, "the stone the builders rejected has become the cornerstone", and "a stone that causes people to stumble and a rock that makes them fall".

"They stumble because they
disobey the message"!

1 PETER 3

Peter kicks off this chapter with some very specific marital advice. It's mostly reasonable albeit a bit "male centric" in nature. "Wives submit to your husbands" seems to be a common theme in Paul and Peter's teachings. I do not like how Peter follows up his statement in that he says the reason is so that any husband that doesn't believe the word will be won over by the behavior of their wives. "Not from outward adornment, like elaborate hairstyles and the wearing of gold jewelry or fine clothes—but by the unfading beauty of a gentle and quiet spirit". **I think that goes for both men and women. Act like Jesus so they will be attracted to following Jesus.**

He tells husbands to treat their wives with respect "as the weaker partner". I love the respect statement but "weaker" is a questionable word in this context.

"Finally, all of you, be like-minded, be sympathetic, love one another, be compassionate and humble. Do not repay evil with evil or insult with insult. On the contrary, repay evil with blessing, because to this you were called so that you may inherit a blessing". **Now _that_ is timeless advice.**

"Whoever would love to life and see good days must keep their tongue from evil and their lips from deceitful speech. They must turn from evil and do good; they must seek peace and pursue it. For the eyes of the Lord are on the righteous and his ears attentive to their prayer, but the face of the Lord is against those who do evil".

Peter also tells us that even if we suffer for doing what is right, we will be blessed. Very importantly, he tells us how to respond to people who ask about the hope that we have; how we have demonstrated that hope in our lives. "Do it with gentleness and respect". That is so good. The best way for us to win people over to Jesus is with gentleness and respect. Because that is how Jesus acts! We don't need to be confrontational and combative!

1 PETER 4

Peter says that people who live like pagans of the past will be surprised that we don't join them and their behavior. But they will ultimately have to give account for their behavior.

"The end of all things is near. Therefore, be alert and of sober mind so that you can pray. Above all, love each other deeply, because love covers a multitude of sins. Offer hospitality to one another without grumbling. Each of you should use whatever gift you have received to serve others, as faithful stewards of God's grace in its various forms. If anyone speaks, they should do so as one who speaks the very words of God. If anyone serves, they should do so with the strength God provides, so that in all things God may be praised through Jesus Christ. To him be the glory and the power for ever and ever. Amen".

This message about spiritual gifts is important. God made us to serve Him, and we need to continuously perform introspection to identify what is the best way for us to attract others to God's kingdom!

Peter also says that we will be subject to a "fiery upheaval" for being a Christian. He tells us to "rejoice inasmuch as you participate in the sufferings of Christ, so that you may be overjoyed when his glory is revealed". We need to embrace the sufferings and "praise God that we bear that name". **This is very important. If we know this world is not "of God", we need to recognize that if we align ourselves with God, we will be persecuted. We need to ask ourselves if we are willing to wear our God jersey, no matter what.**

1 PETER 5

"To the elders of the flock, I appeal as a fellow and elder and a witness of Christ's sufferings who also share in the glory to be revealed. Be shepherds of God's flock that is under your care, watching over them—not because you must, but because you are willing, as God wants you to be; not pursuing dishonest gain, but eager to serve; not lording it over those entrusted to you, but being examples to the flock. And when the chief Shepherd appears, you will receive the crown of glory that will never fade away". **I know Peter was speaking to the assigned elders, but we all need to take a humble servant's heart to care for the flock.** He tells younger people to "submit to your elders" because "God opposes the proud but shows favor to the humble". He tells us to "be alert and of sober mind. Your enemy (Satan) prowls around like a roaring Lion looking for someone to devour". **We need to resist him and stand firm in the faith!**

2 PETER

This letter was most likely written by Peter to the same group of people that received Peter's last letter. While some of them are similar, this letter addresses some of the false teachings that had arisen. Since Jesus had not returned for the second coming (A.D. 68) some were saying that Peter and Paul should not be trusted. Peter encourages us to grow in Christian values!

2 PETER 1

"His divine power has given us everything we need for life and Godliness through our knowledge of him who called us by his own glory and goodness. Through these he has given us his very great and precious promises, so that through them you may participate in the divine nature and escape the corruption in the world caused by evil desires. For this very reason, make every effort to add your faith goodness; and to goodness, knowledge; and to knowledge, self-control; and to self-control, perseverance; and to perseverance, Godliness; and to Godliness, brotherly kindness; and to brotherly kindness, Love. For if you possess these qualities in increasing measure, they will keep you from being ineffective and unproductive in your knowledge of our Lord Jesus Christ...if you do these things, you will never fail, and you will receive a rich welcome into the eternal kingdom of our Lord and Savior Jesus Christ".

Peter then defends his account by saying, "We did not follow cleverly invented stories when we told you about the power and coming of our Lord

Jesus Christ, but we were eyewitnesses of his majesty". **This is critical! Peter is saying we saw it with our own eyes, and we heard God proclaim, "This is my Son". He says that the prophecy of the prophets was not by their own interpretation, but "from God as they were carried along by the Holy Spirit".**

2 PETER 2

This chapter is full of the important lessons and warnings about false teachers, which were everywhere during Peter's time, and they are everywhere now.

"They (false teachers) will secretly introduce destructive heresies, even denying the sovereign Lord who bought them—bringing swift destruction on themselves. Many will follow in their shameful ways and will bring the way of truth into disrepute. In their greed these teachers will exploit you with stories they have made up. Their condemnation has long been hanging over them, and their destruction has not been sleeping".

"Bold and arrogant, these men are not afraid to slander celestial beings; yet even angels, although they are stronger and more powerful, do not bring slanderous allegations against such beings in the presence of the Lord. But these men blaspheme in matters they do not understand. They are like brute beasts, creatures of instinct, born only to be caught and destroyed, and like beasts, they too will perish".

All of this is why it is so important to know the truth, and the truth is found in the only the real truth source—the Bible, which details the life of Jesus and what he said. False teachers are everywhere, and more than making up stories, they twist the lessons of Jesus and make it sound very easy to be a follower of Jesus, which it is not. They make it sound so easy so you will follow their message, (not the truth of Jesus) which will give them money and power. We need to know the truth so we can recognize and combat the lies. The lies that make following Jesus sound easy and

the lies that speak of earthly gain are the most dangerous because they are so attractive. They are truly wolves in sheep's clothing. Be on guard.

"They will be paid back with the harm they have done. Their idea of pleasure is to carouse in broad daylight. They are blots and blemishes, reveling in their pleasures while they feast with you. With eyes full of adultery, they never stop sinning; they seduce the unstable; they are <u>experts in greed</u>—an accursed brood".

"These men are springs without water and mists driven by a storm. Blackest darkness is reserved for them. For they mouth empty, boastful words and, by appealing to the lustful desires of sinful human nature, they entice people who are just escaping from those who live in error. They promise freedom, while they themselves are slaves of depravity—for a man is a slave to whatever has mastered him. If they escaped the corruption of the world by knowing our Lord and Savior Jesus Christ and are again entangled in it and are overcome, they are worse off at the end than they were at the beginning. It would have been better for them not to have known the way of righteousness, than to have known it and then to turn their backs on the sacred command that was passed on to them. Of them the proverbs are true: 'a dog returns to his vomit,' and, 'a sow that is washed goes back to her wallowing in the mud'". **We need to recognize liars and stay away from them! This is the clearest explanation of what false prophets do, why they do it, and how to combat it.**

2 PETER 3

This is Peter's heartfelt plea to be ready for Jesus' return. He tells us that people will scoff at this notion, and it will get worse as time goes by, almost like, 'Where is your Savior, I thought you said he was coming?' Peter says, "But do not forget this one thing, dear friends: with the Lord a day is like a thousand years, and a thousand years are like a day. The Lord is not slow in keeping his promise, as some understand slowness. He is patient with you, <u>not wanting anyone to perish</u>, but everyone to come to repentance". **Jesus**

wants our hearts so he begs us to repent so he can spend eternity with us.
"You ought to live holy and Godly lives as you look forward to the day of
God and speed its coming. That day will bring about the destruction of the
heavens by fire, and the elements will melt in the heat. But in keeping with
his promise, we are looking forward to a new heaven and a new earth, the
home of righteousness".

1 JOHN

This letter was written by John in probably around 90 A.D. while John lived in Ephesus. It was a letter to the Church there where a group had split off from the church and began to espouse "advanced" views. John wrote the letter to help them discern truth from error. The new church claimed Jesus never came and he was not the Messiah. They felt their own spiritual elitism bypassed morality and love as marks of one's spiritual maturity.

1 JOHN 1

"The life appeared (Jesus); we have seen it and testify to it, and we proclaim to you the eternal life, which was with the Father and has appeared to us…This message we have heard from and declare to you: God is light; in him there is no darkness at all. If we claim to have fellowship with him and yet walk in the darkness, <u>we lie</u> and do not live by the truth. But if we walk in the light, as he is in the light, we have fellowship with one another, and the blood of Jesus, His son, purifies us from all sin". **That tells me that God is the key to true friendship.**

That is a powerful claim that John makes right out of the gates— make no mistake, this is the truth, you know it, so don't live a lie. "If we claim to be without sin, we deceive ourselves and the truth is not in us. If we confess our sins, he is faithful and just and will forgive us our sins and purify us from all unrighteousness. If we claim we have not sinned, we make him out to be a liar and his word has no place in our lives". **This is John attacking**

the beliefs of the people who split from the church—if you think you are
not sinners, you are liars.

1 JOHN 2

"My dear children, I write this to you so that you will not sin. But if anybody does sin, we have one who speaks to the Father in our defense—Jesus
Christ, The righteous one. He is the <u>atoning sacrifice</u> for our sins, and not only
for ours but also for the sins of the whole world". **This is the beauty of following Jesus. There is always someone to close the gap on our sins—which He
will do. John explains that we must walk the walk—not just talk the talk.
"Whoever claims to live in him must walk as Jesus did". <u>Live like Jesus</u>!**

"Yet I am not writing you a new command, but an old one…its truth is
seen in him and in you, because the darkness is passing, and the true light is
already shining. Anyone who claims to be in the light, but hates his brother
is still in the darkness". **This is once again, validation that following Jesus
is about one thing—love. You cannot follow Jesus and be a hater.**

Do not love the world

"Do not want the world or anything in the world. If anyone loves the
world, love for the father is not in him. For everything in the world—the
cravings of sinful man, the lust of the eyes, and the boasting of what he has
and does—comes not from the father but from the world. The world and its
desires pass away, but the man who does the will of God lives forever". **These
teachings about not loving the world are so difficult for us to comprehend
and integrate into our faith. I live in this world, why would I hate it? John
is telling us that the things of this world are not "of God", and when we
choose those things, we are choosing them over our promised inheritance
in heaven which IS from God. Love of the things in this world is a trap that
keeps us from recognizing God's promised inheritance for us.**

John continues his theme of "Jesus is the only way" by warning that
anyone who professes anything different from that is from "the antichrist".

"Who is the liar? It is the man who denies Jesus is the Christ". **For our purposes, this tells us that we are either "for Jesus" or "against him".**

1 JOHN 3

"How great is the love the Father has lavished on us, that we should be called children of God. And that is what we are. The reason the world does not know us is that it did not know him. (So, when we feel like an outlier in our beliefs, that is why!) He tells us that in Jesus there is no sin because sin comes from Satan. "The reason the Son of God appeared was to destroy the devil's work. no one who is born of God will continue to sin, because God's seed remains in him".

This is a tricky message to understand. As humans, we do sin. I think John is saying, "as followers of Jesus, we don't consciously sin with forethought. And when we do sin, we seek repentance."

"This is a message you heard from the beginning: We should <u>love</u> one another…do not be surprised, my brothers, if the world hates you…anyone who does not love remains in death". **This is how we should seek to be recognized as a follower of Jesus—how much we love others.**

"This is how we know what love is: Jesus Christ laid down his life for us. And we ought to lay down our lives for our brothers. If anyone has material possessions and sees a brother in need but has no pity on him, how can the love of God be in him"? **We need to love with our mind, our heart, and our actions!**

"And this is his (God's) command: To believe in the name of his Son, Jesus Christ, and to love one another as he commanded us. Those who obey his command live in him, And he in them. And this is how we know that he lives in us: we know it by the Spirit he gave us".

1 JOHN 4

Much of this chapter is a repeat of the other chapters in 1 John. False prophets, the antichrist and the love of God and our neighbors. He says to not believe every spirit because "many false prophets have gone into the world. This is how you can recognize the Spirit of God: every spirit that acknowledges that Jesus Christ has come in the flesh is from God, but every spirit that does not acknowledge Jesus is not from God". Jesus tells us that because we are from God "the one who is in us is greater than the one who is in the world…this is how we recognize the Spirit of truth and the spirit of falsehood".

Then John hits "Love" hard! "Dear friends, let us love one another, For love comes from God. Everyone who loves has been born of God". He also says that God loved us first and showed it by sending his one and only Son. "Dear friends, since God so loved us, we also ought to love one another… God is love. Whoever lives in love lives in God, and God in him. In this way, love is made complete among us so that we will have confidence on the day of judgment: because in this world we are like him. there is no fear in love. But perfect love drives out fear". **That is so powerful. Love. Love. Love. If we live in love, we have nothing to worry about. That means we are living with God, and he has our back.**

1 JOHN 5

John reiterates that it is all about Jesus. By loving God and obeying his commands, we overcome the world and, "who is it that overcomes the world? Only he who believes that Jesus Christ is the Son of God".

"God has given us eternal life, and this is life in his Son. He who has the Son has life; he who does not have the Son of God does not have life".

"This is the confidence we have in approaching God: that if we ask anything according to his will, he hears us. And if we know he hears us—whatever we ask—we know that we have what we have asked of him". **The** concept of "confidence in approaching God" is so reassuring! If we are sinners, how can we approach God with confidence. Because he loves us, and he begs us to come to him. When your child does something wrong, don't you smile when they come to you and tell you about it?

2 JOHN AND 3 JOHN

These letters were written in the late 80s and early 90s. They were written at the time when Gnosticism was being taught as the key to salvation. Gnosticism is the teaching that professes knowledge is the key to salvation, not faith in Jesus. John consistently warns against false prophets who spread these lies.

2 JOHN

One of the lines that John repeats in both 2 and 3 is "walking in the truth". **That is such a poignant way to describe what following Jesus is all about. Knowing that something is true is different than living like something is true. Again, we need to walk the walk.**

"Many deceivers, who do not acknowledge Jesus Christ as coming in the flesh, have gone out into the world. Any such person is the deceiver and the antichrist. Watch out that you do not lose what you have worked for, but that you may be rewarded fully".

John tells us that if we "run ahead" but don't continue teaching the truth—<u>we do not</u> have God. He goes on to say that anyone who comes to us with lies—we should not except into our house—which is very specific direction. Jesus' command is that we "walk in love".

3 JOHN

This letter is to someone named Gaius.

"I have no greater joy than to hear that my children are walking in the truth". "Do not imitate what is evil but what is good. Anyone who does what is good is from God".

This letter dedicates several lines that are specific friends of theirs (Diotrephes) that are too narrow in scope for this summary.

JUDE

Jude's letter is a plea to avoid false teachers. At this time, there was a group of teachers known as Antinomians. They twisted the concept of God's grace to mean that because we are saved by grace, we now have no moral applications and can do whatever we want—especially from a sexual standpoint. Jude implores us to resist this teaching.

"For certain men whose condemnation was written about long ago have secretly slipped in among you. They are Godless men who change the grace of our God into a license for immorality and deny Jesus Christ our only sovereign and Lord. Though you already know all this, I want to remind you that the Lord delivered his people out of Egypt, but later destroyed those who did not believe". He also mentions Sodom and Gomorrah and the immorality that occurred there—<u>they were destroyed by fire</u>!

"In the very same way, these dreamers pollute their own bodies… these men are blemishes at your love feasts—shepherds who feed only themselves. They are clouds without rain, blown along by the wind; autumn trees without fruit and uprooted—twice dead. They are wild waves of the sea, foaming up their shame; wandering stars, for whom blackest darkness has been reserved forever…these men are grumblers and faultfinders; they follow their own evil desires; they boast about themselves and flatter others for their own advantage".

"But you, dear friends, build yourselves up in your most holy faith and praying in the Holy Spirit, keep yourselves in God's love as you wait for the mercy of our Lord Jesus Christ to bring you to eternal life".

Jude's depiction of false teachers is incredible. The imagery and descriptions are so accurate. There are so many false teachers today. They flatter us to gain our alliance, then ask for our money, and flatter us more to retain that alliance. It is incredibly dangerous and sometimes difficult to spot, which is why we need to stay on guard.

The concept of "do whatever you want because you have been saved" still exists today. We need to understand a subtle truism of following Jesus. We don't attempt to live upstanding lives because we <u>have to</u>, we do it because we <u>want</u> to, because we committed ourselves to living the life that he lived.

That life is love.

THE STORY OF JESUS IS A VERY SIMPLE ONE.

Mankind was separated from God because of our sinfulness. Because he loved his creation (us), God sent his only Son to earth to absorb our sin by dying on the cross and rising from the dead three days later. That act of selflessness, rebuilt our relationship with our Heavenly Father and allowed us to be "one" in relationship with him. While Jesus was here on earth, he demonstrated love where ever he went, and he asked us to do the same. He asked us to believe him when he said he was the Son of God, and to follow Him in our words and actions. In doing so, He promised us the joy and peace that is only found in the Kingdom of God here on earth. And He also promised that if we did so, we would spend eternity in Heaven with Him. God, the Creator of the Universe, loves each and everyone of us so much that He did all this so we could be with Him. That's all He wants. For us to be with Him. And He gave us the map to get us there.

GOOD NIGHT!

THANK YOU

Jean you are the greatest life partner that I could have ever been gifted from God. You are the wind in my sails, my lighthouse in a storm, the rudder on ship that races out of control, and the person that feeds my ego by encouraging me and laughing at my ridiculous jokes. You literally encourage me in everything I do, and I have no idea where I would be without you. You walk with love every minute of every day. You have made our family's life very fun, and to travel this life with you has brought a joy that I never thought possible. I will always love you.

Jake, Sam, and Julianne, you changed my life, and you helped me understand love. There is no possible way I can ever explain to you how much you are loved. Understanding that love is what put God's love for me (and us) in perspective. I love you because you are my kids, and we are his. And I'm so proud of each of you. Not because of what you have accomplished, but because of who you are as people. If you are the only three people who ever read this book, it will have been worth the effort. Thank you for your willingness to read your Dad's notebook!

My Mom and Dad built a God centered family in a God centered home from the moment that every one of their kids were born. They taught me that living your life with a "God first" mindset is the only way to traverse this world. They sacrificed beyond comprehension, and I will be forever grateful to God for placing me in the family of my Mom and Dad.

Tim, my brother, you introduced me the concept of having a personal relationship with Jesus Christ in 1988, and I can't ever thank you enough for that. I know it took me a while because I can be a slow cooker. But you helped flipped my leaf and because of your faith, you have changed generations of our family.

My siblings Tim, Donna, and Tricia and I are in many ways closer now than we were when we grew up together in the 60's 70's and 80's. Donna and Tricia, you are faith filled women of God and you inspire me every day.

Dan Coughlin (Cogs) and Mike Feder (Feds, resting in Jesus' wonderful peace since 2012), you guys have been the greatest life brothers anyone could ask for. Every year we embarked on a Dream Weekend where we set our goals for the next year. Somewhere in that journey we realized that the only way to do that was to put our priorities in order and that meant setting our "God Goals" first. You guys changed my life, and Cogs, you continue to do so.

To my life brothers in Men's Ministries in Aurora, Illinois, Gallatin, Tennessee, and Scottsdale, Arizona. You taught me that iron sharpens iron, and men need men. We go through life trying to impress a world that challenges us and sometimes beats us down and we keep it all to ourselves because we tell ourselves we are above it all. We are not. It's about transparency, authenticity, vulnerability and being a part of the brotherhood of Jesus warriors. And to all the other men who have been my wing men on this journey of following Jesus, thank you. You know who you are!

To Felice Kriceri. When I had 630 pages of handwritten notes and was wondering how to get it transcribed, I asked you if you knew anyone who could do it. And I will never forget what you said, "yeah, me". If you hadn't said that I'd still have 630 handwritten pages! You walk around this earth with a generous heart, just like we are told to do. I appreciate you in a big way.

And I'll save the best for last. To Jesus. You gave me the gift of you. And I believe you promised me two things if I followed you: True peace on earth and eternity in Heaven with you. For that, I am eternally grateful. Literally. I'll see you soon because life is short. Eternity with you will be a long, long joyful time.

ABOUT THE AUTHOR

The author of THE Book is God.

The author of THIS book, which is commentary on THE Book, is Jeff Hutchison.

Jeff Hutchison is an executive leader in the Medical Device industry and has led sales organizations for both Fortune 500 as well as start-up Companies. His expertise is in sales and marketing of new medical device technologies.

Jeff is the founder of Team G6 Consulting, which focuses on developing leaders and teams. He has published several articles on sales strategy, leadership, and team development and is an accomplished speaker at business and non-profit events. Team G6 was named after Galatians 6:9 which says "Let us not become weary in doing good, for at the proper time we will reap a harvest if we do not give up".

In life, that means work hard, do the right thing, and don't give up! In Galatians, it means don't get tired of spreading the Good News of Jesus, because you will eventually reap a harvest of listeners, because the story is so incredible.

Jeff has been married to his wife Jean for 33 years and they live in Gallatin, Tennessee and Scottsdale, Arizona. Together they have two sons, Jake and Sam, and one daughter, Julianne. Jeff's greatest love is traveling the world with his family and his fondest memories are coaching his kids' baseball, soccer, and basketball teams when they were growing up. He is an avid runner, golfer, biker, pickle baller, hiker and traveler.

Jeff Hutchison
teamhutch@comcast.net
teamg6consulting.com